CHRISTIANITY AND CONSERVATISM

D0334368

CHRISTIANITY AND CONSERVATISM

edited by

Michael Alison

and

David L. Edwards

Hodder & Stoughton

LONDON SYDNEY AUCKLAND TORONTO

UNIVERSITY OF CHICHESTER

British Library Cataloguing in Publication Data

Christianity and conservatism.
1. Great Britain. Society. Role of Christian church
I. Alison, Michael   II. Edwards, David L. (David Lawrence)
1929–   CTC 322.1CHR
261.10941

ISBN 0-340-52949-0

Copyright: *Introducing a Dialogue* © David L. Edwards; *The Two Cities* ©
Lord Hailsham of St Marylebone; *The Tension of the 1980s* © Ronald Butt; *The
Church of England in Opposition?* © John Gladwin; *Is There any Word from the
Lord?* © Lord Blanch of Bishopthorpe; *Wealth and Poverty in the Bible* © J. R.
Porter; *Conservatism before Conservatism: Political Theology in an Anglican
Confessional State* © J. C. D. Clark; *Do British Parties Need Philosophies?* ©
Edward Norman; *Poverty and Wealth Creation* © Lord Harris of High Cross;
The Feeding of the Billions © Michael Alison, MP; *The Conservative
Quadrilateral* © Brian Griffiths; *How Well Have Britain's Poor Fared?* © Frank
Field, MP; *The Limits of the Market* © John Atherton; *Christians, Conservatives
and Europe* © Timothy Raison, MP; *Conserving the Family* © John Gummer,
MP; *Responsible and Accountable* © Ruth Etchells; *Towards an Understanding* ©
David L. Edwards; *Appendix* © Margaret Thatcher, MP, 1990

First published in Great Britain 1990

Published by Hodder and Stoughton,
a division of Hodder and Stoughton Ltd,
Mill Road, Dunton Green, Sevenoaks, Kent TN13 2YA
Editorial Office: 47 Bedford Square, London WC1B 3DP

Photoset by Rowland Phototypesetting Ltd, Bury St Edmunds, Suffolk

Printed in Great Britain by Clays Ltd, St Ives plc.

Contents

Preface

by the Prime Minister

NOT for two thousand years has it been possible for society to exclude or eliminate Christ from its social or political life without a terrible consequence. God is not easily mocked. And it is one of history's supreme ironies that the first political conspiracy to make the attempt saw instead the very foundation of the Christian religion, leading on to the flowering of Christian civilisation.

Thus we are told in the gospels that the Herodians and the Pharisees conspired together to trap Jesus in his words, so as to secure his arrest and execution. So great was the imagined political threat which Christ represented, that two groups – not normally on the same side – made common cause to try to do away with him. For they perceived in Christ an authority which, threatening the authority of Rome and Jerusalem alike, transcended their own precious partisanships. So, burying their differences, they came together to Christ with their famous trick question about paying tribute to Caesar.

They got the famous answer: 'Render therefore unto Caesar the things which are Caesar's; and unto God the things that are God's.' It did nothing to assuage their fears; rather the reverse. So they pressed ahead with Christ's arrest and execution. Yet their fears were well-founded. Something – somebody – transcendent had burst in upon their life and times, and the very plot and deed of crucifixion started an irreversible growth.

Today the very memory of the Pharisees and the Herodians, even of Imperial Rome itself, has fled away into the mists of history. Yet that ancient encounter between the founder of Christianity and his opponents was only lately brought most vividly back to my mind, and to that of millions of others, by Vaclav Havel in his first speech as the new President of Czechoslovakia. Havel reminded the world that the great Jan Masaryk had written that 'Jesus, not Caesar . . .' should be the lode star. And he added, on his own account: 'Our country, if that is what we want, can now permanently radiate love, understanding, the power of spirit and ideas.'

What a glorious vision the new President expressed, after the long dark night of totalitarian secular tyranny which had, until so recently, engulfed Czechoslovakia and its neighbours! It was the Christian faith which kept alight the flickering flame of hope in those societies, and which now sheds its rays on their various national pathways to the future.

It is against this background that I contribute with enthusiasm this short Preface to the present collection of diverse essays under the broad title of *Christianity and Conservatism*. It will be apparent from what I have written that my very last intention is to support any project which might belittle Christianity by partisanship, or exalt Conservatism by some whisper of the transcendent. But, as a number of the essays make clear, a historical turning-point has been reached for our nation, and the way ahead must be carefully and judiciously charted. For many centuries Christianity, here focused in Anglicanism, was part of the very woof and warp of our society and its institutions. Indeed Anglican clergy held the top offices of state long before the Tory party came into existence. This intimate association between Church and State was profoundly creative in the advance to national consciousness.

In our own age new freedoms have come with growth and maturity; old associations have been left behind. Christianity has indeed done much to promote this evolution. But paradoxically, it has become vulnerable to the risk that it might itself be marginalised. For from freedom has flowed pluralism. Can Havel's vision of a secular society transformed by the power of the spirit, and of Christian ideas, be realised in today's world? That is the question which these essays set out to answer, from the perspective of one of the great political traditions in our society.

MARGARET THATCHER

1

Introducing a Dialogue

David L. Edwards

FOR some years I used to recite the stately prayer which has been said by the Speaker's Chaplain at the beginning of each day in the proceedings of the House of Commons in Westminster since the seventeenth century. It is a prayer for a wise agreement and the key to wisdom is seen as impartiality, 'setting aside all private interests, and partial affections'.

The prayer is, however, often the prelude to fierce controversy in the House. There is of course a long history of this; the very arrangement of the seating seems designed to encourage adversarial politics, although it is due to the rectangular shape of the chapel which the House inherited from the Middle Ages as its meeting place. Particularly during the 1970s and 1980s, the confrontation between the Conservatives and Labour could be a war of words, almost between two nations, with MPs declaring any private financial interests but also exhibiting prejudice and partiality. It seemed that any hope of agreement had been overwhelmed by the need to be radical in response to new realities – among them the poison of inflation; the human cost of the decline of the old industries; the contraction of the manual working class; the new, and to many of the British uncongenial, importance of training and information; the emancipation of women to be workers; greater expectations about social security, health care and old age;

the growth of international competition and investment; the slow and problematic birth of a union of the states of Europe; the vigour of local loyalties and protests; the horror of defence in the nuclear age; and the dreadful prospect of polluting and exhausting nature. No soft answers have seemed possible for these new questions. How can a government curb inflation without increasing unemployment? How can it stimulate the economy without stimulating a credit boom, thereby bringing back inflation, and without sucking in imports, thereby wrecking the balance of payments? How can it control the economy when the flow of capital is international? How can it finance a developing welfare state without destroying incentives by taxation? How can it afford a health service with ever-increasing numbers of old people, costs of drugs and surgery and demands for competitive wages? How can it 'go into Europe' without surrendering the national identity that great wars have been fought to preserve? How can it share power with regional or local government without dissolving the nation or enraging those who must pay local taxes? How can it deter aggression without being willing to annihilate civilisation? How can it combine the economic growth demanded by all the peoples of the world with a prudent care of the environment? The new radical realism which confronts such challenges has been accompanied by scorn for the proposals of rival groups. This has been a mood on the New Right, on the New Left, and even in attempts to 'break the mould' by renewing the Centre. Any hankering after a consensus or 'social contract' in 'one nation' has often been denounced as camouflage for nostalgia, laziness and general wetness. The need, it has been said, is for a clash of convictions. There must be a battle between parties offering the electorate either a clear alternative to the government or else the doctrine that there is no alternative.

This confrontation has not been ended by the discrediting of Communism in the spectacular Soviet and European changes of 1985–90, or by the fact that the Labour Party, having discovered when in power that the IMF was a more reliable support than the TUC, and having discovered when in opposition that its constituency activists (not to mention Militants) tended to be further to the Left than the electorate, has moved to the middle ground. For Socialism remains on the agenda. In terms of British books, Anthony Crosland's assumption in *The Future of Socialism* (1956) that capitalism had been defeated is now a period piece, but Brian Gould still sees the future of the Labour Party as *A Future for Socialism* (1989). However 'Socialism' may be defined – for Mr Gould, it seems to be essentially 'social justice' including worker participation in the control of a company and limits on the profits of shareholders, but also greater individual and local choice – it is always said to be something that cannot be got from the Conservative Party. In the spring of 1990, when this book goes to the printer, the future of Conservatism seems to be uncertain and many Conservatives are said to be looking forward to a kinder, gentler regime (echoing President Bush's promise), with a more manifestly 'caring' approach to those in need. However, it is certain that Conservatives do not care to be thought likely either to bring back State Socialism or to move forward to Mr Gould's decentralised, red-rosed, variety. 'Conservatism' may be defined in a variety of ways – as the defence of individual freedom under the law, of small communities or of the authoritarian state – or it may be left carefully undefined in favour of a pragmatic handling of a government's given problems. But it is, all Conservatives agree, something for which all Conservatives will fight. As another General Election approaches, the collapse of the parties of the Centre in the polls encourages both the main parties to go fishing for moderates; but British politics is still usually presented to the public as a clash of ideologies. That is strikingly different from the situation in most of the European Community or in the USA, where the differences between Christian Democrat and Social Democrat, or between Democrat and Republican, are differences within a social consensus.

The old House of Commons prayer for unprejudiced and impartial wisdom may also seem odd in the light of the recent history of the Church of England, which the Speaker's Chaplain modestly represents. A 1990 report from a church committee, *Living Faith in the City*, tried to give an objective account of what is believed on the Right: 'Policies based on common obligations, corporate responsibility and social justice are rejected as leading inevitably to a loss of personal freedom, the growth of bureaucratic vested interests, waste and economic stagnation.' It is, however, not hard to predict which side of that balance the report will proceed to favour, particularly since 'economic stagnation' has the appeal, or at least offers the consolation, of being environmentally friendly. It seems to be assumed in that report that the Conservative Party, although it has not yet rejected massive public expenditure for the sake of 'common obligations, corporate responsibility and social justice', has actually fallen under the spell of the ideology of the New Right and has rejected the policies which created the welfare state. The Thatcher Government tries to 'recast British society', the report says, and therefore it needs a 'moral input' from 'the Church'. The contrast between such a view of Conservatism – a view which is distant, cool, hostile or patronising – and traditional Anglican attitudes could scarcely be greater. In the past it has often seemed that the English Churches, particularly the Church of England 'by law established', would quietly obey the Crown and support the government of the day while concentrating on their own timeless religious concerns. For example, the Speaker's Chaplain's prayer for wisdom was answered in his own case by confining his public words to the unvarying recital of the same psalm and prayers each day.

More elevated spokesmen of the Church of England were given more freedom, as is still shown by the presence of bishops in the House of Lords, but if a political preference was expressed by the average bishop it could be expected to be a discreet blessing on the Conservative Party – or on the

Liberals when they were by modern standards Conservative. The little joke of uncertain origin about the Church of England being 'the Conservative Party at prayer' has often been repeated because it contains some truth. Did not the Tory Party trace its origins to the defence of 'Church and King' against Popery, Dissent and Treason? Did not this party still intend to conserve a Christian society, a cause to which rotund quotations from Burke and Disraeli were appropriate? Did not the Speaker's Chaplain's set prayer voice the Establishment's support of Christianity when it included 'the maintenance of true religion' among the purposes of Parliament (as it still does)? There was also the tradition of idealistic Christian Socialism propagated most influentially by Archbishop William Temple's *Christianity and Social Order* (1942) and celebrated in Maurice Reckitt's *Maurice to Temple* (1947), as there was a tradition of specific complaints about some government policies. Gatherings such as the Church of England's old Church Assembly registered concern about unemployment and bad housing. But there was nothing that looked like a systematic attack on a Conservative government and the critical voices were not so significant as the fact that most regular Anglican churchgoers could be relied on to vote Conservative.

After the Second World War the mood changed somewhat. As a student I listened to the lectures by Professor V. A. Demant published as *Religion and the Decline of Capitalism* (1952). The welfare state and the mixed economy with its public and private sectors were established as modifications of the traditional social order. They owed much to the vision of the Christian Socialists but also had continuity with the paternalism of the Tory/Conservative tradition and of the Liberal Government of 1906. On the whole the Church of England supported the new Establishment – but so, on the whole, after the initial 'bonfire of controls' and despite tensions and conflicts with the unions, did the Conservative Party led by Churchill (author of *Liberalism and the Social Problem* in 1909), Butler, Eden, Macmillan, Douglas-Home and Heath. The answer to unemployment and poverty seemed to be the distribution of subsidies and benefits after high taxation. Public expenditure grew to a Keynesian level since Beveridge's hope that 'social insurance' would soon finance itself proved utopian. Later the answer to inflation (caused in part by the unthinkability of lower wages to take account of overmanning and higher energy prices) was a prices and incomes policy; if labour was being disciplined, so was the market. When in 1976 the General Synod of the Church of England did me the honour of debating a document I had been asked to write on *The State of the Nation*, these were the 'social contract' answers which I attempted to develop, for I had not yet learned that a prices and incomes policy, however admirable ethically, is not realistic since human beings are human. The British Council of Churches' report on *Britain Today and Tomorrow*, edited by Trevor Beeson (now Dean of Winchester) in 1978 after extensive consultations, envisaged a future which was also a development of the consensus sometimes known as Butskellism, although with more emphasis on local participation and local co-operatives. I remember the joke that Britain tomorrow was to resemble Yugoslavia.

However, in 1979 a government was elected which was not what the British Council of Churches wanted. It was radically reforming, even revolutionary. Although elected to the Conservative leadership in 1975, Mrs Thatcher has been inspired by convictions which are not conservative in the everyday sense of that term epitomised by a Duke of Cambridge's famous remark that the right time for change is when it can no longer be resisted. On the contrary, in some spheres she has sharpened up the traditional Conservative belief in strong government, curbing the might of the trade unions, changing the time-honoured practices of the professions, disciplining or abolishing local authorities and imposing the poll tax. But in the main she has used her power to enforce policies close to those of the nineteenth-century Liberal apostles of entrepreneurial capitalism and free trade, who in their day were regarded by Conservatives as ungentlemanly. The effect has been described by a

Neo-Marxist thinker, Professor Stuart Hall, who himself advocates for the Left *The Hard Road to Renewal* (1988). He argues that 'Thatcherism' aims at 'hegemony', which implies: 'the struggle to contest and disorganise an existing political formation; the taking of the "leading position" (on however minority a basis) over a number of different spheres at once – economy, civil society, intellectual and moral culture; the conduct of a wide and differentiated type of struggle; the winning of a strategic measure of popular consent; and, thus, the securing of a social authority sufficiently deep to conform society into a new historical perspective'. Whether Mrs Thatcher is so similar in her aim to a Marxist revolutionary as Professor Hall claims may be questioned. Essential to her position is her belief that she is only setting the people free to do what deep down they want, not imposing an ideology, and it is certain that in some important spheres she has followed, rather than led, public opinion. Public expenditure has stopped growing but has not been slashed drastically because it is recognised that the public still wants most of the welfare state. Trade union power has been reduced, but mostly in ways which the Labour Party has itself come to accept as being desirable 'in place of strife'. In these and other spheres, Mrs Thatcher may be said to have acted on behalf of a consensus which continues; and where she has pioneered, it has sometimes meant the uncovering of a new consensus, as in the general disillusionment with nationalisation as a panacea or as in the popularity of extending the ownership of homes and shares or as in the spread of the new mood that hard and enterprising work deserves financial encouragement. But what is also certain is that she has changed the terms of the British political debate. Her prescription of strenuous competition to cure what used to be called the 'British disease' of inefficiency has meant that in politics others have had to compete with her. Her proclamation of uncompromising convictions has meant a firm, and if necessary isolated, stance unusual in Conservative history.

One of the departures from tradition under her personal

hegemony has been that most spokesmen of the Church of England, and of other British Churches, have constituted a kind of opposition to her government. The General Synod which, descended from obscurer bodies, had been born in 1970, cut its teeth by chewing up many of the policies of her government; and the influential church report on *Faith in the City* (1985) did not conceal a lack of faith in 'Thatcherism' as an approach to urban and national renewal. As expressed by such church leadership, the political affections of 'the Church' have seemed definitely partial. This phenomenon has often been analysed in the press and books on it include *Church and Politics Today* edited by George Moyser in 1985. It is not surprising that there has been a counter-attack from Christians with other political convictions who also claim to belong to 'the Church'. In her pamphlet *Another Gospel?* (1988) Rachel Tingle was therefore concerned, 'not only that leaders of the Anglican Church are increasingly advocating one-sided and dangerously simplistic prescriptions to complex problems but, perhaps even more importantly, that they are making it almost impossible for those who disagree with them to express their concerns and alternative views in such a way that they will be given due consideration'.

Obviously the polarisation of politics in the much-analysed 'Thatcher years' should not be attributed entirely to the character of the Prime Minister or to the zest of other politicians for political battles. In response to vitally important problems in the economy and in the work of government, disagreements have been profound and profoundly serious. But these serious arguments have been accompanied by an exchange of half-truths, slogans, bogus panaceas and personal insults which has left most of the electorate unimpressed. While there has been no enthusiasm shown for any coalition, in general elections the Conservative vote has been in decline since 1931 and the Labour vote since 1951 and in recent elections no party has persuaded as many as half of the voters. Living in recent years at some distance from Westminster – in the rural peace of

Norfolk or amid the urban deprivation of the London Borough of Southwark – I have felt the force of the popular suspicion that despite the entertainment value of the gladiatorial fights in the Commons (now featured on TV) the great economic and social problems of a new age may require a different treatment. A wisdom may be needed of which no one party has the monopoly, even if one does not agree with all the low opinions which politicians proclaim about their adversaries. Dwelling among the grass roots or street litter I have also often wondered whether it is wise for statesmen and churchmen to be quite so divided and out of touch with each other. Perhaps they are out of touch with the real problems? Like many others, I have suspected that a calmer study of the new realities of our society might result in the discovery of more common political ground and that a common Christian faith, or reverence for Christian ethics, might help political antagonists to respect each other and even to lay aside all partial affections in favour of the common good. Many of us have not been able to forget the prayer for reconciliation (attributed to St Francis of Assisi) which Mrs Thatcher used on the doorstep of No. 10 before first entering the house as Prime Minister.

In 1987 I seized the opportunity of a debate in the General Synod on a somewhat abstruse report on *Changing Britain* (which stressed that politics is about fundamental values essential to 'human flourishing' including 'interrelatedness') to plead for a deeper dialogue between the Church of England and the Conservative Party. I said:

> No doubt conversation about the questions of the day between bishops, Tory MPs and other leaders is important and does go on. No doubt many Anglicans are also Tories, so that dialogue goes on *within* minds and consciences. But surely priority should be given to a systematic and (yes!) philosophical dialogue about what Conservatism is and what Christianity is . . . Those headlines about *Maggie in New Clash with Bishops* are so sad in the light of Conservative history, where certainly religion and politics do mix and mix creatively.

To my surprise the Archbishop of Canterbury mentioned this proposal to the Prime Minister, who wished it well. She was to make her own Christian convictions and their relevance to her policies plain in her speech to the General Assembly of the Church of Scotland in May 1988 (printed in this book as an appendix). Meanwhile she asked the Right Hon. Michael Alison, MP, formerly her Parliamentary Private Secretary, then Chairman of the Houses of Parliament Christian Fellowship and now the Second Church Estates Commissioner, to organise a dialogue in consultation with the Head of her Policy Unit, Professor Brian Griffiths, and others. The dialogue has been wholly independent, with its costs met from private and anonymous sources, and not all the contributors would identify themselves as Conservatives. (My own views, for what they are worth, are at variance with much that is said to be Conservative, as may be seen in my *Christians in a New Europe* (1990) or in the 1990 collection of essays which I have edited on *Robert Runcie*.) But it says much about the historic relationship between Church and Party that there has been this degree of encouragement from high places. It also says much about a common willingness to tackle difficult controversies for the sake of the welfare of Church and State that the contributors have co-operated. With many existing duties they have been willing to prepare essays, to listen to criticisms, to revise some opinions and generally to persevere in a time-consuming project which included two residential meetings at Newick Park in Sussex. The main regret of our group has been that one of the wisest of our number, Canon Graham Routledge of St Paul's, died before he could develop his preliminary draft for a chapter. At Cambridge he had taught law, but we have not forgotten the force of his plea that the basis of the Church's message in any generation should be the New Testament's understanding of love.

The essays now presented are obviously subject to many limitations in time, space and ability and are intended to open, rather than close, the dialogue. Each contributor could have said much more here and has said it elsewhere. The sole purpose is to help the fair-minded reader to see what the most important issues are and where he or she sees the truth, which ought to inspire political thought and action in the years to come. No attempt has been made to standardise these contributions to the debate, in argument, tone or detail.

Any impression that we are a pressure group hoping to produce a political programme which all Christians should accept ought to be dispelled when Lord Hailsham, whose distinguished career in the law and politics has included the chairmanship of the Conservative Party (1957–59) and office as Lord Chancellor (1970–74 and 1979–87), introduces this dialogue. He expounds the distinction between the City of God (about which he generously believes that the clergy may know something) and the City of this world, where the ideal – at any rate for Britain – is freedom under the law, an ideal which falls short of heavenly perfection, sustained by a commonly accepted morality which is not exclusively Christian. He offers some brief but trenchant comments on clergy who pontificate about politics in the earthly city and seems to imply a wish to distance himself from some laymen who seem to think that they can preach better than the clergy on what Christianity involves politically.

Ronald Butt then surveys in more detail the tension between the Church and the Party in the 1980s. He was asked to discuss the nature of the concern which many Conservatives and many who are active lay members of the Church (as he, like Lord Hailsham, is) feel about the attacks directed at Conservative policies from church circles. He has done so with the industry and skill of a leading journalist who cares deeply about these questions, putting the recent relationship between the officers of Church and State in the context of history and probing the meaning of statements by Dr Runcie as Archbishop of Canterbury, and by other eminent churchmen, in the context of the impression conveyed to the public. He defends Mrs Thatcher's own exposition of the links between religion and politics and considers the lessons to be learned for the future from the controversies surrounding her government. Mr Butt is a leader writer and columnist of *The Times*, and he and his Editor have consented to the reproduction at the end of his essay of an article which he wrote in that newspaper on 1 February 1990 about the latest in a series of church reports which have contributed to the strained relationship.

One of the churchmen whose comments on government policy he criticises, John Gladwin, offers in the next chapter his own memories and interpretations of events in which he was involved as Secretary of the General Synod's Board for Social Responsibility from 1982, before his move in 1988 to Sheffield to be Provost of the cathedral in the midst of that city. He may set some Conservative fears at rest by being thoroughly Anglican in his disclaimer of infallibility but also by showing why he called his book *The Good of the People* (1988). And it may interest future historians to have these reflections alongside those of a former chairman of the Board, Bishop Hugh Montefiore, in his book on *Christianity and Politics* (1989), or those of the Archbishop of York, Dr John Habgood, in *Church and Nation in a Secular Age* (1983).

The Anglican tradition takes the Bible as authoritative in some sense, and when political attitudes are commended to Christians the Bible is often quoted. But in this dialogue two questions have to be faced. Can a person preoccupied by the political problems of this age find any light in a Bible completed almost two thousand years ago? Can the Bible be said to teach a 'bias to the poor' if 'the poor' are defined in the terms of the twentieth-century political debates, as has often been argued by critics of contemporary Conservatism in Britain and by Christians in other countries who seek liberation from capitalism? Answers to these questions (yes to the first, no to the second) are suggested by scholarly churchmen in two essays. Lord Blanch was Bishop of Liverpool from 1966 to 1975 and Archbishop of York from 1975 to 1983. Canon Porter taught the Old Testament in

Oxford and was Professor of Theology at Exeter from 1962 to 1986. It is hoped that these two deeply pondered essays will stimulate a more attentive consideration of the Scriptures. It is no accident that the emphasis in them is on the Old Testament, which is more political than the New, but the next essays deal with periods when Englishmen who regarded themselves as Christians associated a veneration for the New Testament with politics which could not be called Socialist.

These periods are surveyed provocatively in two essays by historians. Dr Jonathan Clark, a Fellow of All Souls College, Oxford, takes us into the world which shaped most English minds between the Reformation and the Reform Act of 1832. That world must now seem at least as strange as the world of the Bible, and Dr Clark was encouraged to document his essay lest readers should find it difficult to believe that such a world existed. But he asks us to remember that English Christians once did their theology and political philosophy within an 'Anglican confessional state' and that no theology or philosophy equally coherent has yet emerged in this country. 'Pluralism' has been accepted as the basis of our democracy, and was the cry of Eastern Europe in 1989, but the meaning of that word is often obscure. It may be that at the end of the twentieth century we can learn some lessons from England before 1832. At the very least we can learn that our own political philosophy is not inevitable for Christians.

The modern period is tackled by Dr Edward Norman, a former Reith Lecturer for the BBC and Lecturer in History at Cambridge. He was Fellow and Dean of Peterhouse from 1971 to 1988 and is now Dean of Chapel at Christ Church College, Canterbury. Boldly he asks whether in the post-1832 society Conservatism has been, or ought to have been, a party with its own strong and clear philosophy or 'convictions'. Is its proper role to be, rather, the party of scepticism about all plans for this-worldly Utopias? This apologia for scepticism may be connected with the warnings in Lord Hailsham's opening chapter (and with his statements of the

Conservative case in earlier years). It is also in accord with the main theme of Lord Quinton's lectures on *The Politics of Imperfection: The Religious and Secular Traditions of Conservative Thought in England from Hooker to Oakshott* (1978) and Lord Blake's history of *The Conservative Party from Peel to Thatcher* (revised in 1985). But Dr Norman also argues that, while political parties ought to be somewhat sceptical about their capacity to put the affairs of the world right, the Church ought to proclaim a spiritual (rather than moral) religion with its own absolutes, and would find a surprisingly extensive response if it did so. For this chapter scholarly documentation seemed less necessary, since the period has been covered by Dr Norman's own *Church and Society in England 1770–1970* (1975) and by works such as G. I. T. Machin's two volumes on *Politics and the Churches in Great Britain, 1832 to 1868* (1977) and *1869 to 1921* (1987) and *Church and Politics in a Secular Age* (1988), a mainly sociological study by Kenneth M. Medhurst and George H. Moyser. All four books were published by the Oxford University Press.

Like other studies, *Church and Politics in a Secular Age* judges that in recent years the bulk of church opinion has remained 'moderately conservative'. But an explanation of the alarm voiced by the bulk of church leadership may be found in the fact that under Mrs Thatcher's leadership the Conservative Party seems to have been the party not of 'Church and King', or of anti-utopian scepticism, but of 'Freedom under the Law and the Market'. Is that 'unjust' or 'wicked', as some churchmen have alleged? Or does a compassion for the low-paid or the poor which frustrates the free working of market forces in the end, when it contributes to an unrealistic public expenditure in a wide variety of good causes, lead to poverty and bankruptcy for all? Does this 'caring' encourage dependency and so turn out to be 'the kindness that kills' (to use the title of the symposium edited by Digby Anderson in 1984 in order to denounce 'the Churches' simplistic response to complex social issues')? To get social justice, do we first need to create wealth in which all may participate? Is wealth needed if the polluter is to be made to pay for, and to stop, damage to the environment? And is the market, not Marx, the modern secret of wealth? These are the questions discussed in the next group of essays.

Lord Harris of High Cross became the first Director of the Institute of Economic Affairs in 1957, long before the attacks on over-government associated with that small think-tank were fashionable. In this book he concisely but powerfully explains why competition in the market has proved itself the most effective means of creating wealth. At the beginning of the 1990s it appears that this lesson is being learned in the Soviet Union and Eastern Europe and in much of the Third World, as well as in the Atlantic world. Will it be learned in the churches? Then Michael Alison recounts how a market-oriented capitalism, for all its defects, has already been indispensable in enabling a spectacular increase in the population of the world. At a time when the future is often viewed with gloom, he holds out the prospect of a promised land in which there will be not only survival, and even material plenty, but also a spiritual opportunity. Thus he outlines a liberation which is an alternative to that advocated by the theologians now dominant in (for example) Latin America. His vision is closer to the thought of Christian defenders of 'popular' or 'democratic' capitalism in the USA.

In practice, however, is such a market-led, capitalist Conservatism a creed of greed? Does it advocate selfishness, irresponsibility, materialism and secularism? That is often alleged. Responding to a challenge by the Bishop of Durham, Brian Griffiths outlines a type of Conservatism which might be acceptable to Christian consciences. He was Professor of Banking and International Finance in the City University, London, before he moved to Downing Street as the Head of the Policy Unit in 1985, but he is also noted as a Christian thinker, being the author of *Morality and the Market Place* (1989) as well as *The Creation of Wealth* (1984).

Equally thoughtful – as will be expected by readers who recall his books, on *The Politics of Paradise* (1987) and, in contrast, *Losing Out* (1990) – is an essay by Frank Field, Director of the Child Poverty Action Group from 1969 to 1979, MP for Birkenhead since 1979, Chairman of the House of Commons Select Committee on the Social Services and the Labour Party's shadow spokesman on church affairs. He examines afresh the question: how well have Britain's poor fared under Mrs Thatcher? Inevitably much of his discussion is both technical and controversial (and in his own essay Professor Griffiths takes issue with him), but his conclusion is that the living standards of those dependent on benefits have fallen while most people have prospered, although many complaints fail to distinguish between absolute need and a 'poverty' felt because it is relative to generally rising standards, as when pensions are adjusted to inflated prices but not to average incomes which rise faster than prices. What seems to be established beyond doubt is that an 'underclass' emerged in the 1980s, composed in particular of the very frail elderly, of single mothers on welfare and of the long-term unemployed, in many ways excluded from the citizen's life. If the wealth created by the market is supposed to trickle down, it does not appear to have trickled down far enough. Here is a challenge to the Conservatism of the future.

The value of dialogues between Left and Right is also illustrated by the essay by Canon John Atherton of Manchester Cathedral, who was Director of the William Temple Foundation from 1979 to 1984 and author of *Faith in the Nation* (1984). He belongs to, and praises, the tradition which he calls 'Social Christianity' and in which one element has been Christian Socialism. He refers to the US Catholic Bishops with their pastoral letter on *Economic Justice for All* (1986) as well as to Anglican, Protestant and ecumenical exponents of this tradition, which is by far the weightiest element in modern Christian thinking about social problems. But he acknowledges frankly that he has learned through dialogues such as ours to accept the market as the main mechanism for the creation of wealth. It is needed before wealth can be used or distributed. What, then, he asks anew, are the limits which should be imposed on the market by moral agreement or political regulation?

Canon Atherton's revisionism may mark a turning point in the acceptance of a limited capitalism by 'Social Christianity'. It may be linked to the policy review by the Labour Party at the end of the 1980s. It may also be seen as a British version of a political philosophy (the 'Social Market' in Germany) which has been highly influential in the European Community. The essay about the EC is by the Right Hon. Timothy Raison, MP, formerly Editor of *New Society* and Minister for Overseas Development. He reflects on the origins of the Community in the post-war hopes of eminent Christian Democrat statesmen as well as on some of the problems now surrounding the embodiment of these hopes (after development through very remarkable economic advances) in the European Social Charter. He keeps in mind Lord Hailsham's point that no political institution is identical with the City of God but shows that Christians seeking that perfect city have not held themselves aloof from matters such as the agenda of the Commission in Brussels. Mr Raison, who wrote a booklet called *What is Conservatism?* back in 1964, points here to the new context in which that question must be answered if – as has been commonly agreed since the 1975 referendum – Britain's future lies in the European Community. As the 1990s begin it is often said that 'Europe' – more precisely, the Community's development into an economic, monetary and political union – may split the Conservative Party. But this essay appears to suggest that the continent may be united without the party being divided.

Before I submit a very brief attempt to sum up some of the lessons learned in our dialogue, an essay by the Right Hon. John Gummer, MP, now Minister of Agriculture and formerly Chairman of the Conservative Party, a prominent member of the General Synod, urges us to cultivate the soil from which a healthy society springs – a stable and loving

family life. The essay by Frank Field also considers some of
the problems in this area. Although the gravity of these
problems cannot be denied and controversy (even between
Christians) is inevitable, there will be admiration for the
courage and energy with which Mr Gummer advocates the
placing of legislative and fiscal teeth in ideals about family
life which are often mouthed. And an essay by Ruth
Etchells, Principal of St John's College, Durham, from 1979
to 1988, contributes insights into the spiritual foundations
of politics. It is often argued, by Mrs Thatcher and others,
that the exercise of personal choice in the free market
increases the citizen's sense that he or she is responsible
and accountable for his or her own actions. This may be
understood as responsibility and accountability to one's
own conscience or 'better self', or to the family or community, or to the nation or humanity, but in Britain there
remains a widespread belief that the ultimate reality judging us is God. In a democracy the government as well as the
individual is held to be accountable, but here again it is
widely believed that a government has a duty to promote
'justice' for reasons which go beyond being answerable to
the electorate. Miss Etchells takes us into the profound
question: what does it mean to say that a person, or a group
such as a nation, is responsible and accountable to the God
who is revealed in Christ?

Whether the Conservative Party is elected to rule Britain
for a hundred years, or is replaced in government soon after
the publication of this book, it will be profitable to reflect on
the questions raised by the 'Thatcher years' and explored in
the essays which follow.

2

The Two Cities

Lord Hailsham of St Marylebone

EVERY good sermon deserves a text, and since this, at least in a sense, is a sermon, it shall have one. I take it from the adventures of the ubiquitous and immortal Albert Haddock to be found in *Misleading Cases in the Common Law* by A. P. Herbert and first published in 1927 where it is attributed to Mr Justice Boom sitting in the Divisional Court of the King's Bench Division. (I seem to remember that, in later editions, the passage I quote was attributed to Lord Justice Frog, and finally to the Lord Chief Justice Light, both sitting, it may be assumed, in the Court of Appeal. But I prefer it in its original form.) The learned judge had first described the facts, which were that the intrepid Haddock, having first been bet the small sum of one pound that he would not do so, removed his jacket and proceeded to jump off Hammersmith Bridge and to swim in a leisurely fashion towards the Middlesex bank. Unfortunately, before he reached the shore, Haddock found himself arrested by the river police and they charged him with a number of offences to which he made a variety of convincing answers, but was unlucky enough to say that he had done what he had done 'for fun'.

This, not unnaturally, infuriated the Divisional Court of the King's Bench Division who dismissed his appeal against conviction in unequivocal terms as follows:

In addition to his particular answers (all of which might otherwise have had substance) the appellant made the general answer that this was a free country and a man can do what he likes if he does nobody any harm. And with that observation the appellant's case takes on an entirely new aspect . . . For it would be idle to deny that a man capable of that remark would be capable of the grossest forms of licence and disorder. It cannot be too clearly understood that this is not a free country and it will be an evil day for the legal profession when it is. The citizens of London must realise that there is almost nothing they are allowed to do. *Prima facie* all actions are illegal, if not by Act of Parliament, by order in Council, by Departmental or police regulations or bylaws. They may not eat where they like, drink where they like, sing where they like, or sleep where they like. And least of all may they do unusual actions for 'fun'. People must not do things for fun. We are not here for fun. There is no reference to fun in any Act of Parliament . . .

To this last sentence the learned judge might have added 'or in the Bible'. But it cannot be too often said that the late 'APH' secured a First Class in the Oxford Honours School of Jurisprudence, and that he was seldom more serious than when he was being at his most witty, and, some would say, at his most outrageous.

Of course, what he was really doing was reminding his readers that what distinguishes a free society from its opposite is the general proposition that no act or omission is illegal unless it is prohibited by some positive rule of customary or statute law, and that what distinguishes good law from bad is not the intrinsic morality of the act or omission but the social consequences which it actually does or is likely to produce and the difficulty or otherwise of securing compliance. In other words, a just society is precisely a society the purpose of which is to promote freedom under law, by which I mean freedom responsibly exercised under the regulation of just laws policed and administered by independent and impartial courts. This ideal falls, of course, a good deal short of absolute freedom, and even further short of Christian morality, but at the same time it provides a salutary contrast to the rule of the saints, whether the saints be represented by Savonarola, Habbakuk Mucklewrath, Comrade Stalin or Ayatollah Khomeini. It remains in moderate and pleasing contrast to the kind of society predicated by the current Moderator of the General Assembly of the Church of Scotland or, for that matter, by the Alternative Service Book of the Church of England. These draw the picture of a dualism between the 'common good' or the 'good of the community' and the 'interests of the individual', the 'profit motive', 'market forces' or whatever. In this dualism the good of the community must always be placed first in priority, and the individual enjoined for the good of his immortal soul always to subordinate his own 'interests' to this purely imaginary abstraction of the 'common good'.

A moment's reflection will show that this imaginary picture is false precisely because it is based on a totally false perception of the nature of law and the true purpose of political authority. The 'community' is made up of individuals – individuals liable to sin, and much in need of grace, repentance and forgiveness. But one of the main purposes of law and lawful authority in any moderately decent society is precisely to protect the rights of the individual, or the minority group, against the rulers of the state – the weak against the strong, the rich, the powerful and the many, even if these, as is very frequently the case, represent a majority or a dominant interest.

Like all dualistic philosophies of politics the fallacy consists in drawing a sharp line between the individual viewed as an atomic entity and the community viewed as a separate entity, equally atomic in character and set over and against the individual. The community consists of individuals. But it also consists of a vast number of minor communities such as the family, the nation, the religious denomination, the school, the regiment, the limited liability company, the town, the county, the region, the university, the study group, the profession, the Boy Scouts, the Mothers' Union or the pigeon-fanciers. Indeed, there is an endless variety of ways in which free men, women, and children can fall (or organise themselves) into groups, and these internal communities by no means form the ultimate entities into which the human race is combined or subdivided. Each and all of these relationships must be recognised by law or custom. Each and all of them are on occasion placed in opposition to one another and, when they are in opposition, each and all must be regulated by some sort of rule, which we dignify by the name of law and to which, to a greater or lesser extent, we must give some degree of compulsive force if we are to live together in peace and harmony without falling into one or both of the equal and opposite evils of anarchy and tyranny. Cicero was nearer the truth, and for that matter to the essentials of Christianity, than the Moderator or the ASB when, in defence of natural rights, he wrote (*de Legibus* 1.43): *natura propensi sumus ad diligendos homines, quod fundamentum juris est* (we have a natural propensity to love our fellow man, and that, after all, is the foundation of all law). *Per se*, the worship of the individual, the state, the class, the community, the religious denomination, is a form of idolatry, and therefore a breach of the first and great commandment, which of course is 'thou shalt love the Lord thy God with all thy heart, and with all thy soul, and with all thy mind, and with all thy strength' and 'him only shalt thou serve'. The second is of the same sort, which is, 'Thou shalt love thy neighbour as thyself.' But 'thy neighbour' remains an individual, made in the image of God, and the individual so created is also a member of a vast number of different and overlapping associations, natural and voluntary, none of which is entitled to an absolute or undivided fealty.

We seem to have travelled a long way from our inimitable friend, Albert Haddock. But we must take an even further detour before we may come full circle. St Augustine of Hippo drew a familiar distinction between the City of God and the City of this world. This distinction has a respectable pedigree, and has spawned a host of legitimate or illegitimate offspring from then until the present time. It goes right back to the gospels: 'My kingdom is not of this world: if my kingdom were of this world, then would my servants fight'; 'Render unto Caesar the things which are Caesar's; and unto God the things that are God's'; 'the kingdom of God is within you'. These are not words to be treated lightly. But they must be viewed in context. Augustine's *Civitas Dei* is a voluntary association and we do not all belong to it. We elect, or are elected, to belong to it. But, like the unitary family, the *Civitas terrena* is a natural society. In the nature of things we have a father and a mother and, in practice, a nationality. We do not choose our parents nor our domicile of origin nor, in the first place, our nationality. We are all members of these, and other, societies which we did not choose to join and whose laws and customs we are expected to observe.

But there are two, and related, further distinctions in Augustine's Tale of Two Cities. The *Civitas Dei* is governed by the laws of morality. It assumes free-will in its members, and operates on their consciences, which it enjoins: 'Be ye perfect even as your Father in heaven is perfect.' In other words, nothing is an acceptable goal short of moral perfection. In contrast, the City of this world deals in sticks and carrots, that is, suasions and disincentives such as we usually apply to donkeys. It certainly does not aim at perfection. *Pace* Lord Atkin in Donoghue v. Stevenson, there is no law which says: 'Thou shalt love thy neighbour as thyself.' Far more than the *Civitas Dei*, the *Civitas terrena* is concerned with externals rather than with motivation. It usually limits its prohibitions and commands to acts of external conduct. Its criteria characteristically involve the social consequences of acts and omissions. It presupposes a conventional morality, and a level of acceptance far lower than that prescribed by the *Civitas Dei*. It is based on the art of the possible, and its limitations are confined within the bounds of enforceability.

There can be no one-for-one relationship between the absolute morality of Antigone and the prohibitions of

Creon, and, lamentably, the unfortunate individual, the toad under the harrow, must sometimes choose which of the two divergent laws he means to obey. Nevertheless it would be wrong to suppose that the state, the *Civitas terrena*, has no concern with virtue, nor that the standards of virtue that it recognises are or should be incompatible with the standards of virtue prescribed by the *Civitas Dei*: 'I am come to fulfil the law, every jot and tittle, and not destroy it'. No one who belongs to the Church of England, enslaved so long to the ludicrous doctrines of passive obedience and the Divine Right of Kings, can afford to assert that we have no obligation ordinarily to obey the laws of the state whether we agree with them or not. When Mr Bumble said 'The Law is a Hass', he was protesting against a law which prohibited him from committing particularly mean and nasty frauds against the innocent and the unprotected.

Where, it seems to me, that the modern cleric goes astray is in his failure to come to terms with parliamentary democracy, which does in fact provide some rational and moral basis for respect for authority irrespective of differing political opinions. No more arguments, please, about Hitler or 'unjust laws'. Some laws are so obviously unjust that we cannot obey them. But they are few and far between in a free society, and when, for conscience' sake, we have to disobey, we must accept the consequences without too much posturing in front of the cameras.

It was said the other day that the Archbishop of Canterbury came to No. 10 Downing Street and protested against leading Conservatives criticising bishops (one of whom has denied the Virgin Birth and the physical resurrection) when, in the name of religion, they enter into the realm of controversial party politics. He might, at least in my case, have added to the category of those being criticised moderators past and present of the Kirk's Assembly, and indeed the professional clergy of all religious denominations.

It has, however, to be pointed out, with due deference, that nothing in the training, education, or intellectual attainments of the professional clergy as such justifies the belief that they are any more qualified than the average voter of any religion or none to pontificate on controversial political questions, and that every time they do so both the average voter and, for that matter anyone else interested, is entitled to give them a riposte to each of their various claims. The only basis for their intervention in a parliamentary democracy into the stormy seas of party controversy is their undoubted right as citizens of the *Civitas terrena* in a free society to talk as loudly as they choose on any subject they choose, however muddleheaded or nonsensical their political views may be, and to invoke the sacred name of St Albert Haddock as they jump off Hammersmith Bridge. But they should remember three very simple propositions before they do so. In the first place, every syllogism requires a minor as well as a major premiss, and if the minor premiss, which usually consists in factual analysis or questions of degree, is wrong, the conclusion is vitiated. Secondly, they also owe a duty, which they do not always perform, to put the dignity and sanctity of their own calling above their private and idiosyncratic views, however much weight (or the reverse) these may be entitled to command. The same also applies to synods, conferences, and other gatherings operating in the field of religion. Their function is to save souls and preach the Gospel, and they should get their priorities right before they offend the consciences of their neighbours by public utterances such as some of those made by the Bishop of Durham.

The third proposition which bishops should bear in mind is that they have a clear duty not to misrepresent their opponents. Contrary to what they suggest, no political party, least of all the Conservatives, believes in the untrammelled rights of the individual or the uncontrolled operation of market forces. Speaking as a Conservative I can say with confidence that we believe in freedom under law, by which, as I have said, I mean freedom responsibly exercised under just laws impartially administered. Most Conservatives believe that, over the past forty years, and under the influence of Socialist collectivism, the pendulum has been allowed to swing too far against the freedom of the individual and in favour of the intrusive state. This may or may not be right. But it is not necessary either to be a Christian or to abandon Christianity to believe this, and, in as much as this is a matter of factual analysis and judgment and not a matter of faith or morals, I doubt whether the professional clergy have very much of value to add to the debate. If they do so, they should, I think, remember that the longest single period in the life on earth of the founder of our religion was spent in a carpenter's shop, which operated, so far as one can tell, for profit (but without sin) either under his reputed father or under his own management. Most political judgments are matters of degree, fact and opinion and have no bearing at all on the salvation of individual souls or the verities enshrined in the Nicene Creed, always provided that those who make them arrive at their conclusions honestly, humbly and in good faith. To say of an honest political leader, however wrong he or she is believed to be, that his or her policies are 'wicked' is, apart from anything else, a sin against charity, and therefore against the light. It should also be remembered that at the inn the Good Samaritan spent his own money, and did not complain that the Treasury did not provide the extra *denarii* required out of the rates and taxes. In the *Civitas terrena*, the City of this world, we are all equals, and sky pilots should remember that if anything they are less equal than many others.

3

The Tension of the 1980s

Ronald Butt

PERHAPS the most remarkable thing about this book is that the idea for it should ever have been conceived. Fifty, thirty or even fifteen years ago it would have been taken as axiomatic that the Conservative Party regarded the Anglican Church as providing the moral cement of society. Correspondingly, the Anglican Church could look with a certain tacit satisfaction on the Conservative Party as implicitly committed to uphold the general tenets of the Christian religion. Of course, there were religious sceptics among Conservatives, many of whom could be regarded, in the words with which Lord Melbourne was said to have described his own position, not as pillars of the Church but as buttresses supporting it from the outside. Nevertheless, to Conservatives generally, whatever the degree of their personal theological commitment, Christian values provided a necessary ethical and spiritual foundation for the body politic. A broad community of interests and understanding enfolded the Tories and the Christian sect which had been established by law as the Church of England.

Between the Conservative Party and other Christian denominations, however, there was no such direct historical tie. During the nineteenth century, religious Nonconformity was more closely associated with Liberalism and it also played a part in the evolution of the Labour movement. Although a few nineteenth-century Anglicans were categorised as Christian Socialists, most notably the theologian F. D. Maurice and Charles Kingsley, it was essentially from the chapels of Nonconformity that the emerging Labour Party drew religious support. This, however, was not so much a product of theological theory as of the matter of fact that chapels and Methodism were the religious habitat of many of the working people who provided Labour's early leadership. Nonconformity was therefore disposed to be critical of the Anglican-Tory connection as well as of the particular religious forms of the Church of England. The fact remained, nevertheless, that a belief in a society broadly guided by Christian moral principles, as they had been long understood, was engrained in Conservative thinking, which took it for granted that Church and State should walk hand in hand.

Overt religious scepticism or positive rejection of Christianity were more often to be found on the other side of politics. Despite the origin in Christian principles of one strand of Socialist tradition (the generally respected Archbishop Temple of Canterbury was one of a number of ecclesiastics in our own century who have exemplified this tradition) many in the Labour Party, and perhaps the majority of its intellectuals, have explicitly rejected Christianity on rational grounds closely related to their politics. An intellectual espousal of agnosticism, if not atheism, has been an essential concomitant of their Socialism. To some, who were not restricted only to those most fully committed to Karl Marx, religion was simply the opium of the people, used to distract them with the idea of a heaven hereafter from the more attainable condition of a Socialist heaven on earth. To many more, religion was simply irrelevant to the true goal of a fairer society. That remains a fair description of the attitude to religion of many and perhaps the majority of 'activists' in the Labour Party today. The difference in historical attitudes is perhaps symbolised by the fact that whereas the Conservatives have always begun their annual party conference with a religious service, the Labour Party has never done so.

The comparatively neat symmetry of the relationship between religious and political attitudes has, however, been shattered during the ten years since Mrs Thatcher formed the first of the three Conservative governments in which she has been Prime Minister. As prominent churchmen have increasingly tended to compromise on the theological and ethical doctrines which have been regarded as essential to Christianity for about two thousand years, many of them have been more willing to declare publicly their religious conviction that the economic and social policies pursued recently by the Conservatives in power have been inimical to Christian ethics. They have been prepared to give ground on traditional Christian teaching, particularly in respect of personal morality, in order to ensure that the Church should not be too out of step with what is regarded as the prevailing climate of secular (including non-Christian) opinion. Yet many in the prevailing school of thinking in the Church have displayed remarkable religious certainty in asserting that the policies pursued by the Conservative governments elected since 1979 have been morally flawed and have tended to promote a selfish and callous society incompatible with Christian principles. On this matter, churchmen have spoken as though with a kind of *magisterium* and as if they had the revealed authority of the Church for censuring the Government.

This tendency has been persistently criticised by Dr Graham Leonard, the Bishop of London, most forcefully in an interview in the *Daily Telegraph* of 20 September, 1989. Here he observed that, on the one hand, there had been 'the attempt to *domesticate* God: to make him amenable to what we think are the best ways of solving the world's problems. In worship, it is this lack of awe and reverence which has been most noticeable . . .' On the other hand, 'all kinds of things on which Christians may legitimately differ have been made of first-order importance'. This, he suggested, had been 'the great undermining of the Church of England', which had hitherto insisted on fundamentals.

Dr Leonard illustrated the point by observing that to be opposed to apartheid was not inevitably to be in favour of sanctions against South Africa: 'and yet sanctions have been presented as though they were an article of faith necessary for salvation'. He drew the conclusion that the Church was now seen as 'almost a hobby, something for insiders' which 'unchurched' many people. 'I think that it's become increasingly difficult for ordinary lay people to feel a love and loyalty for the Church of England.'

I have quoted the Bishop of London at some length because, such is the current mood within the established Church (and also, in varying degrees in some of the other Churches), that any criticism of churchmen's attacks on the government is usually dismissed, with some contempt, as representing nothing more than the sensationalism of the media and the self-interested complaints of the politicians criticised. It is said to be only right for the policies of government to be subjected to moral judgment by the clergy. There is, nevertheless, also a significant segment of opinion, clerical and lay, within the Church which shares the Bishop of London's view of the matter. But those who do so feel overwhelmed by the weight of contrary sentiment in the places of power in the Church – and particularly in the House of Bishops.

The Politics of Durham and Canterbury

The most prominent exemplification of a critique which apparently puts the 'Church' into a position that can be identified with that of a secular political outlook hostile to Conservative policy has, of course, been that of the Right Rev. David Jenkins, Bishop of Durham. The climax of his long-running attack on the Government's conduct of public affairs was perhaps reached in a radio interview on Easter Sunday, 1988, in which he described the Government's economic and social policies as 'wicked'. A number of Dr Jenkins' fellow bishops left no room for doubt immediately afterwards that, even if they regarded his choice of words

as ill-advised, they were generally sympathetic to his sentiments, particularly insofar as these appeared to be directed
particularly at changes that had been made not long before
in the social security system.

Yet these alterations in the allocation of social security
benefits had been made on the grounds that they were
necessary to concentrate the limited amount of available
money more effectively where the need was greatest. Of
course, any such changes were bound to mean that some
beneficiaries under the former arrangements would lose to
some extent in order that others in greater need should
receive more help. This could only have been avoided if
more extra money could be found, and it was the Government's economic judgment that, given the importance of
resisting inflation in the public interest, this was not feasible. On this premise, the changes in social security
arrangements were seen by the Government as justified by
the obligation incumbent on them to govern and to determine priorities in the general public interest.

In other words, the ministers responsible regarded themselves as acting in the light of a *moral* duty to make the social
security system function more equitably. Their political
critics, on the other hand, disputed the Government's
general social policy, arguing on both economic grounds
and on social principle that more money could and should
be found. That, of course, is largely a technical dispute
about feasibility and it is the kind of argument about public
policy that is proper to party politics in a parliamentary
democracy. But the ecclesiastical censure of the Government's decisions and policies on this and similar occasions
could be regarded as an improper gift of the moral weight of
the Church's approval to one side of what should be a
strictly political dispute. In this particular instance, the
Labour opposition seized eagerly on Dr Jenkins' words to
support its case. Defending the Bishop's 'right to speak out
as he did,' the Labour Party's deputy leader, Mr Roy
Hattersley, said: 'Wicked is too mild a word to describe this
knowing, deliberate, calculated cutting down of the poor's

lifeline. I call it downright immoral.' (In Mr Hattersley's vocabulary the more eschatological word 'wicked' apparently ranks as less strong than the looser everyday word 'immoral'.)

The Bishop had thus, whether intentionally or not, placed himself (not for the first or last time) on one side of a political dispute, which on this occasion was concerned with how economic resources should best be used to meet the criterion of need accepted by all parties. (In October 1989, during the Conservative Party's annual conference, Dr Jenkins also denounced administrative changes the Government intended to make in the Health Service. He described them as 'sheer fraud', voicing his own suspicion that they might be a prelude to privatisation of the NHS, despite the Government's categorical assurance that they were not.) But if Dr Jenkins were no more than an exceptionally outspoken representative of a few prominent Left-sympathising clergymen (in the manner, say, of the late Dr Hewlett Johnson, known to the media of the time as the Red Dean of Canterbury), that would have been of no great importance. The particular significance of the Bishop of Durham's repeated, politically-charged, interventions, which, however, have not been made in declared party-political terms, is that he has been only the most trenchant spokesman of what has increasingly appeared to be the dominant climate of opinion among the upper Anglican clergy.

For example, in March of the same year, 1988, the Archbishop of Canterbury, Dr Robert Runcie, said in a speech to the Free Church Federal Council that the Church had become increasingly 'exposed and isolated' because many politicians had 'retreated from the middle ground'. He interpreted this 'middle ground' as that which most politicians of all parties had, until recently, occupied and he defined it in terms of attachment to the 'welfare state'. He observed that, 'Conservatives like Rab Butler and Harold Macmillan had no major difficulty with the idea of the welfare state,' and added: 'Christian leaders such as

Archbishop Temple spoke for almost all Christians and almost all parliamentarians in welcoming the welfare state's common Christian principles. *But the Churches today, while they still hold to these convictions, find the wider political consensus has disappeared.'*

Although the Archbishop made no direct reference to the present Government, he could hardly have made clearer his opinion that it was the Conservative administration led by Mrs Thatcher which had abandoned a consensus based on Christian principles, leaving the Church of England in a lonely position defending it, only to be attacked by the errant politicians for doing so. He appealed to his Free Church audience in these words: 'What I want to say today is that we in the Church of England deeply need and value your support for our maintenance of the ideal of a social consensus and the welfare state.' Significantly, he added: 'In the Free Churches you have a longer tradition of being a "loyal opposition". If we in the Church of England are sometimes so perceived, please help us to get used to this prophetic perception.' The Archbishop's use of the word 'perceived' was not uncharacteristic of his mode of expression. It avoided the need to acknowledge outright that the Church had now indeed become a 'loyal opposition' by suggesting only that it was *'perceived'* (by others) to be such. But the whole tenor of his remarks indicated that the Church accepted the role of loyal opposition with some enthusiasm. Being interpreted, his words could only mean that the Archbishop welcomed, on behalf of the Anglican Church, a new role of opposition-mindedness on political issues. By clear implication, he was accepting that this was directed particularly against current Conservative social and economic policy as it had never been before against the policies of either former Conservative or Labour governments.

A further insight into Dr Runcie's mode of thinking was his observation that politicians had abandoned the middle ground, though the Church had not, which seemed to carry the implication that the middle ground is the ground which both the Church and all good politicians ought to inhabit. In ecclesiastical politics, Dr Runcie undoubtedly tries to keep the Church on the middle ground, if that is the appropriate description of the ground on which sufficient consent can, by gradualist methods, be obtained for what he regards as desirable change. Whether the middle ground is always the moral place to be in secular politics is, however, debatable and it is certainly clear that it is no more practicable for all good politicians to inhabit it than it is for everybody to receive an 'average' income. There may well be times in politics when it seems right, in conscience, to take issue with what has been the 'middle ground' of a former consensus which no longer meets changing needs.

Dr Runcie spoke, moreover, as though this role of loyal opposition had been made necessary by a Conservative repudiation of the principles of the welfare state established after the end of the Second World War. Yet the framework of the welfare state has not been altered and no politician now in power has suggested that it should be. Indeed, the Government has been repeatedly attacked by its opponents for seeking to justify its policies by brandishing figures of increased expenditure on welfare, in order to side-step the charge that it has undermined the welfare state by funding that is inadequate in terms of need. The true significance of the figures on social service spending and the propriety of the Government's use of them is, of course, open to legitimate political debate. But whether the Government is to be praised for spending more on welfare in real money terms, or censured for failing to meet rising need by assigning a declining proportion of the gross national product to welfare, its actions have been only on the margin of the welfare state. The basic and central principle and structure of welfare provision have remained unchanged, whether in respect of health care, pensions, unemployment support or social security.

Yet the Archbishop of Canterbury's argument did not merely imply that there had been a fundamental departure from the welfare state in principle. His criticisms, like those of other churchmen who share his general view of the Government's policies, conspicuously lacked any significant acknowledgment of the reality that, since resources are finite and potential needs are limitless, the details of welfare allocation have to be adjusted from time to time to meet new priorities in changed circumstances. It is particularly noteworthy that ecclesiastical criticism of the Government's alleged parsimony towards social spending, compared with the accepted attitudes prevailing before 1979, has made little or no allowance for the exceptional inflationary circumstances (and the resultant social and economic disorder) in which the Conservative Government took office in 1979. Nor has criticism from inside the Church acknowledged the changed public consensus in 1979, which had come to recognise a new, urgent and overriding priority for government: the eradication (or at least the substantial reduction) of the inflation which had eroded the living standards of so many people and had reached a point at which social stability itself was being undermined. Harold Macmillan and Rab Butler may indeed have had no difficulty, as Dr Runcie put it, with the welfare state. But they also had no gargantuan inflation to deal with comparable to that which confronted the incoming Conservative Government of 1979 – as, indeed, it had the previous Labour Government under the then Mr James Callaghan.

Attacks on the Conservative Government's policy, far from being confined to a few bishops, had become so frequent at all levels in the Church by the beginning of Mrs Thatcher's third term of office that, in an attempt to restore some kind of understanding between churchmen and politicians about the Government's thinking, she invited a number of bishops to Chequers for discussions at the end of 1987. This meeting did not become public knowledge until the following February. It then emerged from some who had been present that, whereas the churchmen considered that there had been a backsliding in *public* morality with regard to social provision, the Prime Minister saw the essential problem as a decline in *personal* morality, for the

revival of which there was now an urgent need. She therefore expressed the hope that the Churches would play a
part in encouraging a personal moral revolution alongside
the economic revolution that was in progress.

The first publicised response of some of the bishops to
this meeting seemed to be guardedly receptive. There was
some agreement that the time was perhaps ripe for a
renewed emphasis on personal morality. But the *rap-
prochement*, if that is the right word for it, did not last long.
In a pre-Easter and post-Budget interview with the BBC TV
programme *Panorama* on 29 March, 1988, the Archbishop of
Canterbury returned to his former theme with, if anything,
added emphasis. He did so in the light of reductions just
made in the taxation rates for higher-rate taxpayers. What
he said was an appropriate prelude for the louder trumpet
blast of condemnation of 'wicked' Conservative policies
(referred to above) which was to come from Dr Jenkins a
few days later.

On the matter of personal morality, Dr Runcie demonstrated the disposition for compromise and the refusal to
assert absolutes that has persistently characterised his public utterances in that respect. Saying that he was often asked
to 'give a lead', he replied that he would give one – 'but it
may not always be popular'. It would, he said, 'be a lead
against rigid thinking, a judgmental temper of mind and a
disposition to oversimplify very complex problems'. He
rejected the accusation (made against him in the unhappy
Crockford's Preface) that he was a pragmatist who wanted to
put off questions until someone else made the decision. 'I
am not a pragmatist, but I do recognise that it takes time
and unique patience before you find solutions which are
generally acceptable in the life of the Church,' which, he
added, had to live in unity with Christ amid a variety of
religious and other opinions. (What those words seem to
suggest is that the task of the leaders of the Church is not so
much to promote absolute standards on which personal
morality should be based as to move 'the Church' gradually
towards solutions which are acceptable to its people but

which also do not sit too uncomfortably or provocatively with the ideas of the wider society. It is perhaps a concept with which St Paul might have had some difficulties.) 'That's our vocation,' Dr Runcie continued, 'and despite the difficulty of following it at the present time, when so much is polarised, so much is sensationalised, so much is politicised, it is something I am determined to lead the Church through.'

Many Christians lament the sourness of the controversy between the leaders of the Church and not only the present Government but also those in the Church itself who wish to stay closer to traditional Christian moral teaching than many bishops apparently think necessary. To those who do so, Dr Runcie's charge of sensationalism and politicisation seems misdirected. This accusation can be said to apply at least as much to the abrasive utterances of some senior churchmen as it does to complaining politicians, unhappy laymen or even the media. As for the discussion of personal morality, Dr Runcie's own most generally noted contribution to it on this particular occasion was his statement that a stable homosexual relationship would not be a bar to ordination if it was 'maintained in affection but without the acts which are condemned in the Bible'. His listeners were given no guidance as to the test, confessional or otherwise, by which he proposed to ensure that these conditions were satisfied.

Dr Runcie was, however, much more concrete in the matter of political and social morality. His words left little room for doubt that the discussions at Chequers had not altered the cast of his thinking. The Church, he said, 'might have a moral duty to oppose some of the immigration policies and policies on South Africa. It might have a duty to question the kind of use of the taxation system to reward success rather than to meet social needs which are urgent and crying.' This statement was couched in terms that demonstrated very clearly what it is about the excursions of Church leaders into politics that causes so much deep offence.

In the first place, although Dr Runcie's remarks clearly implied criticism of the present Government's policies in the areas he named, they also wore a camouflage of imprecision. Thus, in speaking of the 'moral duty' that the Church *'might'* have to oppose *'some'* of (the Government's) policies on South Africa, he left wholly unclear the circumstances in which this threat of opposition might be carried out. Of course, the General Synod of the Church of England had already expressed its general support for sanctions, in opposition to the Government's judgment that sanctions would hinder rather than promote the peaceful end of apartheid. But the difference of opinion was over political means, not ethical ends. By suggesting that the 'Church' might come out more assertively against the Government's policies for South Africa, Dr Runcie was making a vague threat of the Church's disapproval of the general direction of policy without being specific about what would actually earn outright condemnation. Since then, the progress made within South Africa towards dismantling apartheid suggests, albeit tentatively, that the Government's political judgment on peaceful ways and means has perhaps been shrewder than that of 'the Church'.

But the Archbishop's remarks also raised a further question. What should be taken as representing the mind of 'the Church' collectively when political matters are at issue? Is it the General Synod or is it the voices of those bishops who choose to speak *ad hoc* in any given situation? (If the latter, which voices are to be taken as the more authoritative where there is conflict? Are (say) the Bishop of Durham's and the Archbishop of Canterbury's pronouncements to be preferred to those of the Bishop of London, and how does the status of any of these compare with the latest votes of the General Synod?) Is it, indeed, feasible at all for 'the Church' to make pronouncements on political matters with any kind of collective authority? Or are the utterances of bishops and other clergy on political topics no more than off-the-cuff personal opinions by individuals, which should deserve no more weight than is given by the quality of their argument and their personal reputation with the public?

Likewise, the Archbishop's observations about taxation begged some very concrete questions, most notably in his reference to the 'kind of use of the taxation system to reward success'. In context, this seemed to relate to the then recently-reduced rate of income tax for higher earners. To the Government, tax-reduction was justified not because those who had already achieved success needed further reward for its own sake, but on the grounds that the policy would encourage more generally the spirit of enterprise and effort, and the attempts to achieve success which are of benefit to society as a whole, including the poor. Whether this justification is correct or not is obviously a matter of political and economic opinion. It is largely a technical question, the answer to which is disputed. But Dr Runcie gave no indication that he even recognised and acknowledged the existence of the technical economic argument advanced in favour of the policy. Nor did he suggest that the Church itself could offer technical reasons for opposing it. His words simply seemed to take it for granted that the policy of cutting taxes for higher earners had the sole purpose of 'rewarding success' as such and that, therefore, the Church might have to oppose it on the moral grounds that it was at the expense of urgent social needs. He assumed a connection between the tax cuts and 'crying' social need which was unmet. Yet though he was clear enough in the *general* direction of his criticisms, he made it quite plain that he did not wish to commit himself by pointing a finger of condemnation at any *particular* current policies. He went on to state that he had not said all this 'over a particular issue at this moment'. Yet even after this qualification, he again used words which suggested that he was having it both ways, adding: 'Nevertheless the Church has to be concerned about those who have been the casualties of success in other quarters and those left behind, particularly in such areas as health and education.' In effect, he was saying that he was not referring to anything specific while also identifying, even though in broad terms, the 'left behind' health service and education as being among 'the casualties of success'.

To many, this general approach seems unacceptably political. Nobody questions that the misgivings of Dr Runcie and other clergy about the Government's policies are rooted in their perception of the best way to approach their Christian purposes. Their attitude is based on their Christian concern for those in need. The reason for questioning what they say is not mistrust of their motives or intentions. It is rather that they seem to have been so heavily conditioned by the received opinion of the pre-1979 secular consensus on *political method* that they can now see no technical, economic or political approach to the problems of meeting need other than to return to the assumptions and methods politically dominant in the years before 1979. In practical terms, this approach often comes perilously close to an endorsement of the thinking of the political parties opposed to the Conservatives. It is certainly a fact that leading figures in those parties, whatever their own religious agnosticism, have been quick to call these clerical pronouncements to their own aid.

It is almost as though adherence to pre-1979 social and economic assumptions and practices has become an article of faith in the thinking of the most influential churchmen, to be used as a point of reference in almost all political eventualities. Demands for social spending seem to override all other considerations and those who are in need are seen simply as the direct sufferers from the success of others. Little merit, or benefit for *society as a whole*, appears to be discerned in material success or endeavour. In many ecclesiastical messages, sermons and parish magazines, both are often described pejoratively as 'materialism'. Nor has it been only in the last few years that criticisms have been directed by the Church at both the Government's policies and at the ethics of the materialistically 'successful' society which the Government's policies have encouraged. Since virtually the beginning of the Conservatives' present period of office, there have been clerical attacks on the Government's policies, including, for instance, on the British Nationality Act, the policy on sanctions against South Africa, nuclear defence, the handling of the miners' strike, monetarism and, most persistently, social policy, inner city deprivation and unemployment.

The report *Faith in the City*, produced by the Archbishop of Canterbury's Commission on Urban Priority Areas, was in many ways the high-water mark of systematic criticism of the Government's policies. Published in 1985, just before unemployment began what was to be a dramatic and consistent fall as a consequence of renewed economic growth, the report acknowledged that the Church of England had neither the mandate nor the competence to 'solve' the problem of unemployment. But it asserted nevertheless that 'as the national Church' (whatever precisely that means at a time when the Anglican Communion is smaller than that of the Roman Catholic Church in England) it had 'a particular duty to act as the conscience of the nation. It must question all economic philosophies, not least those which, when put into practice, have contributed to the blighting of whole districts, which do not offer the hope of amelioration, and which perpetuate the human misery and despair to which we have referred.' The Church, according to the report, must question the *morality* (their italics) of these philosophies from its own standpoint. Referring to the assumption of current economic policies that 'prosperity can be restored if individuals are set free to pursue their own economic salvation' (a curiously loaded and sardonic turn of phrase) the report, which was much criticised for its political slant, asserted categorically and in italics that: *'We believe that at present too much emphasis is being given to individualism, and not enough to collective obligation.'*

How widespread has been the propagation of these ideas from the pulpit is impossible to quantify and it is certainly disputed. But on a purely impressionistic judgment, the views of the clerical critics seem to have had some considerable success in moulding the outlook of many in church congregations. In an article on 'Politics and the Church', which appeared in the *Yorkshire Post* of 18 October, 1983, a 'country rector in the Ripon diocese' who (significantly) 'thought it prudent to remain anonymous' was reported as saying that, 'average Anglican preaching today is rather like *Guardian* readers talking to *Telegraph* readers'. (It was not the only occasion on which variants of this simile have appeared.) Since 1983, however, just as the *Daily Telegraph* has modified its former right-wing position, so also there are signs that the kind of social vocabulary to be heard from the pulpit, and expressed in *Faith in the City*, is now echoed more frequently among the more active members of the laity. How far this is because they have been conditioned by the tide of clerical opinion, and how far it indicates that laymen who are uncomfortable with the prevailing view in the Church are less inclined to put themselves forward for active roles, can only be a matter of guesswork.

Churchmen who make political or economic pronouncements which are subsequently invalidated by events are, however, always in danger of putting their credibility at some risk. This was demonstrated by the then Bishop of Lincoln, the Right Rev. Simon Phipps, when he spoke to the General Synod on unemployment in November 1984. Having acknowledged the success of the Government's policies in bringing down inflation, he blamed these policies for the side-effect of unemployment. Asserting that 'it was not enough just to say, as the Government does, that the revival of the economy, on the basis of greater efficiency, will produce the jobs required to reduce unemployment,' he went on to say that the free market could not 'bear the full implication of our employment situation' and advocated a new initiative which might well include a 'judicious element of reflation . . .'

In retrospect, those remarks illuminate with singular clarity the nature of the general tension between the Church and the politicians in power. They were made in good faith and in moderate terms by a bishop with a long-standing interest in industrial relations. But they advocated a particular kind of economic action which, in the light of subsequent developments, would certainly seem to have been misguided. For the new and more 'efficient' economy to which the bishop referred *did* in fact produce more jobs and, soon afterwards, unemployment began to fall steadily, so much so that in many parts of the country there developed labour shortages. What the Bishop of Lincoln had done was to take a position in a strictly economic argument about the best means of reducing unemployment, and to appear to lend the spiritual weight of a bishop's words to the economic opinions of the Government's political opponents, which, as it happened, were shortly afterwards disproved by events.

Furthermore, there is some ambiguity about what 'the Church' regards as the main target of its general criticisms. How far is it speaking against the Government's policies as such and how far is it addressing the personal shortcomings of those who benefit most in material terms from the Conservative Government's encouragement of individual success? In his remarks (referred to above) made at Easter 1987, Dr Runcie seemed to have the Government's policies firmly in his sights. But in a later interview, addressed to businessmen and given to the *Director* magazine in October 1989, he appeared to be concerned mostly with the individual consciences of those who enjoy the most material benefit from those policies. Saying that he 'believed in wealth creation', Dr Runcie also asserted the incontestable Christian principle that there is 'no *automatic* connection between wealth creation and a happy society'. But he also went on to make the more sweeping statement that he 'sensed' an increasing danger in society that the successful, like the Pharisees, most of whom also led 'lives of exemplary moral rectitude', were being tempted to make uncharitable and untrue judgments about the unsuccessful, the unemployed and the poor, as though their condition were their own fault and as though success was 'a sort of blessing or reward for righteousness'. Whether there is sufficient evidence to support Dr Runcie's impression that this kind of attitude is increasing is debatable. Even so, if he had said no more than that, his remarks could be regarded as simply a reminder to the rich of their moral obligations to the poor and of the particular spiritual risks that wealth inevitably brings. But he did not leave his argument there.

For one thing, he clearly seemed to be using his warning against the pharisaical temptations of the self-righteously wealthy as a rebuke to those who argue that the Church should do more to stress *personal* as distinct from *social* morality. In other words, he appeared to regard the call for more stress on personal morality as pharisaical, that is to say, as uncharitably censorious. The Church, he said, often met the challenge from a 'section of our political and commercial leadership' that they had 'made people wealthy' and that it was 'the Church's job to make them good'. That, said Dr Runcie, was not the Church's view of its task, which was to 'make people godly', godliness and goodness not being the same thing. The Archbishop elaborated this by saying that 'Jesus reserved his most astringent criticism for the Pharisees, most of whom, far from being unscrupulous and double-dealing, led lives of exemplary moral rectitude . . . He disliked their self-righteous and judgmental attitudes.'

Yet it is far from being the case that those who stress the need for greater personal morality are generally either well off themselves or self-righteously pharisaical. Dr Runcie's words travestied the real source and nature of the criticisms made against church leaders for their failure to offer more certain guidelines to assist personal responsibility. It is not from the politicians and the 'commercial leaders' who have 'made people wealthy' that such criticism generally comes. Nor is it usually the materialistic high-earners in their thirties (whom Dr Runcie specifically said he suspected of lacking a sense of responsibility for the 'left-behinds' and whom he seemed particularly to cast in the role of judgmental Pharisees) who complain that the Church speaks with insufficient firmness on standards of personal morality. The criticism that the Church compromises and pulls its punches in this respect is far more deep rooted than that and comes from many ordinary people who are not much concerned with the argument between the Conservatives and the Church on political matters. Those who ask the Church to be as forthright and active in its teaching on personal morality as it is on social and political action do not generally do so because they are self-righteously condemning the sinner, but because they believe that if the Church were more precise in giving firm principles for guidance it could help at least some people to avoid the sin and its consequential unhappiness.

Complaints that the Church has lacked conviction in advancing clear and unambiguous principles of personal morality are motivated in large measure by the practical consideration that a Church which (to give a single example) retreats from its ancient teaching on divorce and remarriage, and now even wishes to allow the marriage service to be conducted by clergy who have been ordained when they themselves are already divorced, is failing to give, even to its own flock, the guidance which can help to overcome the temptations which multiply unhappiness. That is not an argument of self-righteous Pharisees. The case against the Church is that, through an over-indulgent sense of compassion, it appears to set the seal of its tolerance on the conduct of those who feel entitled to adjust their morality as they go along to suit their own interest. But Dr Runcie was content to dismiss emphasis on personal morality as pharisaical; he did not address himself to the concern of those who fear that the Church's attitude comes near to conniving at flexible standards of personal morality which diminish human happiness. He preferred to dismiss the concern for personal morality as pharisaical.

So, while the Church rebukes the Government for insufficient social concern, it is itself rebuked by many for allowing its own standards to be modified under the influence of the contemporary ethical fashion of moral subjectivity, which often leads to the break-up of family life, denying children the stable background which is the basis of a kindly and healthy society. It must, of course, be added straightaway that between the charge that the Church gives infirm guidance on the personal conduct required of a Christian and the separate allegation that churchmen are too prone to intervene in politics, there is no essential connection or even logical contradiction. If the Church's political interventions could be shown to be justified intrinsically and objectively, they would not be invalidated by any shortcomings in its message to individuals. Nevertheless, it is clear enough why some people should feel with regret that the Church now devotes to social activity too much of the fervour it would once have directed to personal morality.

One final observation must be made on the Archbishop's remarks to the *Director* magazine. Though his comments were on this occasion mainly directed towards well-off individuals who were insufficiently charitable to the poor, Dr Runcie still did not altogether leave the Government out of it. Though he emphasised that the 'tensions' between Church and Government were not as evident as they were made to seem in the popular press, he also observed that there were 'some differences between us'. Remarking that 'the present Government supports a view of society in which an individual's rights and duties are enhanced,' and acknowledging that this was also part of the Christian ethic, he added that, 'the Church always balances this with its understanding of Christians belonging to one another'. That, he said, gave 'a corporate dimension to our faith and ethics, which is bound sometimes to be at variance with a highly individualistic approach'. This remark can only have been intended to imply that the Government lacked sufficient understanding of the 'corporate dimension', which, however, the Church could supply. Dr Runcie made this point by remarking that the Church was in daily contact with people in 'areas where the Conservative Party had little support'.

Mrs Thatcher's Creed

I have dwelt on Dr Runcie's comments on the tensions of the 1980s not only because he is the Primate of All England but because he has expressed himself on these matters in greater detail than anyone else, seeking with candour and moderation to explain the Church's critical position. It is also in the light of these tensions that the controversial speech given by Mrs Thatcher to the Church of Scotland in May 1988 must be assessed. That speech is printed as an appendix to this book and its gist can be summarised very briefly as follows: Christianity concerns the spiritual rather than the social but the two are not separate. Human beings must work to create wealth, but making money must not be a selfish activity. Christians can disagree about social institutions but, whatever these institutions are, they should be based on the acceptance of individual responsibility. There must be laws providing for such social needs as health, education, pensions and help for the elderly, the sick and disabled. But the intervention of the state (through taxation, for instance) should never be so great as to remove all personal responsibility. What matters most is how individuals use their money; it is a Christian duty for individuals to help their fellow men: '. . . it is not the creation of wealth that is wrong but love of money for its own sake.'

Though Mrs Thatcher's statement of her convictions included a strong assertion of individual responsibility to the poor, it unleashed upon her bitter attacks from within the Church as well as in the House of Commons. A public letter signed by the chairman of the General Synod's Board for Social Responsibility, the Bishop of Gloucester, and by its secretary, Prebendary (now Provost) John Gladwin (whose chapter follows this one), declared that social harmony was threatened by 'deep divisions and injustices' in society. It asked whether it was not 'unrealistic' to claim that the needs of the poor could be met by individual acts of charity. The letter also stated that 'justice and generosity apply to governments as well'. Yet (whatever the merits of the general line of economic argument advanced by 'the Church') it is hard to discover in Mrs Thatcher's address any suggestion that the needs of the poor *could* be met *completely* by individual charity, which the phrasing of the letter seemed to imply was her position. On the contrary, she referred specifically to the obligations of the Government to provide for those in need.

Likewise, when the letter went on to say that there was a duty to resist the popular myth that the poor were feckless, greedy and lazy, it was surely attacking a myth that was more in the imagination of the writers than in that of most of those who have been critical of the Church's political utterances. Mrs Thatcher was reminded in the letter of the analogy between the difficulty of a camel trying to pass through a needle's eye and that of a rich man seeking to enter the Kingdom of Heaven. Yet her address had emphasised the spiritual obligations of the rich to the poor. Indeed, her main point seemed to be that though society, through the state, had a fundamental obligation to the poor, it should not take so much on to itself by means of taxation that it both stifled individual initiative in wealth creation and also left no scope for individual voluntary giving. It may well be that her critics dispute the proposition that it is morally desirable to leave plenty of scope for voluntary giving. If so, it was open to the writers of the letter from the Board of Social Responsibility to do so. They did not, however, argue this. Instead, the letter asked the astonishing question whether 'governments accept upon behalf of us all in society a responsibility to play – and to be seen to be playing – a crucial and inescapable part in the fight against these enemies of the human, namely poverty, unemployment, victimisation and distress'.

Taking the words used at face value, this hardly seems to be a question with rational meaning, bearing in mind the scale of social spending to which any government, Conservative or Labour, is committed today. This obligation is indeed 'inescapable' in the sense that no government can, or seeks, to escape it. So the question of whether governments recognise a need for them to play 'a crucial and inescapable part' in fighting poverty and unemployment seems simply to ignore the political facts for the sake of making a rhetorical point. Whether or not *enough* funding is provided for social purposes at any particular time is certainly a debatable question, the answer to which depends on what constitutes enough and on what proportion of resources should be made available for the purpose. Ultimately, however, answers to the question must hang on differing opinions about how relative needs are to be assessed, given limited resources.

It is hard to read the words used by the Board for Social Responsibility in any sense that does not condemn them of exaggeration for the purpose of making a point against the particular way in which the present Government has judged it economically appropriate and socially fair to formulate policy. The statement that 'justice and generosity apply to governments as well as individuals' also prompts the comment that 'generosity' is never quite the right word to apply to government funding, since the money disbursed belongs not to the politicians disbursing it but to the taxpayers to whom the politicians are answerable. Indeed, perhaps the least of the reasons for a government to be generous is 'to be *seen*' to be playing a part fighting poverty since it is only too easy for politicians to bid for electoral popularity by being seen to use public money.

The letter from the Board also asserts that 'wealth acts as a barrier to the Kingdom if it encourages total self-reliance and independence, tempting people to believe that they are masters of their own destiny'. It is, of course, a statement of the obvious that wealth brings particular temptations, just as poverty or intellectual superiority do; and the temptations of wealth are perhaps the greatest of all because they are so often not recognised for what they are. Yet a logical inference from the words used seems to be that it would be positively desirable for every individual to have some degree of financial dependence. That, however, would seem to indicate a particular kind of political relationship between the individual and the state and to raise questions about desired political systems which would seem to go far beyond the remit of the Board. They are certainly matters too fundamental to be considered here. The letter, it is true, prefaced its observations with the proviso that none could take exception to Mrs Thatcher's stress on personal responsibility. It also conceded that wealth was not evil in itself. Nevertheless, the tone of the letter as a whole was deeply, if politely, critical of Mrs Thatcher's attempt to explain her political philosophy and of her emphasis on the charitable function of each individual. As a coda to these reactions to the Prime Minister's speech to the Church of Scotland, it should perhaps be noted that the Methodist Conference in the same month went on to 'declare its sense of outrage' at the way the Government's policies were increasing the wealth of the rich 'at the expense of the poor'.

Church and Politics

Several broad questions and issues emerge from the differences between the Government and the Church which have been described in this account. Does criticism of the approach of churchmen carry any implication that they should hesitate to speak at all on secular public and political affairs? Given that it is proper for them to do so, what constraints should they impose on themselves? Further, since churchmen have, through much of history, been much more directly and closely involved in politics than they are today, what precisely are the objections to their present mode of doing so? Finally, are there any grounds, in the criticisms directed at the Government led by Mrs Thatcher, for believing that current Conservative social attitudes are intrinsically flawed (or more flawed than those of other political parties) if judged by Christian criteria?

Perhaps the best starting point for considering these questions is a brief reference to the kind of direct role that churchmen have played in politics in the past, which was once very extensive. Throughout the period we call mediaeval, ecclesiastics were political office-holders. They were literate; they were not preoccupied, as lay magnates were, in furthering dynastic ambitions, or (with a few notable exceptions) in trying to control the king; and they could be rewarded cheaply with benefices which already belonged to the Church. They were therefore very suitable for employment as ministers of the crown. With very few exceptions, all the Chancellors and Treasurers of England from the Conquest to the Reformation were bishops, or sometimes deans or archdeacons. These episcopal Chancellors, however, acted strictly as lay politicians, and were judged as such, even though the speeches with which they opened parliaments were usually a mixture of policy statements and sermons. Such disputes as occurred between Church and State before the Reformation largely affected their rival jurisdictions, rather than questions of morality, whether social or individual. There is no evidence, for example, that the clergy ever openly registered objections in principle to the barbaric punishments of the time, even to hanging, drawing and quartering. Suppressing their Christian compassion, they connived at the burning of heretics. They stood aside from the state's right to determine its own penalties according to the brutal customs of the age. In their capacity as Lords in Parliament they were content simply to withdraw from the proceedings when there was a trial of a crime carrying a punishment of blood. Nor is there any evidence that they were particularly concerned with poverty as a *political* issue rather than as a condition which the Church itself had a duty to try to alleviate. Likewise, when ecclesiastics were involved in political disputes in the post-Reformation period (Archbishop Laud, for instance), these were largely concerned with differences of doctrine, principle and order in religion, though they also overlapped with political differences. That the rich must not oppress the poor remained, of course, a theme of Christian preaching, but the social

divisions in the nation, including the stark divisions between the condition of the poor and that of the rich, were
generally accepted.

It was not until the later eighteenth century that some
churchmen of an evangelical persuasion began, hesitantly
at first and in a politically cautious manner, to take an active
interest in remedying some social ills, notably slavery, by
political action. In the nineteenth century, there was also
concern to apply Christian moral criteria to dealing with
certain specific social questions in a political context; Bishop
Samuel Wilberforce's concern for education, the preven-
tion of cruelty to women and children, the reduction of
hours in factories and the more humane treatment of
prisoners were examples. But it can hardly be said that the
clergy were more active than lay Christians (Lord Shaftes-
bury, for example) in seeking remedies for social ills by
political pressure. Above all, there was nothing that gave
the appearance of a crusade by the Church against the
general policies of the government in power or the basic
social structure. The Christian Socialism of F. D. Maurice,
for example, was essentially a product of his theology; it
was an attempt to apply broad Christian principles in
society without prescribing detailed action. Even for those
other, and few, nineteenth-century Christian Socialists
who advocated state control of the economy, the concept of
a Christian society came first. In the twentieth century there
have been some well-known individual members of the
clergy who were identified with particular political positions. But there were no open suggestions from sources
which could be said to represent the Church *as such* that one
political party's set of policies for managing the nation's
affairs conflicted with Christian principles, with the apparent implication that those of an opposing party might be
more virtuous.

It was not until after 1979 that a barrage of complaints and
condemnation which could be interpreted in this way was
aimed at the policies operated by the Government. The
change was particularly great by comparison with the

immediately preceding years, when there had been no comparable complaint against the economic and political practices which had allowed inflation to erode the value of money and social stability, or against the strikes and industrial disorder which caused so much hardship. Nor had any objections on moral grounds been directed against the attempts to remedy inflation by prices and incomes policies (despite their general failure) as there have been against the (generally more successful) attempts to cure inflation by monetarist methods. Before 1979 there was no condemnation of the fall in living standards of those (emphatically not the rich) who had been least able to protect their earnings and savings from losing their value.

The contrast is sharp between the quiescence of the Church on social and economic policy before 1979 and clerical attacks since 1979 on the Government's attempts to solve economic and social problems by a free market, disciplined by the control of money and lower taxation. The opinions of the most influential churchmen appear to have been set hard during the sixties and seventies in adherence to the then conventional methods of economic management, despite the fact that these were no more than the products of one particular school of economic thinking (as fallible as any other) just as today's different policies are. Yet it would have been at least as logical to condemn the policies which before 1979 caused inflation, on the moral grounds that they were equivalent to the social crime of robbing the people by clipping the coinage, as it was to condemn the cure of inflation after 1979 on account of the temporary side-effects of higher unemployment.

It is important to make it clear, however, that the references to the passivity of churchmen in past centuries in the face of barbarities, social or penal, of lay government and society are in no way intended to suggest that it was right for the Church to be as passive as it apparently was. On the contrary, it must be a sign of frailty that the clergy have not been more inclined over the centuries to stand out against cruelty and poverty, or to condemn needless war instead of blessing it, as they often did. The point of these references to the past is simply to show just how sharp a change of ecclesiastical stance is represented by the present disposition of the Church to act politically as a 'loyal opposition'. The change can only be explained by reasoning circumstantially. In the first place, it was much harder in more arbitrary times to contradict the lay power in its own sphere of influence than it is today, when democratic government is an easy target, always assailable by a few quotable remarks which, when uttered by prominent Anglicans, can be guaranteed to make headlines.

The more fundamental explanation, however, is that the leadership of the Church has generally found it no more easy than the laity does to rise above the limitations of contemporary thinking and intellectual fashion. In the more distant past, it passively accepted the tortured deaths and the brutal symbolism of the heads on London Bridge. Centuries later it accepted passively the gibbet as penalty for minor offences and it turned late to the question of slavery and the poverty of the slums. When it has espoused reform, it has usually gone with a generally rising tide. Today, it is true, its thinking is not so much *strictly* up-to-date as heavily conditioned by the social and political ideas of the sixties and seventies. Several reasons can be suggested for this attachment to yesterday's fashion. One is that the formative years in the thinking of many of today's senior clergy were the sixties and seventies. They still adhere to the ideas they formed then. Another explanation is the Church's preoccupation with sociology (for whatever reason) which is itself still dominated by the thinking of the sixties. More broadly, these assumptions have remained strong in the particular parts of the secular intellectual classes with which many of the clergy seem particularly comfortable, notably in the universities, the media of communication and social pressure groups.

None of the foregoing, however, constitutes an argument that churchmen should speak exclusively on ecclesiastical affairs or confine themselves to theology in its strictest sense, avoiding all comment on wider issues. There are, indeed, times when they should be bolder and more independent of secular thinking of all sorts. But if this is so, what kind of constraints should they impose on themselves – and about what should they speak? It is clear that the Church has a duty always to exhort any government to act justly, to safeguard liberty, to express in general terms the duty of society as well as of individuals to care for the poor, the sick, the disabled and the unemployed, and to work for peace. The Church can also properly remind the body politic that, although the success of the most able works for the general good, the majority of people will not achieve 'success' in the conventional sense – and the community must therefore make sure that they are treated fairly. The unambitious and (in commercial terms) the less enterprising make contributions to society which cannot always be assessed in earnable wages. Society also has its duty to those who are for personal reasons inadequate. Further, when any specific social problem becomes apparent, the Church can legitimately remind any government not to lose sight of it amid other political preoccupations.

On those principles, the Church would have been perfectly entitled to remind the present Government of where it felt need was particularly acute and required more attention, just as it would have been justified before 1979 in preaching to individuals, trade unions and governments that inflation required urgent attention as a social evil. What is generally ill-advised is for churchmen to enter political and economic arguments about how precisely such problems should best be dealt with, censuring one set of policies and implying support for another. They can speak freely on moral ends but will be wise to be wary when entering into controversy about ways and means. Above all, it can surely never be right to speak intemperately with broad-brush words and ill-thought-out concepts, or with generalised imperatives which seem to carry overtones of a higher spiritual sanction for economic or political opinions which may be ill-informed.

This said, it is impracticable to try to differentiate with sharp precision between the general social causes and matters of principle to which church leaders should draw attention, and the detailed policy prescriptions over which they should exercise self-restraint. When and how they decide to speak is a matter for their consciences and, hardly less important, their judgment. Each case has to be judged in its own terms. It could, for instance, be argued in some circumstances that to make a general statement of principle on policy without referring to any of the details involved would rightly be censured as indulgence in loose and easy generalities. Misgivings about the way in which 'the Church' has criticised the present Government's actions in no way implies that there is nothing which it should criticise. It is very clear, for instance, that on the margins of the new 'enterprise society' new problems of social hardship have arisen and it is right for the Church to stress the importance of meeting them.

The significant charge against the recent incursions of church leaders into politics is perhaps less that they have spoken outside their proper remit but that the quality and logic of their argument and intervention has often been poor, superficial and imprecise. Indeed, if they had been effective and persuasive, the case against their interventions would have been much less strong. As it is, they have often given the impression of taking sides against the elected government without substantiating their position clearly and convincingly. On occasions, they have conveyed the impression that they were censuring policy on moral grounds while denying they are doing any such thing. On certain issues they have persistently had to fall back on ephemeral politicised formulae (the tactics used in reaching a compromise position on unilateral disarmament was a case in point), so discrediting the Church with the public and dividing churchmen needlessly.

A notable case of misjudgment has been the General

Synod's opposition on moral grounds to the Immigration Acts, including that of 1968 under a Labour Government. Reflecting the intemperate opinion of pressure groups involved with immigration policy and the rooted position of what is called progressive opinion, the General Synod declared these measures to be discriminating against black and brown people. It could do so, however, only because the people who were pressing in excessive numbers for admission happened to be black or brown. Yet the social problems arising from the concentration in urban areas of immigrants from a very sharply different culture would have been virtually the same whatever their colour, and the number would have had to be restrained whatever their racial origin. As it was, the fact that those affected by the Acts were brown or black made it easier to make a false equation between immigration control and racism. Worse, the attacks on these measures took inadequate account of the social purpose behind them: to prevent the exacerbation of racial tensions in urban areas. This was a classic case in which the idealistic theory was preferred, whatever the adverse social consequences, to sensible practice. The issue has illustrated very well the recent tendency for spokesmen for 'the Church' to pronounce in favour of one side of a political argument without giving due weight to the considerations on the other side which are no less concerned with the public good.

When 'the Church' acts in a crudely partisan way it throws away what could be its greatest value in secular public affairs: its opportunity to speak as a trusted, well-regarded referee whose measured words have a special place because it is recognised to be wise, disinterested, sensible and willing to take account of the merits on each side of an argument. It is often only too clear that statements are made which are hasty, ill-reasoned and uncoordinated within the Church itself. If the quality of thought were better, there would have been far less reason to take exception to the Church's interventions on public questions. Above all, the Church should not appear to be throwing the weight of its spiritual authority behind what are inevitably ephemeral political positions. Those who are taken to be speaking for the Church should (to adapt the words used by the Bishop of London about sanctions against South Africa) be particularly careful not to speak as though higher (or lower) taxation, higher (or lower) public spending and looser (or tighter) monetary control are articles of faith; they are nothing more than temporary expedients which need constant adjustment as circumstances change. In other words, the Church should try to avoid sounding judgmental on matters over which it has no special qualifications to judge.

Where it is surely entitled to be more judgmental (in the light of its own founding spirit) than it now chooses to be is in respect of personal morality. But here too it has been inclined to take too much of its inspiration from the secular climate. It is reluctant (as its compromising attitude to marriage has shown) to sail into the wind. Secular ethics today are governed by an obsessive adherence to a non-judgmental social and moral subjectivism. And who can seriously deny that the Church has been influenced by the fact that the greatest social solecism at the end of the twentieth century is to express even a hint of moral disapproval of any form of personal choice, behaviour or relationship, unless it can be categorised as racism or as non-egalitarian? How far this is because many senior churchmen are themselves, through the schools and universities which shaped them, the products of the secular climate must be a matter of opinion. But in both their apparent doubts and their certainties, they are very much people of the secular, largely non-Christian, age.

The final question to be asked is whether it is possible to see anything intrinsically hostile to the Christian tradition in the general direction that Conservative politics have taken during the past decade. Here the cardinal point of reference should surely be that it is a fallacy to see the individual and society as fundamentally at odds with each other. Mankind is born to live in society, which expresses his common nature. Yet the individual is often seen as a largely selfish agent for his own interest, in stark contrast to the official agents of a disinterested and beneficent society acting on behalf of the 'better parts' of all the individuals who comprise it. That was the assumption during the years in which state collectivism dominated thinking on political and social matters, and it still seems largely to colour the opinions of churchmen.

The positive contribution of Socialism to the modern world has been a heightened awareness of the importance of collective responsibility on behalf of the individuals in society. But the adverse consequences of a theory which asserts the superiority of the state collective over the individual have become steadily clearer, not least in Eastern Europe. Its greatest flaw is discouragement of personal responsibility, without which no society can be truly moral. It is as true of adults as it is of children that the best way of encouraging them to behave responsibly is (having provided the right teaching) to give them responsibility. If the state takes from all individuals responsibility for the things that matter most – their children's education, the health care of their family, the provision of housing and the chance of saving for the future – ill will follow.

More people will seek to evade illegally the high taxation required to pay for the state's management of all that matters, or will squander their energy in avoiding it by asserting the letter of the law. The black economy will flourish and social benefits will be more often abused. If there is discontent with the state's monopoly services, there will be no means by which any part of the population can point towards the possibility of attaining higher possible alternative standards by contracting out into self-provision. There will be no neutral measuring rods of efficiency and of helpful service; the servants of the state will be the only judges of the services they themselves provide. Above all, if the state is assumed to have taken over the moral duty of providing all the welfare that matters, many individuals will be less willing than they might have been to work or give charitably. That would be a very serious loss because individual knowledge and personal understanding can often discern need far more effectively than is possible for a bureaucratic apparatus. The development of the hospice movement is telling evidence of this. It is also a reminder of the efficiency with which individuals can form their own collectives outside that of the state. For individual concern to be diminished would, therefore, represent a grave loss to society. Besides, who would dispute that individual giving to others, either of service or money, can often be much warmer and often much more innovative than what is available from a larger and more impersonal bureaucracy?

None of this challenges the basic role of the state and of the community in welfare. What matters is the balance between the moral obligations of the individual and those of society to others. In the post-war years the balance tipped increasingly away from the individual; since 1979, the Conservative Government has sought to redress an imbalance. In doing so, and in its attempt to secure acceptance of the market as the best mechanism for making responsible choices, it acts on a theory which (agree with it or not) has a basis in morality. It is not a theory representing an absolute; only foolish adherents suppose that it provides all-purpose solutions or needs no qualifications. Like all political ideas, it offers only a partial insight into truth. But it is important for the Church to recognise more full-heartedly than it has recently seemed willing to do that there is a rational and ethical basis to what the post-1979 Government has attempted. Though it is true that Conservative politics represent the self-interest of the better off, just as Labour politics represent that of the poorer, this does not invalidate the argument that it is to the general good to encourage individual responsibility and to restrain the power of the state to diminish it. So far as possible, it is sensible to try to work *with* the grain of human nature rather than against it. When the Church is tempted to decry the emphasis on success and materialism, it should remember that most of the greatest scientific and technological advances which have benefited mankind have been achieved by individual effort.

Indeed, churchmen should not censure 'materialism' quite as glibly as they often do; the word needs definition before use. The early glass in great cathedrals or in the windows of the rich was the preface to the glass that has long kept out the cold for everyone. Central heating, not long ago the luxury of the very few, now warms millions. These benefits in their early days could also be called materialism. The Church should acknowledge more full-heartedly that, within its own teaching, there is a case for restoring more scope to the individual to take responsibility for himself and for others. It is a case much more philosophically powerful than might be supposed from the general tenor of the ecclesiastical rhetoric of the eighties.

A KNEE-JERK SERMON

A review in *The Times*, 1 February 1990

THE overriding political danger ahead of the Government is that it will either not defeat inflation decisively in the next year or that, if it does, the cost of victory will turn growth into recession and the fall in unemployment into a renewed rise. That is not an economic climate in which it is easy to assuage public discontent with the condition of many public services and the level of investment in them. In a tactical sense, therefore, the progress report from the Archbishop of Canterbury's Advisory Group on Urban Priority Areas, *Living Faith in the City* (the sequel to *Faith in the City*), might be said to be well-timed. Moreover, although it has followed its predecessor into the fray against the trend of government policy, it has done so with greater circumspection. The Government's commitment to the renewal of the inner cities is acknowledged, though with criticism of the resources allocated and the methods of deployment.

Yet the report reveals deplorably slipshod and illogical thinking and its words ought not, because they are softer in parts, to escape critical analysis. As good a place as any to begin is the following sentence: 'In brief, the Government's claim is that by more selective targeting and more central control a smaller total of public expenditure can be used more effectively to encourage a higher level of private sector investment, leading to more rapid and sustainable local economic regeneration.' But that implies that the Government sees selective targeting and central control as a way of spending less. In fact, the Government's claim is only that they are the best way to get value for a given amount of money, the supply of which cannot be infinite. Nor would anyone suppose from the sentence quoted that the Government is actually spending much more in real terms; the implication seems to be that it is spending less.

The report goes on to criticise as inadequate the policy of encouraging a higher level of private-sector investment to benefit the priority areas. Then, having it both ways, it adds that it does not 'seek to prejudge the political choices between free market and interventionist solutions to these problems and the range of practical courses in between these extremes'. But to contrast the 'free market' and 'interventionism' as opposites in this context is absurd; the money given to stimulate the private sector is itself interventionism. The truth is that the term 'free market' has become both a buzz-word and a bogey in the church circles which consider these matters. They know that it is something that they must come to terms with. But they stay convinced that what they call 'interventionism' (which must be direct) is the way of virtue. Recalling that *Faith in the City* tended to recommend interventionist policies as the best practical way, the report remarks that it could not say this was wrong 'in the deplorable situation that exists in Urban Priority Areas today'.

So too, on poverty and employment the report recalls

the belief of *Faith in the City* that 'too much emphasis was being placed on individualism and not enough on collective obligation'. It records the fall in unemployment without acknowledging that this has been due to the free-market policies it derides. It adds that the number still unemployed is much higher than would have been tolerated until a few years ago but does not mention the concealed unemployment which formerly led to inflation paid for by everyone. Indeed, nowhere does inflation come into the argument at all, which is what makes the report so purblind. Instead, the report attacks attempts to draw a distinction between absolute and relative poverty, declares that society is becoming 'more unequal', seems to reject targeting social benefits and declares that current economic and social policies are intended to 'recast' society.

It states: 'Policies based on common obligations, corporate responsibility and social justice are rejected as leading inevitably to a loss of personal freedom, the growth of bureaucratic vested interests and economic stagnation.' From the first part of that sentence, you would hardly think that the public spending announced in this week's White Paper for the next year will be 39 per cent of the gross national product; that by far the largest spending item is £56 billion on social security; or that health will take £22 billion, and that both represent increases in real terms.

The report proclaims that 'economic and social policy has therefore come to elevate individual freedom as the paramount goal and the dimension of the community has been neglected' and states that for a considerable number of the poor 'the picture looks bleaker than it did in 1985'. Yes it does, but only because inflation has returned to plague us. But the report has nothing to say about this, or how money is to be found for the potentially never-ending rise in potential claimants on the public purse.

One sentence alone makes common sense. The report declares that over the next five years those who take poverty seriously must talk about the principles of the welfare state and the philosophy behind the move from universal to targeted means-testing benefits. Quite so. And that means talking about ways and means. If the Church insists on setting up committees on political economics, let it do so properly, talking about where the money it wants to spend is to come from and stop treating it as a kind of manna. If it wishes to play in the game of political economy, it had better set up its own committee of ways and means.

4

The Church of England in Opposition?

John Gladwin

'CHURCH DAMNS TORY REFORMS' (*Sunday Times*, 28 January 1990) is the sort of headline that covers a multitude of sins. 'Church' usually means the Church of England and a story may be started by anything from a minor report of a sub-group of the General Synod to a statement issued from Lambeth Palace. Once the Church of England is news, almost anything will do to keep the pot boiling. This is not to suggest that there is nothing on the boil. There has been plenty brewing over the past decade much of which has been distasteful to those responsible for public policy. The controversy does, however, reveal considerable ignorance about the mysteries of the inner workings of the Church of England. So let us begin our story by setting out some of the facts about different levels of authority and work in the Church.

It helps to distinguish between statements issued by individuals on their own behalf and those issued in some representative way. The views of a bishop may be of interest because they come from someone in a senior position. They are, however, that person's views – no less and no more. A statement issued by the House of Bishops of the Church carries far more weight. This represents the corporate mind of the leadership of the Church at that moment on the issues at stake. Interestingly, the House of Bishops rarely issues statements on matters of social and political concern.

Again, we need to distinguish between the views of working parties set up to look at issues within a specific brief and the formal opinion of the agencies to which they are accountable. Nobody, for example, considers the views of the Warnock report on Human Embryology to be official government policy. The views are important because they represent the considered judgment of a specialist group arrived at after careful deliberation. Similarly, reports of working parties in the Church of England must be given due weight as the careful work of skilled people. They are not, however, to be seen as Synodical policy until adopted as such. There are three stages through which reports proceed before being adopted by the General Synod. First, a working party produces a report and it is made available for people to consider. Second, the Synodical body responsible for the working party forms its own judgment on it. Third, that body (such as the Board for Social Responsibility) seeks the backing of the Synod itself for these views. The further an opinion progresses up this ladder the weightier its status becomes.

Throughout we need to distinguish between the views of representative bodies and persons – be they the Archbishop of Canterbury or the Board for Social Responsibility – and the opinions of church members at large. In the end Christians with strong convictions have to respect the mind of the whole Church, which may or may not wish to receive and support the views adopted by its leaders. One of the great tests is its acceptability to the whole Church. My guess is that one of the reasons *Faith in the City* carried so much weight is that it was widely welcomed by the Church as a whole.

All these distinctions are easily and understandably forgotten by those who frame newspaper headlines or shape broadcasting programmes. It is important that both the Church and our political leaders understand what is going on at these times and take due account of it. From the

Church's point of view, I have always taken the view that all publicity is good publicity and that no publicity is disastrous. If we are doing our work well we shall touch upon sensitive issues. That what we do and how we do it is often simplified by the media to the point where these distinctions are lost is a pity, but not something we should lose too much sleep over. When people take no notice of us we should start to worry!

So why has everyone taken so much notice of the Church of England over this past decade? What has such a cautious and conservative body like the Church of England done to warrant this perception that it is a new opposition to the Government? Whatever has been happening that leads to the creation of (for example) huge TV billboard posters depicting the Prime Minister spanking the Archbishop of Canterbury?

Mrs Thatcher came to office in 1979. Dr Runcie was enthroned in Canterbury in 1980. The relationship of the Church of England to Her Majesty's Government is symbolised and personalised in these two persons. The relationship of Church and State in the 1980s belongs to them in a very particular kind of way.

It has been suggested that a difference of opinion between the Prime Minister's Office and 'the Church' over the nature of the service held in St Paul's Cathedral following the Falklands War in 1982 marked the beginning of the public nature of the conflict. The roots of these concerns go much deeper but it would not be unfair to see this as the beginning of the public awareness that the Church and the Government were uneasy with each other. The insistence of the Archbishop of Canterbury, strongly encouraged by his ecumenical colleagues, that the service include acknowledgment of the Argentinian losses and avoid a triumphalist note, was reported as not meeting the Prime Minister's expectations.

The close relationship of the Church of England and the Tory tradition goes back a long way into our history. In the latter half of the nineteenth century the Conservative Party and the Church of England shared a commitment to the establishment of the Church of England in the face of the pressure from the Dissenting Churches, supported by the Liberal Party, for disestablishment. The significance of this issue has declined throughout the twentieth century and with it the necessity for the Church of England to be seen to be closely associated with the politics of the Conservative Party. However, some of the sentiments of the past live on and this adds a sharper edge to the distress felt by leading Conservatives when their Government and its policies are seen to be under attack from the Church of England.

Following hard on the Falklands Service controversy came the report of the Working Party of the Board for Social Responsibility, *The Church and the Bomb* (1981), which came down in favour of unilateralist policies with regard to nuclear weapons. The report aroused enormous interest, specially when its conclusions were leaked to the media shortly before its official publication and provoked hostile Conservative comments. Almost inevitably, the conclusions of the Working Party, chaired by the present Bishop of Salisbury, were taken as the position of the Church of England as a whole. Perceptions are *all* in this business. The fact that the full Board, under the chairmanship of the Bishop of London, rejected its Working Party's conclusions did little to remove the feeling that the Church of England was 'unreliable' on defence. The debate held in the General Synod in February 1983 was televised and reported across the world. The Church's Synod, led by the Bishop of Birmingham, decided on a classical middle route between the position taken by the Board and that of its Working Party. It came down, among other things, in favour of 'no first use'.

The Church and the Bomb is a classic document in the tradition of Anglican social thought. It examines the detail of the issues on defence, weapons-technology and strategy and then seeks to uncover the theological and ethical questions which arise from them. The problem of nuclear deterrence was high on the agenda of Christians at the time. These were the years of the deployment of a new generation of weapons – SS20s and Cruise and Pershing missiles. The security of our world seemed to be under fresh threat. The literature produced by the Churches at this time was considerable. The World Council of Churches published a report, *Before It's Too Late* (1983). Of a somewhat different theological approach was the statement produced by the Catholic bishops of the USA, *The Challenge of Peace: God's Promise and Our Response* (1983). This set out the classic Catholic theological approach and sought to discern its meaning for the issues of nuclear strategy.

It became increasingly clear that in rejecting the unilateralist approach the Church of England had not done enough to provide an alternative theological and strategic understanding. It was through an examination of the political processes of peacemaking and an endeavour to think of these in a theological setting that the Church found a new way forward which may well prove much more useful in the present highly mobile situation of East-West relations. The 1988 report, *Peace-making in a Nuclear Age*, attracted much less publicity than *The Church and the Bomb*. Its substance, however, may be much longer lasting. A statement produced by both unilateralists and multilateralists, it provides a fascinating theological framework for the politics of making peace. It was warmly received by the Synod but has received little or no attention from Conservative thinkers. It was *The Church and the Bomb* which set the tone of the relationship of Church and Government on these issues. It has proved difficult to alter that whole climate.

One of the outcomes of the Falklands service and of publication of *The Church and the Bomb* was the increased media interest in the comment of the leadership of the Church on political issues. The General Synod became a much more public body. It is interesting to compare the General Synod in this respect with the British Council of

Churches. The BCC had frequently passed strongly-worded motions antagonistic to public policy. They were rarely reported in the media. It was the opinion of the Church of England which mattered. This was seen as an unusual source of opposition to Government. From now on the Church of England was news. In due season, however, this rubbed off on others. More recently, both the General Assembly of the Church of Scotland and the Methodist Conference have hit the news for exactly the same reason – perceived hostility by a historic Christian community to public policy.

It was in the late summer of 1982, at the time of the leak of *The Church and the Bomb,* that I took up the post of Secretary to the Board for Social Responsibility. I quickly gained a sense that the leaders of the Church of England found themselves in the unexpected situation of attracting increased public interest in their views. They were not always at ease in this environment. Bishops dislike conflict and often lack experience of the rough and tumble of the world of public affairs. Moreover they were concerned not to adopt the role of official opposition to Her Majesty's Government. Their difficulties were increased by the collapse of effective political opposition as represented in the results of the 1983 General Election. The lack of a credible parliamentary opposition led to the search for other bodies to voice the concerns of those anxious about the direction of public policy. There were some who saw the Church as having potential here. These feelings were strengthened by the fact of the episcopal presence in the House of Lords at a time when the House had become a focus for opposition to Government legislation. Bishops were lobbied both locally and nationally to oppose such Bills as the abolition of the Metropolitan Authorities and especially the GLC. Even the Bishop of London, seen to be one of the leaders of the Church in sympathy with Conservative ideas, opposed this Bill. The bishops had a difficult tight-rope to walk, balancing on the one hand a concern to represent widespread anxieties put to them from their local communities, and on the other hand avoiding becoming lobby fodder for the opposition.

These were issues of major public concern which seemed to require comment from the representatives of the Church. The historic interest of the Church on issues such as local government, housing policy, education and social care left the bishops little alternative. Their silence on the episcopal bench in the Lords would have been seen as a major dereliction of duty. Yet to speak out on so much controversial and radical legislation of the Thatcher Government was bound to be interpreted in a political light. I suspect that the distance of time will lead to the judgment that they fulfilled their role, in a very difficult political climate, with integrity.

This growing public interest in the views of the Church came at a time when the Government was engaged in a programme of radical reform. The Thatcher Government called into question the assumptions of previous decades. It challenged the balance of the public and private sector and launched into a massive programme of privatisation. It challenged the concept of universal benefits and provision built into our system of welfare and public services. It altered the balance of power between employer and trade unions and reduced the powers of local government. It is interesting to note that only some aspects of this reforming programme attracted deep concern in the Church. There was little comment, for example, about privatisation; some, but not extensive, comment about legislation regarding trade unions, and very little about the drift of taxation policy. There was much more concern about the impact of policy on social provision and on the power of local government. This may be because of the historic concern of the Church for the poor and the way the Church is rooted in local communities. Bishops are frequently in close touch with the leadership of their local communities.

The salt which stung the wound was provided by recession and the massive growth of unemployment. The devastation of regions of our economy, the impact on the young and on older people now out of paid employment, hit the Church. Parishes could not be unaware of the awfulness of the experience and its devastating impact on families and households. The Government kept on playing the tune: 'there is no alternative'. The Churches, stirred up by what was happening to people, replied: 'there has to be an alternative!' In a sense that led to a dialogue of the deaf. The Government held to the theme that economic sense dictated policy, however unpleasant its consequences. They accused their opponents of not understanding basic economic reality. The Churches, in contrast, were concerned for the moral and spiritual health of the nation and lived daily with the damage done to people by such policies. It seemed that economic reality and moral concerns were in deep conflict.

That leads straight into the next major source of conflict between the Government and the Church, namely the publication of the report of the Archbishop's Commission on Urban Priority Areas, *Faith in the City*. It was immediately perceived as a direct assault on government policy. Conservative ministers and supporters, probably not having read the report, dismissed it, one criticism being that it was 'Marxist theology'. Of all the criticisms that can be made of the report, that one really cannot be made to stick. Indeed, the criticism of it from the Left is that it does not deal at all adequately with the major structural issues of class and power in our society. Nevertheless, as with the immediate perceptions about *The Church and the Bomb*, the damage was done. The attempt from within the Government at rubbishing the report only served to establish it in the popular mind as a direct assault on public policy and as an important work. It was sold out within days.

The subsequent history surrounding *Faith in the City* reveals a much more complex set of relationships, between the concerns of the Church and the policies of the Government. There were indeed proposals made which did not fit with the objectives and philosophy of the Government, for the report did look to more public involvement through both local and national government. But the Government underestimated the commitment of the report to the regeneration of local urban economies. Subsequent discussion between ministers and church leaders, and between government departments and the central councils of the Church, has led to some interesting collaboration on significant projects for regeneration in urban communities.

Furthermore, there can be little doubt but that the widespread impact of *Faith in the City*, well beyond the borders of the Church, acted as a stimulus to the Government to consider its own approach. Mrs Thatcher's much-publicised declaration following her election victory in 1987 that something needed to be done for the inner cities was evidence of the Government responding to concerns which had been raised by the Church. The setting aside of programmes and ministers for urban regeneration was all part of this response. Indeed, it would be possible to maintain that the growth of partnership schemes between local authorities, urban development corporations and local business agencies is the sort of co-operative approach to issues which would gladden the hearts of the members of the Archbishop's Commission.

We ought not to underestimate the impact on the members of this creative Commission of their visits to key cities in England. Many were clearly shaken by the extent of the deprivation seen and by the debilitating struggle of community groups to provide support for people in distress. All of this was experienced at a time of high and persistent unemployment and at a time of rate-capping and severe restrictions on local authority spending. People in our urban areas did not understand public policy. They saw it as a direct attack on the poor. This was true both for economic policies which led to high unemployment and for social policies which cut the funding of public and voluntary bodies. A basic achievement of *Faith in the City* was to raise these concerns to a level which required the Government to respond. There can be little doubt that the Church and the wider community in our urban areas found great encouragement and support from this report. A voice rooted in religious life and values, and independent of the political realm, had spoken up in a decisive way. This voice was echoed in many parts of the community. It said what many others clearly wanted said and represented the concerns of many responsible persons and agencies in our society.

It is not the case that a committee foisted such concerns on the rest of the Church. The General Synod debated *Faith in the City* in February 1986 and gave it an enthusiastic welcome and a fair wind. An office was set up to further its concerns and when the time came for this to be phased out the Synod insisted on its continuance. The Church Urban Fund was established and appealed to church members to finance a multitude of local projects – an appeal which got a very large response. The General Synod of the Church of England can hardly be called a radical left-wing body. Nevertheless throughout this period it has not been afraid to endorse opinions which are clearly critical of public policy – sometimes by massive majorities. A lot of this is a result of the initiatives of individual members of Synod, who have the power to table motions. It was a Private Member's motion which produced the virtually unanimous support in the Synod for maintaining the value and character of Child Benefit, the unanimous expression of concern about the Social Fund and the sharpening up (even in the face of the opposition of the Archbishop of York) of the Synod's opposition to the Community Charge.

Every single piece of legislation on immigration has been criticised by bishops of the Church from the early sixties onwards. Archbishop Michael Ramsey, for example, was a strong public opponent of the Labour Government's 1968 Immigration Act. The opposition was rooted in moral and religious concerns. The legislation was seen as a thinly disguised attempt at restricting coloured immigration. The use of the concept of 'patriality', which in effect gave access to Britain to white people from the Commonwealth and kept at bay Commonwealth citizens who were black, was seen to be particularly offensive. However much politicians protested their innocence, it seemed to church people that this was a simple device aimed at keeping black people out. The patriality principle has affected all subsequent legislation including the 1981 British Nationality Act. By huge majorities in 1983 the Synod reiterated the Church's sense of unease about the legislation – but to no avail. The Government was not prepared to yield any ground on these matters. In this the Church of England had the full support of the leaders of the Roman Catholic Church in England and Wales, of the Church of Scotland and of the major Free Churches. The Churches simply do not believe that it is possible to have good race relations in the community if a policy is pursued through a law which divides families and through an administration which persistently doubts the integrity of black people seeking to join their families settled in the UK.

Another example of social concerns in the Church of England relates to welfare policy. The welfare state has its roots in the reform of the poor law in the nineteenth century and in the development of public services by both local and national government policy. The rationale for major public services, aimed at tackling root problems of poverty, ill-health, illiteracy, poor housing and unemployment, was set out in the 1944 Beveridge Report. It fell to the 1945 Labour Government to give this shape in the central provision of services. The philosophy was to pay for services out of common contributions so that all who had need of them had access to them free of charge when they needed them. These foundations were built upon by subsequent administrations, both Conservative and Labour.

The post-1979 Government has, however, seemed to many to question the principles upon which the welfare state had been created. They appeared to want to move away from ideas of increasing equality through the redistributive effect of welfare services and move towards public provision providing a safety net to protect the poorest.

Thus they have looked with distaste on universal benefits available to all irrespective of personal circumstances. Child Benefit, one of the most effective of such mechanisms, has been frozen. Targeted benefits are the favourite alternative.

The 1987 report of the Board for Social Responsibility, *Not Just for the Poor*, is a major Anglican contribution to the contemporary debate about the future direction of welfare policy. It has promoted continuing discussion in the Church. Michael Bayley's book *Welfare – a Christian Option* (1989) carried on the debate. The BSR report looked at the Christian tradition and its teaching on duty towards the poor, at the major philosophies and social movements which had influenced recent experience and at the options before our community today. It came down in favour either of direct public provision of services or of major public funding of services provided by others. It rejected both universal exclusive state provision and minimalist concepts of welfare provision. The Synod supported these judgments. That provided the central councils of the Church with a broad basis on which to examine each specific proposal from Government. It will shape the way the Synod responds to the present debate over the reform of the Health Service.

The BSR saw *Not Just for the Poor* as a major contribution following on from *Faith in the City*. It stood in a tradition of encouraging public policy to provide effective and human defences in our society to protect its most vulnerable members. The anxiety felt by the Church that the Government's reforms of the welfare state are not going to improve the lot of the poorest and will not effectively tackle the problem of poverty may be seen in all of this work.

A contrasting approach to the issues of poverty is to be found in a pamphlet written for the Conservative Political Centre in 1989 by Mr John Moore, until recently Secretary of State for Health and Social Security. This was entitled *End of the Line for Poverty*. In it he attacks the concept of 'relative poverty', which has gained such credence in recent years, holding that as society gets wealthier so it will define people as poor who are, in fact, not poor, for we have long since abolished the absolute poverty of Dickensian times. The 'poverty' people talk about today is not real poverty. The implication is that a relative concept of poverty confuses inequality with poverty. They are not the same thing. Thus far, Mr Moore is making an interesting point – though he fails to recognise that there are many people in our society who, for example, have central heating in their homes but do not have the resources to use it. Possession and use are also not to be confused. It is, however, when he proceeds to maintain that it is in capitalist and free-enterprise societies that poverty is abolished that the argument loses touch with reality. Was not Dickensian England a capitalist and free-enterprise society? The classic error of this argument is the jump from what might be a proper statement about the sort of economies which create wealth to the assumption that this will sort out the problems of its distribution. Wealthy societies can have horrendous levels of poverty. Welfare policies are meant to ensure a proper measure of redistribution and protection so that all can have access to the basic services necessary for a decent human life in society. This debate is bound to continue.

What are we to make of this story of differences between the Church and the Government? What conclusions may be drawn? First, we would do well to recognise the widespread ignorance on both sides of this debate. Conservative politicians do themselves no credit when they try to lecture the Church on social thought when they clearly have little idea of the depth and history of serious Christian social thought in this country. Similarly, the Church does itself no credit when it has manifestly failed to understand the philosophical stable from which Conservative thought proceeds. The issues are far too serious for the debate to be led by the mutually ignorant.

Second, there has been a failure to understand each other's concerns. The Church is open to criticism for failing to enter into serious debate about the philosophy and direction of economic policy. For example, the attack on

Faith in the City that its proposals were not costed had some effect. More recent attempts by the Industrial and Economic Affairs Committee of the BSR and by other bodies to open up a serious debate about economic theory and practice need to be encouraged. The Church has a tradition of theological and moral concern on questions about money and economic values. Not all of it is well-developed. It needs reviving and updating. The Conservative Party similarly needs to understand the direction from which the Church comes. The Church is likely to raise deep moral questions about any set of policies whose success depends on hurting the poor. Governments have a duty to attend to the consequences of their policies on the weaker members of society. The present administration remains open to legitimate moral criticism for an apparent lack of seriousness in facing up to the damage done to large sections of our society by the changes that have taken place. It is not an adequate response to dismiss these hurts as unavoidable. The argument that growing inequality in a society growing wealthier will lead to the effective abolition of poverty is not proven.

Third, the conflict has raised important questions about the respective roles of Church and Government in the public sphere. Both parties face difficulties. The Church struggles to avoid playing the role of opposition. The legitimacy of church comment on public issues needs to be rooted in the essential worshipping and believing life of the Church. The theological and spiritual rationale for its concerns must be clearly and unequivocably set out. The Government has, in similar fashion, found it hard to recognise that contributions to political matters that go far beyond the immediate institutions of politics are proper and should be heeded for what they are. This is an area where we have made some progress. The days when politicians tell churchmen to stick to 'spiritual' matters, meaning that they should desist from any serious comments on public issues, are over for the moment. The Prime Minister's speech printed as an appendix in this book recognised the role of the Church in this sphere. That surely opens the way for a more substantial debate on the dilemmas of political life today and the sort of moral and religious response which the Church might give.

The task of stating the Christian tradition in response to human life and concerns in its social setting is persistent. Much of what we do is interim and provisional. Both Churches and politicians should be careful not to claim too much for their work. Living with conflict and with real differences of perspective is always helped by a proper humility about what we do.

5

Is There any Word from the Lord?

Lord Blanch of Bishopthorpe
Archbishop of York 1975–83

MANY a hard-pressed cabinet minister, beset with the problems of his department, if he were a religious man, might well in his heart ask the question at the head of this chapter. He is unlikely to send for a prophet or a priest or a bishop and actually formulate it. But a certain king of Judah in the early part of the sixth century BC, desperate for guidance and reassurance, did do just that. His kingdom was at the heart of an acute international crisis which exposed him and his people to sudden invasion and certain defeat. Confused by the conflicting advice of his counsellors, he sent for the prophet Jeremiah and put this question: 'Is there any word from the Lord?' (37:17). Indeed, there was a word from the Lord, but a highly unwelcome one, which was proved true in the event: the kingdom would collapse because it was so full of sin.

The question I am asked to address in this chapter is whether this episode in the life of an ancient Middle Eastern people is of any significance in the decision-making activity of a modern government, grappling with the intransigent problems of a society uncertain of its direction, with heavy international responsibilities and exposed to persistent political and social problems at home. We might put the question in a slightly different way more appropriate to a complex, pluralistic, supposedly-secular society: 'Is there any source of authority outside our political and judicial structures to which we can appeal, for example, in the management of the economy, in the framing of foreign policy, in the running of the prisons, in the ordering of the schools or the financing of the health services?' These are practical questions less threatening than the crisis which confronted King Zedekiah, but troublesome nevertheless and infinitely important for those whose lives are affected by the decisions that have to be made. The sheer complexity of them will overwhelm us unless we can find the formative, creative 'Word' to which we may conform. Such a 'Word' would not banish controversy or undermine our traditional party structures, but it could serve as a pole star when we are in danger of losing our bearings altogether.

I am just a student of Holy Scripture. I have no overt political commitment. Such knowledge as I have of the machinery of government is derived from my observation of it from the cross-benches of the House of Lords. The only political speech I ever made was made at school in the 1930s during a general election – for which side I do not now remember. But in this chapter I am not concerned with political issues as such. I am looking at Holy Scripture to see whether the wisdom of the distant past can be made accessible to a society obsessed with the present and generally lacking in historical perspective. I believe that the Scriptures provide a valuable source of argument, reflection and aspiration which is not irrelevant to the issues which dominate and disturb Western society. We must not be deterred by the distance in time and space of these ancient writings. Whatever our private attitudes to them may be, they are the product of a Judaeo-Christian tradition which has been hugely influential in the forming of our public institutions, our educational practice, our underlying attitudes to life. Secular, pluralistic, we may be, but we remain the inheritors of a tradition which took its rise in the Sinai desert some three thousand years ago. In that sense we cannot undo the past and we would be wise not to ignore it.

Neither is the biblical past so utterly different from our present as we might suppose. War was then an instrument of policy and weary ambassadors shuttled from capital to capital. Babylon had a well-organised civil service and an elaborate filing system. Credit was available in the commercial world. And there was always the taxman. The world which the Scriptures reflect was not backward, primitive, uncivilised. But these Scriptures are remarkable amongst all the other writings of the ancient world in that they regard the world and its history from a particular perspective which colours and informs every aspect of life. That perspective arises from the conviction that Israel had been called by God, that their God was the God of all the earth, and that he intended a society based on peace and justice in which the whole world would ultimately share.

Israel's Law

The Quran is a collection of revelations given to the Prophet Muhammad who died in 632. The Book of Mormon purports to be the record of a series of visions to Joseph Smith in the year 1827. I mention these writings only to point to the difference between them and the Scriptures of the Hebrew people. The Quran and the Book of Mormon are each from the hand of a single person at a particular time; they have a certain uniformity of approach, and the style in each case is consistent. The Hebrew Bible, on the other hand, was at least eight hundred years in the course of preparation, and is associated with an even longer span of history – from Abraham to Alexander, some 1,500 years, with Adam in the background. It is rooted in history and it abounds with the names of people and places. (A modern Concordance will supply you with between four and five thousand such names.) It is far from homogeneous, and comprises poetry and prose, court records and archives, propaganda and piety, hymns and proverbs, laws and customs. It was produced under widely varying political and social conditions. It does not present a uniform point of view, and writers sometimes contradict each other. It began with the recorded experiences of a people in slavery, and subsequently records the story of a people on a long march from Egypt to Canaan. It describes national life under a series of charismatic figures known as judges. It traces the origins of the monarchy, and ventures some reflections upon it. It chronicles the rise of a highly distinctive (if not unique) body of men known as prophets. It records and comments on an experience (mostly adverse) of the effects of monarchy, and treats the subsequent exile of the people in Babylon as a judgment on the apostasy of the monarchs and the people alike. By the intervention of the Persian king, Cyrus, they are permitted to return to their homeland, and to establish a new form of polity under the leadership of the scribal class. The later writings bear witness to the sad decline and bitter divisions in the national life, culminating in the fall of Jerusalem under the Romans, and the beginnings of modern Judaism.

There is nothing singular about such a history. It could be the history of any nomadic tribe looking for security in a world dominated by mighty military and political powers. The fact that Judaism endures to this day and is represented by a small but significant state on the stage of the world is a tribute to their remarkable powers of endurance – and that could be all. We have seen it all before. But what is remarkable about the history of this particular tribe is that it looks back upon its history as recorded in its sacred Scriptures as evidence of the activity of God in its midst – and not just its God, but the God of the whole earth who has a particular function in mind for his chosen people, Israel. That function was revealed in visions to Abraham, was reinforced by the experience of slavery and redemption in Egypt, reiterated by the prophets, rehearsed by the psalmists, and demonstrated by the survival of the nation under conditions of unimaginable suffering and stress.

I am writing this morning in my study looking out on a view of the North Oxfordshire countryside bathed in May sunshine. I am familiar with the story of Israel and I get used to it. But I pause for a moment to contemplate this extraordinary claim that is being made for it: the destiny of mankind was entrusted to the hands of an obscure and powerless Middle Eastern tribe. We may seek to rationalise it but we cannot ignore it. The function of Israel in the history of mankind was, in their view, quite precise. It was to act as the guardians of the Law delivered in summary form to Moses at Mount Sinai which would one day prevail over the whole inhabited earth. For this Law they had to be prepared to suffer and, if need be, to die, if they were to prove equal to their astonishing vocation. So, Moses received the Law; judges were appointed to enforce it; kings were expected to uphold it; the prophets strove with might and main to entrench it in the civic life; priests were its guardians in the Holy of Holies; worshippers gathered round it; psalmists sang about it; and generation after generation of learned men sought to apply it to the everyday life of the ordinary Israelite. It was a precious possession held in trust for the world. It was the ultimate gift of God to mankind. 'How I love your law, more precious to me than gold or silver!'

Other ancient nations had their law codes, the most famous of which is the Code of Hammurabi, emanating from Babylon some three hundred years before Israel received their law in the desert. But no such law code, to the best of my knowledge, was ever set to music. The Hebrews sang the praises of their law; they were enraptured by it; they danced before it. I cannot imagine an English lawyer singing Magna Carta, however important he conceived it to be. This calls for explanation. The Decalogue or Ten Commandments, if we may take it as the core of all subsequent legislation, begins with an affirmation about the author of the Law. He was the only God; he was the jealous God; he was the God who would not have his name taken in vain. But above all, in the pious Israelite's mind, he was the God who had delivered the people from slavery, and had led them through the wilderness. The Law was not just the law of Moses, it was the Law of God, and a God, moreover, who had shown his power and mercy to the people over whom he presided. The law-giver was not a judge remote on his heavenly bench, or a fierce schoolmaster breathing retribution. He was the gracious saviour of the people.

This brings us to the second reason for the Hebrews' intense devotion to the Law. The word 'Law' is a somewhat misleading translation. The Hebrew word *Torah* which stands behind it in essence means 'to teach', and the most striking example of it is to be found in the book of the prophet Hosea, who says of God: 'When Israel was a child then I loved him, and called my son out of Egypt . . . I taught Ephraim to go, and I took them in my arms . . . I drew them with bands of love, and I picked them up and held them to my cheek, I bent down to them and fed them' (11:1–4). The author of the Law was more than a judge; he was a father, teaching his child to walk, encouraging him forward, picking him up when he fell, providing good food and nourishment on the way. So the people had something to sing about when they passed through the dark valley. They had something to be ashamed of when 'they roamed to their hearts' content along the paths of wickedness and ruin, wandering through trackless deserts, and ignoring the Lord's highway'. These were words written by the author of the Wisdom of Solomon (5:7). But they echoed and re-echoed through the life of Israel for centuries before as the people grappled with their sense of shame at their easy-going neglect of God's Law and their offences against his love. There were to be times when the song of the redeemed sounded more like a dirge. But in shame and in joy the Law was to them more precious than gold or silver.

The divine Law was thus based on a relationship, not just on a fiat from on high. But not all God's people treasured that relationship; they were not all saints or prophets or hymn-writers. The relationship therefore had to be articulated in a series of rules which comprise the rest of the Decalogue, intended to curb what the Book of Common Prayer calls 'the unruly wills and affections of sinful men'. It would be hard to deny their importance in terms of social life and government policy within any civilised society. Happy the legislators, for example, who could frame a law which observed the necessary and beneficent balance between the rush and roar of daily life and the 'Sabbath' rest which was commanded for the people of God. There would be less juvenile crime, less drug addiction, if children and parents 'honoured' each other. We could certainly do with less 'murder' in our streets. Marriage could be a more creative and fulfilling institution if the command against 'adultery' were more scrupulously observed. The Home Secretary could sleep more easily in his bed if 'theft' ceased to be a way of life for so many of our population. Justice might be more swiftly achieved, and the investigative branch of the Inland Revenue could be disbanded, if we could be relied on not to give 'false witness'. So these provisions of the ancient Law remain as relevant for us as they were for them. They remain the basis of any ordered society, and government continues to have a responsibility for articulating them in legislation and enforcing them. 'Government under the Law' may mean much more, but it can hardly mean less.

The last commandment of the Law, 'Thou shalt not covet,' deserves a paragraph of its own because of its sheer oddity, and the reader will have to excuse a brief excursus on the meaning of the word in the sacred Scriptures. The New Testament word is frequently associated with sexual desire, but it is capable of an innocent meaning, viz. 'pleasure, delight'. The equivalent in the Old Testament has a similar variety of usage, but in the vast majority of cases it means 'inordinate, ungovernable, selfish desire'. This is the word used in the tenth commandment, and, significantly enough, in the story of the Garden of Eden; it relates to the tree which Adam and Eve 'desired' and to which they succumbed. We find ourselves therefore in the tenth commandment with a prohibition which is concerned not with an action but with a desire, not with overt law-breaking but with inner disposition. Put crudely, if I take a brick and hurl it through a jeweller's window to snatch some precious item inside, I am committing a criminal offence and will have to pay the consequences. But this commandment makes it an offence against the Law of God to stand in rapt desire outside the window, coveting the object inside. Obviously covetousness is an attitude, not an act, and therefore cannot be punished as a crime. Nevertheless, here is a commandment against it. I have looked in vain for any such commandment in, for example, the sophisticated and humane legal code promulgated by an Assyrian emperor and known as the Code of Hammurabi. Others have looked for it in vain in other codes of law. It is not surprising, therefore, that it has occasioned polite but vigorous controversy in the field of Old Testament scholarship, without, as far as I am aware, producing any assured result. Are we free to infer, then, that Israelite law is concerned not only with action but with motive and intent? If so, we are in the presence of a remarkable insight into the springs of human conduct. This interpretation is borne out by the way in which the story of Naboth's vineyard is recounted. Elijah, as the champion of the Law, was rightly incensed at the unlawful and violent means by which the king appropriated his subject's property, and predicted his coming punishment. But the author of the narrative is careful to point back to the primary cause of the offence against God. King Ahab had 'coveted' Naboth's vineyard. It is a curious irony that the twentieth century has been marked by the growth of a giant industry, at the behest of the market, carefully devising images intended to excite an Ahab-like covetousness. This is not just a personal matter, malign though its effects may be in personal terms. It is an acute social problem as well. 'Take the waiting out of wanting' was the way one bank introduced its credit card to the public. I am old enough to remember the giant hoardings which appeared during the Second World War, with the figure of a large white elephant and the words, 'if you don't need it, don't buy it'. Many a modern Chancellor of the Exchequer, in his fight against inflation, might look

back to that government-sponsored advertisement with
amazement and envy.

The 'interiorisation' of the Law incipient in the tenth
commandment was to have a long history in the life of
Israel, as prophets and psalmists strove to get behind the
formal provisions of the Law to intention and motive. So
the author of Psalm 51 taps a universal religious experience
when he cries to the Lord to wash away all his guilt and
create a new heart within. Only so, would the sacrifices
prescribed by Law have any meaning or validity. Jeremiah,
faced with the apostasy of Israel, looked forward to a new
covenant when God would set his law within them and
write it on their hearts (31:33). The experience of Ezekiel is
particularly significant; when he and his people languished
as exiles in Babylon, far from the visible embodiments of
their religion – no land, no king, no temple – he heard a
promise: 'I will put my spirit into you and make you
conform to my statutes; keep my laws and live by them'
(36:27). St Paul, though in a different context, makes the
same contrast when he refers to a letter he had written to
the Corinthian church. He compares 'the letter written
not with ink, but with the spirit of the living God, written
not on stone tablets but on the pages of the human heart'
(2 Corinthians 3:3).

This process of interiorisation found its greatest expo-
nent in Jesus of Nazareth, who, referring to the Decalogue
in his 'Sermon on the Mount', enunciated in memorable
words the whole essence of his ethical teaching: '. . . our
forefathers were told, "Do not commit murder . . ." But I
tell you, Anyone who nurses anger against his brother
must be brought to judgement . . . they were told, "Do not
commit adultery." But what I tell you is this: If a man looks
on a woman with a lustful eye, he has already committed
adultery with her in his heart' (Matthew 5:22, 27). Later in
his ministry he confronted his opponents with this striking
metaphor: 'You are like tombs covered with whitewash;
they look well from the outside, but inside they are full of
dead men's bones and all kinds of filth. So it is with you.

Outwardly you appear righteous to men, but within you are full of hypocrisy and crime' (Matthew 23:27–28). In such words the process of the interiorisation of the Law reaches its apogee – and indeed confronts us all with the unsavoury realities which underlie the smooth and pleasant face we present to the world. A man may smile and smile – and be a villain.

Jesus and the Law

But who was he, this Jesus of Nazareth, who thus presumed to enlarge the implications of that ancient Law given by God through the hands of Moses? His life story can be briefly told. He was brought up by Jewish parents in a little-regarded town of Nazareth in Galilee, in a little enclave of the Roman Empire. His parents were observant Jews, and he attended with them the sacred festivals of their religion. He would have been made familiar with the history of Israel at an early age. He would have become aware of the customs and the practices which marked Israel as a 'peculiar people' – the Sabbath observance, the ritual purification of domestic utensils, the recitation of the *Torah*, the practice of family prayer, and the saying of grace at meals. He attended the local synagogue school, and there his formal education began and ended. He was apprenticed to his father as a craftsman. At some indeterminate point in his life his father died and he, as the eldest son, became head of the family. At about the age of thirty he discovered within himself unexpected powers of teaching and healing. A few local men became his helpers and pupils, and together they constituted the beginning of a renewal movement which rapidly spread throughout the towns and villages circling the Sea of Galilee. The movement excited at first the interest and later the opposition of the Jewish leadership in Jerusalem. Some three years after the beginning of his public ministry, on a visit to Jerusalem for the Passover, he was arrested, tried and executed as a threat to public order. Certain of his followers subsequently asserted that he was alive and had made himself known to them. Nothing that happened in his life was so remarkable as what happened after his death. Within three hundred years the Roman Empire was officially Christian and by our own day a third of the human race are his adherents, at least nominally.

But the question remains. This bleak biography tells us something of what he did and what happened to him, but it does not answer the question, 'who was he?' The question is, strictly speaking, unanswerable, as generations of scholars have found, if we are looking for an answer which can satisfy every rational criterion. In any case, within the context of this chapter I can do no more than refer the reader to the opinions that were voiced about him among his own contemporaries. The earliest impression was that he was a prophet, akin to John the Baptist and the great prophets before him. Some thought he was Elijah returned to life or another Jeremiah. Greatly daring, his closest disciples even permitted themselves the thought that he was the Messiah long-awaited by the Jewish people, who would throw off the Roman yoke and usher in the golden age. But the vocabulary of the gospels reveals the role in which he was primarily regarded by the people at large. The most common name for him is 'Rabbi' (or the Greek word for 'Lord', which means much the same thing). The evidence of the vocabulary is strengthened by many other features of his life and ministry. He was not a Rabbi in the sense that he had been through the Rabbinic schools and had been formally ordained. But it was not unknown in this period for gifted teachers who had established a reputation among their peers to be accorded that title. Moreover it was customary for a Rabbi to attract to himself a group of pupils who would not only listen to his words but accompany him on his travels, learning from his style of life and spirituality. They were called disciples or 'learners'. But he was not a *guru*, plucking beautiful ideas out of the air. He was, and was regarded as, a 'teacher of the Law'. I have it on good authority that the word 'to teach' in the Hebrew invariably means to teach the Law unless it is qualified by another object. This is borne out by the manner of his teaching – vivid, circumstantial, humorous, proceeding more by way of question and answer than by straight discourse. His was a Rabbinic method, although it was generally acknowledged that he spoke with a special authority, often lacking in the official teachers of his day.

These observations on Jesus's role as a teacher would be obvious to any attentive reader of the gospels. But there are many other, less obvious, pointers to this primary role. In addition to the direct quotations from the *Torah*, there are innumerable allusions to it. Many of his most familiar parables are built round some ordinance of the Law, which would have been recognised by his hearers, if not by us. His most famous sermon was the Sermon on the Mount, though it has to be said in parenthesis that it is more than a sermon, rather a series of discourses over a period of days, subsequently gathered together by the writers of the gospels. But the setting, on the mount, invited comparison with the gift of the Law to Moses, also on the mount – a point emphasised by the author of St Matthew's Gospel. But that same author makes an even more telling comparison with the *Torah* by dividing his Gospel into five distinct parts corresponding to the five books of the Pentateuch. All this may reflect a common belief amongst the Jews of that day that the Messiah, when he came, would bring with him a new *Torah*, which would not supersede the old *Torah* of Moses, but would infinitely deepen and enlarge it, and make its provisions known to all mankind and not just to the Jews. This would account for the emphatic utterances regarding his role in his relation to the Law. He had not come to destroy it, but to fulfil it. He insisted that not one jot or tittle of the Law should pass away until all should be fulfilled. He was not convicted of any breach of the Mosaic Law at his trial, but because of his claim, shared by some of his followers, that he was the Messiah. In his view, as for St Paul, the Law was holy and good, and would continue to the end of time. Jesus was not just a gifted teacher but an expositor of the Law, albeit a Law profoundly enlarged in scope and deeply interiorised.

The account I have given of the origins of Hebrew Law and the stages through which it passed – the desert, the kingdom, the prophets, the exile, and its radical reappraisal in the teaching of Jesus – can no doubt be criticised in detail by specialists in the field, but, I think, is not seriously misleading. But the question has yet to be answered – can our hard-pressed cabinet minister still look to it for guidance in the complicated issues which trouble the modern world? He may be a religious man who runs his own life on the basis of this ancient Law. After all, it is part of our heritage. The Decalogue is still embedded in the liturgy of the Church; it appears in the Church of England's Alternative Service Book of 1980 in association with precepts from the New Testament. But could he turn eagerly to it as a 'word from the Lord', as he sits at his desk and picks up the telephone?

I ask the reader for the moment at least to suspend his disbelief while I make two comments. The first is that this Middle Eastern tribe from which the ancient code descends had a genius for religion, not just as a philosophy or an idea but as something to be applied in detail to social and political life. Moreover they did not live their life wholly in the backwoods of Canaan. There were always (from 586 BC) more Jews outside Palestine than within it, and they reached positions of eminence in many of the great nations of the world. Joseph may have been the first to be entrusted with political power in one of the great empires of the ancient world, but he was certainly not the last. The famous Jewish historian, Josephus, had been a commander of the Jewish army, but he was happy enough on retirement to live in Rome on an imperial pension. Philo was an intellectual luminary in the university of Alexandria. Roman emperors had due regard for the influence of the Jewish people in public life and sought as a matter of policy to win their support. The Jews served their God and lived by his

Law in a world every bit as complex as the society in which we live now. They honoured their homeland, but they often felt more at home outside it. Some of them were even prepared to believe that Plato was a second Moses.

The second comment is this. Jesus was sent primarily to the lost sheep of the house of Israel, to revive their love for God and for God's Law, to meet them in their distresses, to bring them consolation and healing. But, necessarily, his ministry could not be confined to them. Galilee had indeed been forcibly Judaised, but the majority of the inhabitants were not Jews. There were Greeks and Persians, Roman soldiers and Syrian merchants. It was a polyglot, polyform, pluralist society, marked by a bewildering variety of religions. The great god Pan was one of them, with a shrine at Banias. But other gods and demi-gods abounded. The slopes of Mount Hermon were littered with shrines erected by the devotees of many religions. And over them all hung the heavy, brooding presence of Roman state religion. So, whilst as we have already seen, Jesus's teaching was conducted largely on the basis of and within the context of the Law, there were timeless, universal truths to which the non-Jewish hearer responded with enthusiasm – the woman of Tyre and Sidon, the centurion from the local Roman garrison, the trader from Syria who happened to be passing that way, a member of Herod's court. It was not only Jews who heard him gladly, but Gentiles, who were quick to discern the note of authority which ran through his discourses, and responded to him. It was, after all, a Roman soldier who is commemorated in the Gospel as one of the first to voice publicly his private opinion of Jesus of Nazareth – that he was a 'son of God'. So the very setting of his ministry in pluralist Galilee marks him out not just as a teacher of the Jews but as the teacher of mankind. He universalised the 'Law of God' to the point at which it ultimately became the moral law of the Western world. The cabinet minister who took it seriously in public life would be following in a long tradition.

Hearing the Word

When King Zedekiah's advisers failed him he turned to Jeremiah the prophet, confident that he would hear a word of the Lord from him. But on what was this confidence based, and is there any counterpart in the modern world? Jeremiah was part of a long tradition of prophecy, stretching over many centuries. The prophet played a role which varied with time and circumstance. Elijah saw himself as a champion of the Law of Israel over and against foreign influences. Amos was a fierce critic of the 'establishment' of his day. Isaiah acted as counsellor to a series of kings. Jeremiah was treated by the defence minister of his day as a traitor who weakened the hands of the men of war. Ezekiel laboured for the unity and integrity of his people in exile. All the prophets were in some measure predictors of the future, not based on a kind of second-sight but on a reading of God's hand in history. But they were above all 'men of God', who were believed to have a direct relationship with God and a perception of his will. But where now is this authority located, and to whom does our hard-pressed cabinet minister turn if he happens to be a conscientious believer – to the Archbishops or the Cardinal or the Chief Rabbi, to the House of Bishops or the General Synod of the Church of England, to a personal confessor? Or does he appeal to what he regards as 'the mind of the Church' in its ecumenical, worldwide aspect? By any such route he is bound to get a diffuse answer which falls very short of being a 'word of the Lord' – though his consultants might think otherwise.

There are, however, other ways of receiving a word from the Lord, and I offer one significant example from my own experience. The Town Clerk of Liverpool when I was Bishop there was a thorough-going Christian man, and a loyal supporter of his parish church. He served on the Parochial Church Council; he occasionally read a lesson and helped with the collection. But he said to me once, during one of the periodic crises which afflicted the city: 'I wish there were a group of people in church in which I could genuinely confide, and receive guidance and support in making the decisions I have to make.' He was looking for a 'word from the Lord', not in the official channels of the Church but in a like-minded sympathetic group of practising Christians who were willing to share his burdens and with him seek God's will. Our hard-pressed cabinet minister has a right to expect some such resource as that, and the Church has a responsibility for providing it.

Many and diverse are the ways of hearing a word from the Lord, given only the desire to hear it and the will to obey it. We need not dredge the distant past for examples. I mention, almost at random, the names of those in this century who have heard a word from the Lord and on that basis have substantially influenced the political and social life of their time. It was a word from the Lord which made Dietrich Bonhoeffer a champion of the Confessing Church against Nazi oppression. It was a word from the Lord to Nicholas Berdyaev, a one-time Marxist, which contributed to the religious renaissance in the USSR. It was a word from the Lord which made Reinhold Niebuhr not only a distinguished theologian but a dedicated social activist in the United States. And, nearer home, it was a word from the Lord which made William Temple's voice heard, if not always appreciated, in Downing Street. But any believer, with no pretensions to fame or influence, who takes seriously the Law of God, received by Moses, activated by the prophets in the life of Israel, preserved and transmitted by the scribes, lovingly expounded and reinterpreted for successive generations by learned teachers, reanimated and profoundly interiorised in the teaching of Jesus – any such believer may be expected to influence his social and political environment if he receives that Law as a word from God. 'Prophecy' in that sense did not begin with Elijah or end with John the Baptist.

If the argument of this chapter has been generally accepted, we shall have concluded that Jesus of Nazareth was not just a wandering preacher, speaking only to the needs of the Jews in the land of Israel. He claimed to be the representative of God and the authoritative interpreter of God's Law, made known by Moses and valid to the end of time. His teaching is recorded in some detail in the gospels, and is embodied at various points in the other documents of the New Testament. No responsible person in public life today can afford to ignore this ancient source of wisdom and insight into the affairs of men. It is valid for all time and in every circumstance, however secular and pluralistic our society may ultimately become. But the New Testament does not stand alone. It stands in a long tradition from the moment at which Abraham left his home in Haran for Canaan. That tradition is marked indelibly by a deep and resounding reverence for the righteous God 'whose mercy reaches to the heavens, and his faithfulness to the clouds, whose righteousness stands like the strong mountains, whose judgements are like the great deep' (Psalm 36:5, 6). The message of the prophet Amos to a wayward people reflects this understanding of the very essence of God's nature: 'Let justice roll on like a river and righteousness like an everflowing stream' (Amos 5:24). To believe that, however difficult it may be to apply it in a highly sophisticated society, is to be delivered from an enfeebling moral relativism and pragmatic politics. But this magnificent moral stance is not just the possession of a favoured few; it is accessible in one form or another to all mankind. Paul the Jew has this to say to us Gentiles: 'The Gentiles who do not possess the Law carry out its precepts by the light of nature; although they have no law, they display the effect of the law inscribed on their hearts' (Romans 2:14, 15). There is a difference between kindness and cruelty, between love and hate, between truth and falsehood, between loyalty and disloyalty which is accepted over most of the civilised world. In biblical terms, there is a law written in the heart which was known in Eden before it was written down at Sinai.

Jesus of Nazareth was recognised by his contemporaries as a teacher of the Law of God, albeit an unconventional, and in some eyes dangerous, teacher. The consequence of the growth of the Church in Europe was that his teaching became integral to Western civilisation as a whole, part of a value-system, which we recognise, though do not always honour, to this day. It is entwined with our political thinking and our social policies. I venture a simple example: the welfare state could be said to reflect the utterance of Jesus quoting Leviticus (19:18), 'you shall love your neighbour as yourself'. In terms of personal conscience and corporate action, the Judaean-Christian tradition has been hugely influential in the formation of Europe. But Jesus was not just or even mainly a teacher of the Law of God, however influential that teaching has proved to be. He was a herald and preacher of the Kingdom of God. That theme is central to St Mark's gospel and appears right at the beginning of his ministry. 'After John was arrested', he says, 'Jesus came into Galilee preaching the gospel and saying the Kingdom of God is at hand' (Mark 1:15). That phrase or its alternative (kingdom of heaven) occurs well over a hundred times in the synoptic gospels. Jesus taught his disciples to pray: 'Thy kingdom come, thy will be done on earth'. He laboured to implant it in the minds of his hearers through a whole range of vivid parables and illustrations. What did the phrase mean? It certainly did not mean the end product of a military campaign or of an ambitious political and social programme. It was essentially God's kingdom or kingship to which he referred, to be achieved by God's hand, in God's time and in God's way. It was sometimes described in terms of growth and harvest, sometimes in terms of cataclysmic events on earth. Jesus did not pluck this 'kingdom theology' out of the air or identify himself with any one contemporary view of the kingdom. He was the beneficiary of a long tradition in the literature of his people. Isaiah had looked forward to the day when the wolf would 'live with the lamb, and the leopard lie down with the kid, and the calf and the fatling together, and a little child would lead them . . . they shall not hurt or destroy in all my holy mountain; for the earth shall be full of the knowledge of the

Lord, as the waters cover the sea' (Isaiah 11:6). The Psalmist envisaged the day when 'all the ends of the earth shall remember and turn unto the Lord and all the kindreds of the nations shall worship before thee, for the Kingdom is the Lord's and He is the ruler over the nations' (Psalm 22:28). The Jewish commentator on this passage is right when he says 'the universal sovereignty of God is the supreme aspiration of Bible doctrine' (*Soncino Psalms*, p. 66). The Christian Church formally affirms it in the Nicene Creed: 'He shall come again with glory to judge the quick and the dead, whose kingdom shall have no end.' Of course, the belief defies description. The kingdom to come lies above and beyond any views we may entertain about the ideal society. It follows that we shall have to be content with strictly interim political and social institutions, and forswear ideological bigotry. It is unlikely that we shall wake up one fine morning and find the whole world Liberal, Socialist or Conservative. But we could wake up one morning and find the whole world transfigured with a strange radiance, and realise that the unthinkable has come to pass – God has entered his kingdom and reigns. Perhaps there is a word of the Lord to our 'hard-pressed cabinet minister', and it comes from the prophet Isaiah: 'My thoughts are not your thoughts, neither are your ways my ways, says the Lord. For as the heavens are higher than the earth, so are my ways higher than your ways, and my thoughts than your thoughts' (Isaiah 55:8, 9). Jesus put it more briefly when he said to Pilate: 'My kingdom is not of this world' (John 18:36). The Christian cry still rings down the ages: 'Thy kingdom come, thy will be done on earth as in heaven.'

6

Wealth and Poverty in the Bible

J. R. Porter

IT would no doubt be generally agreed that one cannot derive precise policy prescriptions for our contemporary society from the evidence of how the people of the Bible dealt with the social and political problems of their own time and this would certainly apply to issues of wealth and poverty. The differences between our world and the world of the Bible are too great to permit of any simple transfer of the laws, institutions and practices of the latter to the former. Further, the biblical evidence reflects a long span of time, in the course of which many religious, intellectual and social developments occurred. It is not surprising therefore that many different approaches to wealth and poverty, to rich and poor, can be detected in the Bible, and any account of the topic must endeavour to give due weight to all of these. This caution is the more necessary since not a few recent studies in this area have tended to concentrate on one particular strand in biblical thinking, to make, one must suspect, a political point, to the neglect of others – so, for example, the evidence of what is called the Wisdom literature is often ignored or undervalued.[1]

---

[1] Such a criticism can be levelled, for example, against the use of biblical evidence in such Board of Social Responsibility Reports as *Let Justice Flow* (1985) and *Not Just for the Poor* (1986).

Nevertheless, it may plausibly be claimed that there are some basic attitudes towards wealth and poverty which underlie Scripture as a whole, which condition its injunctions and practices in this regard and which the religious person may claim should still inform contemporary social behaviour and regulations. We must begin with the Old Testament view of wealth, understood in its basic sense of welfare or prosperity, as a fundamental biblical ideal. It represents God's intention for man and is a sign of the divine blessing, all of which is implied in the biblical doctrine of creation. In Genesis 1:28–29 the particular blessing God gives to human beings is to control the earth, so that it may supply their needs in abundance. It is important to be sensitive to the almost rapturous tone of the language here: man's dominion is described in the language used of the dominion of kings;[2] human destiny is the equivalent of the wealth and splendour characteristic of the ancient Near Eastern monarch, as is brought out in Psalm 8:5ff, which echoes the Genesis passage. Much the same picture is presented by the story of Adam in the garden of Eden in Genesis 2, where we have an ideal of the creation 'in which, from the moment of setting Adam in Eden, God destined man to luxuriate'.[3]

It is to be noted, however, that Adam is set in the garden not just to enjoy it but also 'to till it and care for it' (Genesis 2:15). Man's appropriation and enjoyment of the good things of the world depends on the work he himself puts into realising their potentialities. Work is regarded as an essential part of the human condition, without which human life would be incomplete, throughout the whole of the Bible. It is not confined to agricultural operations, as Genesis 2 might appear to suggest, but includes any type of work which may be demanded by changes in society or

---

[2] See C. Westermann, *Creation* (1974), pp. 51ff.

[3] Anthony Phillips, 'The Attitude of *Torah* to Wealth' in *Heaven and Earth*, ed. Andrew Linzey and Peter J. Wexter (1986), p. 85.

environment, such as the developments into specialised industrial or commercial activities which the growth of civilisation brings about as described in Genesis 4:17–22.

It is against this background that the particular role of the nation of Israel is to be understood. According to the Pentateuch, Israel began as a group of wandering, landless families. But this was not its ultimate destiny in God's purpose, and so one of the central themes running through the entire Pentateuch is the divine promise to the patriarchs that their descendants would be given enduring possession of a land of their own (e.g. Genesis 15:18–21, 17:8). The basis of the nation's existence was this divine gift of the land of Canaan and hence Israel's calling was to leave the desert and its nomadic existence and embrace that gift. Such is the context of what can fairly be described as the creed or confession of faith, whatever its precise date, of Deuteronomy 26:5–11 and, in Hosea, Israel's punishment for her failure to realise that the riches of the land were bestowed on her by her God is that she should become 'naked as the day she was born, parched as the desert, left to die of thirst' (2:3).

What this meant was that the nation was to luxuriate, just like Adam in Eden, in the abundance provided by the land promised and given to it by God. One of the Hebrew terms for 'wealth' is *osher*, of which the basic sense of the root is 'to abound', and it is the abundance of the land of Canaan – 'a land of milk and honey' – which is described and emphasised in a number of Old Testament passages, most fully in Deuteronomy 8:7–10, with its statement, 'It is a land where you will never live in poverty nor want for anything'. And if riches were the sign of God's blessing for the nation, so too were they for those individuals who traditionally represented the ideal and apex of human existence – the patriarchs, Abraham (Genesis 24:35), Isaac (26:12–14), Jacob (30:43), or a king like Solomon (1 Kings 10:14–27). But, further, it is not simply these great paradigmatic figures who are to enjoy the blessing of wealth; it is the

destiny of what might be called the 'average' Israelite too.
So the sign of the ideal state of Israel during the reign of
Solomon is not just the abundance of the national wealth
but the fact that 'Judah and Israel lived in security, everyone under his own vine and under his own fig tree' (1 Kings
4:25); everyone was secure in the enjoyment of his own
property, and it is noteworthy that exactly the same expression is employed to describe the future 'golden age' in
later prophecies (Micah 4:4, Zechariah 3:10). Two other
Hebrew terms for 'wealth' are *hon* and *hayil*, the roots of
which mean 'faculty', 'ability' or 'power'. Thus in the Old
Testament view, wealth is what gives a person the ability to
live a proper life and power over his own destiny, and the
freedom wealth brings is the right of each individual in the
community.

From all this, various consequences follow. In the first
place, for the reason just mentioned, the Hebrew Bible
takes the possession of private property for granted and is
at pains to protect it. It has sometimes been argued that
Israelite law was not concerned with the protection of
property but of persons. However, this is to make a false
distinction, for, in Israel, personal and property rights were
bound up together; it was because such groups as the poor,
the widow and the orphan lacked property that they also
lacked status in the community and so needed protection,
as will be discussed later. In any case, not only is there the
prohibition of theft in the Decalogue, but what is probably
Israel's earliest legal code, the so-called 'Book of the Covenant' (Exodus 21:1–23:19), contains a string of provisions
to safeguard the possessions of those with considerable
substance – fields and vineyards, flocks and herds, houses
and money (e.g. Exodus 22:1–15). Above all, it was having
his own property which conferred full citizenship on a man
and gave him the position of 'elder', with the right to take
part and speak in the legal assembly that regulated the
concerns of the local community.[4] It is the loss of this status

---

[4] See Anthony Phillips, *Ancient Israel's Criminal Law* (1970), p. 151.

which accounts for the sharpness of the prophetic de-
nunciation of the powerful who – probably quite legally, as
again will be argued later – dispossessed the lesser citizens
of their property (Isaiah 5:8–10, Micah 2:1–5).

Secondly, if the powerful ought not to take advantage of
their position to deprive others of their property and its
concomitant rights, the same applied to the state when that
came to be established in Israel. In the Bible, there is a
marked resistance to any interference with private property, not least by enforced taxation, which was regarded as
unjust. As Proverbs 29:4 remarks, 'By just government a
king gives his country stability, but by forced contributions
he reduces it to ruin.' Opposition to the monarchy, as
found in texts probably dating not long after its establishment, was in the first instance on social and economic,
rather than theological, grounds, and one of the main
complaints was against the king's imposition of taxation or
its equivalent forced labour, which prevented the individual from working his own land (1 Samuel 8:11–17; see
also 1 Kings 12:1–15): this perhaps also accounts for the
condemnation of the taking of a census (2 Samuel 24),
which may well have been intended for taxation purposes.

Thirdly, as with Adam, the wealth that God destines for
human beings is the reward for their own efforts to acquire
it – 'that a man should eat and drink and enjoy himself, in
return for all his labour, is a gift of God' (Ecclesiastes 3:13).
The Wisdom literature especially contains a number of
exhortations to work hard and warns that failure to do so
will result in poverty (e.g. Proverbs 6:6–11, 10:4, 20:13,
28:19). However, it would hardly be correct to describe this,
as has sometimes been done, as a straightforward work
ethic: it is not so much work in itself which is the ideal as the
prosperity which it brings and which human beings may
then enjoy.

What has just been said must be balanced by various
other considerations. We may first consider some limitations which are found in the Bible on the individual's
freedom to acquire wealth and his freedom to employ his

possessions as he himself chose. One of these can be described as theological, and again it derives from the fact of Israel's possession of the land of Canaan. As has been stated, this was God's free bounty and so the land and the wealth it produced were ultimately his to dispose of as he willed. This concept is given theological expression in the institutions of the sabbath year and the jubilee in the book of Leviticus, and fully expressed in God's words in Leviticus 25:23: 'the land is mine and you are coming into it as aliens and settlers,' that is, the land of Canaan belongs only to God and the Israelites are there only as 'aliens', permanent, but non-property-owning, residents. During the sabbath year the whole land was to be left fallow as an assertion of its divine ownership, returning to its original state unexploited by man; and the provisions of the jubilee (Leviticus 25:8–55) spring from the doctrine that ownership of property was really vested in God, so that no individual could have an absolute permanent claim on it. However successful a person might be in acquiring wealth by his own endeavours and however much this might be viewed as the ideal, he was never to think that what he owned was under his absolute control: it was always to be understood as a divine gift and the individual was always responsible to God for its proper use (Deuteronomy 8:17–18).

Another kind of limitation can perhaps best be described as social. The Old Testament view of wealth, like so much of its basic social ethics, reflects an age-old and relatively simple society, a pastoral and agricultural community in which each extended family exercised its own autonomy, possessing house and land which provided economic livelihood. Great discrepancy in wealth was not envisaged. Rather, the ideal was that everyone should enjoy the basic necessities of life, an ideal well expressed in the prayer of Agur, son of Jakeh, in Proverbs 30:7ff, which interestingly combines both the theological and social limitations on wealth which we have mentioned:

Give me neither poverty nor wealth,
provide me only with the food I need.
If I have too much I shall deny thee
and say 'Who is the Lord?'
If I am reduced to poverty I shall steal
and blacken the name of my God.

However, these words, reflecting later developments in Israelite society, indicate the possibility of excessive wealth, of great discrepancies in this respect between one person and another. The effect of these developments on the ancient social order will be discussed later when we come to look at the ethical teaching of the prophets.

The words of Agur lead to a consideration of the Old Testament attitude more specifically to poverty. Quite simply, because God has set Israel in so abundant an environment, poverty ought not to exist at all – 'there shall be no poor among you, for the Lord your God will bless you with great prosperity in the land which he is giving you to occupy' (Deuteronomy 15:4). But realistically it was recognised that in the actual world it did exist and would continue to do so, and so, very shortly after the verse just quoted, the book of Deuteronomy has to say 'the poor will always be with you in the land' (15:11). Poverty did not just begin with the new social conditions under the monarchy: all sorts of reasons could bring a man and his family into poverty, even in the simplest and most closely-knit society. But because this was so clearly contrary to the divine purpose, there was a special duty to relieve it as far as possible, a duty laid on any individual Israelite who had the ability to do so.

However, this was not a matter of legal enactment, as can be seen from that earliest Israelite legal code already mentioned, which the other and later Old Testament legal collections presuppose and build upon, the so-called 'Book of the Covenant' in Exodus 21:1 – 23:19. This falls clearly into two parts. The first (Exodus 21:12–22) consists of a series of definite enactments, described in Exodus 21:1 by the legal term *mishpatim*, 'laws'. They seem to be addressed to those responsible for the actual administration of justice, for they deal with civil and criminal matters and provide specific penalties for their non-observance which could be enforced in the courts. What is noteworthy here is the concern to establish strict impartiality in the administration of justice. This section witnesses to the centrality of law, an ideal which marks the whole of the Old Testament. It was to operate in exactly the same way for rich and poor alike, as is expressed in a key verse, Exodus 23:2–3, addressed to those responsible for pronouncing judgment: 'you shall not be led into wrongdoing by the majority, nor, when you give evidence in a lawsuit, shall you side with the majority to pervert justice; nor shall you favour a poor man in his suit'. This always remained a basic principle of Israel's law, for what is said in Exodus 23:2–3 is repeated in much the same terms in Deuteronomy 1:17 and Leviticus 19:15. There was to be no mitigation of strict justice, however harsh the consequences, simply because the guilty person was poor: the thief 'shall repay in full; if he has no means, he shall be sold' – i.e. into slavery – 'to pay for the theft' (Exodus 22:3). At least as far as the law is concerned, the Old Testament appears to know nothing of any inbuilt, legalised 'bias to the poor'.

The second section of the Book of the Covenant, Exodus 22:21–23:19, is very different. Here we find a mixture of humanitarian and cultic injunctions – we shall only be concerned with the former – which envisage no legal redress for their breach and provide no penalties for their non-observance. Rather, they appeal to the moral and social conscience of each person for obedience. In fact, they are a kind of sermon addressed to the nation and this becomes characteristic of the whole of the later legal collections, such as Deuteronomy and the 'Code of Holiness' (Leviticus 17–26). Whereas the distinctive form of the first section of the Book of the Covenant is by way of a statement of a case in the third person singular – 'if a man does so and so, then so and so follows' – here we find a direct address, usually in the second person singular, and sometimes accompanied by motive clauses designed to persuade the hearers to do what is being asked of them (e.g. Exodus 22:21–24). What these humanitarian injunctions appear to seek to do is to go beyond the strict application of the law to a different sphere of justice, to ensure that all in society share in, and are sustained by, the wealth of the people as a whole, to realise God's intention when he gave that wealth to Israel. What is noteworthy is that it is only in this section that we find enjoined the duty of care for the poor and the underprivileged, such as the widow and orphan, and that here the problem of poverty is to be resolved by the action of the individual or perhaps the individual man as head of the family group. But such a person is free to act as he chooses; there is no formal law which can compel him to behave in the ways the author of the section wishes, for whom only an appeal to a person's conscience is available. Even if, as some scholars hold, the injunctions in question in their present form emanate from the royal court, they are still not state law.

At this point, it is appropriate to say something of the role of the Israelite king as an upholder of social justice. The monarch in the ancient Near East was expected to show a particular concern to protect the poor and underprivileged, and the Israelite king was no exception, as several Old Testament passages show: one may instance the description of the ideal king in Psalm 72 or Isaiah 11:3–5. The king had this special responsibility because of his uniquely close relationship with the deity: as God was concerned with the plight of the poor, the widow and the orphan, so, as his intimate servant, was the king. The king's responsibility here was highlighted by the new social and economic conditions which developed during Israel's monarchical period, when there grew up a class of large landowners and rich merchants who were tempted to increase their wealth by forcing poorer groups into actual or economic slavery. The issue for the king was the exploitation of such persons by those more powerful than themselves, and the king's role was twofold: firstly, to rectify any actual flouting of the law when people exercised their right of appeal to him in cases where they had a grievance, but secondly, to set an example of right behaviour for others. It is when the rich use their economic power to destroy the freedom and independence which is every Israelite's heritage that they are attacked in the Bible, not simply for being rich or even very rich. It is when the king, as the wealthiest and most powerful figure in society, fails to carry out his divinely given calling to forward the proper social order for Israel that he is condemned, not because of the position he occupies. This is clearly seen in the prophet's contrast between king Josiah and his son Jehoiakim in Jeremiah 22:13–19. The latter is condemned for his extravagance, injustice and economic oppression while the former who, it is pointed out, was equally a king and equally wealthy, is praised in that 'he dispensed justice to the lowly and poor' and this was because he knew the Lord and what he willed, in a way that his successor failed to do. Again, it is to the monarch's own conscience, his own awareness of his duty, that appeal is made.

It is against the background of the monarchical period that the prophets speak, and various things need to be noted. First, the prophets do not differ from the basic Israelite view that wealth, at least in the sense of a basic self-sufficiency, is good and poverty an evil which ought to be mitigated as far as possible. And they were realistic enough to realise that, in the society in which they found themselves, there was bound to be a disparity of wealth between different groups in the nation. Hence, when they inveigh against the rich, it is not because of their wealth as such, but because of their enjoyment of it while ignoring, or taking advantage of, others' needs. So their attacks on the rich are always accompanied by statements that they are oppressing the poor, and, indeed, these statements always form the climax of the prophetic indictment. For example, Amos rebukes the ladies of Samaria not so much for their idle and luxurious life style or their wealth, but because 'they oppress the poor and crush the destitute' (Amos 4:1).

Similarly, the prophets appear as advocates of the private ownership of property as the right of all Israelites and hence they denounce those who deprive people of their possessions and force them into poverty.

What the prophets base themselves on is not primarily the legal system, as represented by the *mishpatim* of the Book of the Covenant, but rather the general terms of the humanitarian injunctions of the second section of that document. Certainly, they sometimes roundly condemn corruption and sharp practice in the actual administration of the courts, occasions when the high would have been favoured against the low. But such is not their main concern. The problem was that those stipulations of the law which demanded the same impartial treatment of rich and poor alike could be the cause of much hardship, precisely because they required an equal application of the law to those who in fact were not equal.[5] To take the law of theft in Exodus 22:1–3, which has already been mentioned: this would cause no great difficulty for the man who could afford the fine but disaster for the one who could not. Often, the prophets seem to speak not of legal maladministration but of the harshness of the judgments handed down, which the rigorous impartiality of the law necessitated. So what the prophets were conscious of was a conflict between legality and justice, a distinction that can perhaps best be expressed by the two Hebrew terms, *mishpat*, a law or legal ordinance, and *zedekah*, justice or righteousness. What the prophets seem to have desired is that *zedekah* should function, for the benefit of those who would otherwise suffer unduly, in the actual application of the *mishpatim*. We may perhaps see a succinct statement of the prophetic ideal in the words of Psalm 94:14, as rendered in the New English Bible, where it is said of God, 'for righteousness still informs his judgment [*mishpat*], and all upright men follow it'. Righteousness or equity informing law and legal decisions: that sums up the prophetic aim.

---

[5]See Eryl W. Davies, *Prophecy and Ethics* (1981), pp. 98ff.

But how was one to know what was really just in any given situation? What guidelines did Israel have for discerning when 'oppression' was taking place, when the disadvantaged were in fact being unfairly treated? At one time it was thought that the prophets were appealing to the Covenant and its law but it is curious that they hardly ever mention the Covenant, and scholars are now more inclined to believe that they challenge those they condemn to act in accordance with what we might call 'natural law' or 'natural morality', that is, with generally recognised standards of humane and decent behaviour which the human conscience could recognise. As one scholar, speaking of the outlook of Amos, has put it: 'Social morality, understood both as impartiality in justice and care for the rights of the helpless, is not a mere piece of arbitrary divine legislation nor merely a human convention, but almost a part of the order of nature, self-evident to any right-thinking man.'[6]

If this is right, two consequences follow. First, the prophets assume that people can change when they are confronted with the contrast between what they actually do and what in conscience they know they ought to do. The powerful *could* use their power in concern for the welfare and rights of others. The prophets never speak as though some authority, such as the king, should step in to force the rich to behave properly: no doubt they held that on occasion he could and should, but in the first instance the powerful have to realise their obligations and act on them. Secondly, the fact that the rightness of social obligations ought to be so obvious means that neglect of them would incur divine judgment, for God is the creator and guarantor of universal justice. For the prophets, social injustice was what would bring judgment on the nation because the people had no excuse for not doing what was right, and this insight was the root of what was a novelty in the message of the great prophets, the proclamation of doom. To quote again the scholar mentioned above: 'since the rightness of

<hr>

[6] John Barton, *Amos's Oracles against the Nations* (1980), p. 49.

the obligations laid on Israel ought to be as obvious as if they were agreed on by all men, how much worse her guilt is when she also has the advantage of a special personal contact with God to endorse them'.[7] It is this broad basis of natural law which should form the guiding principle for Christian participation in secular politics, not that it is exclusive to Christians, but because they can perhaps understand its implications more clearly than some others.

So far, we have been considering wealth and poverty in the Old Testament in almost purely economic terms but it is important to recognise that, in the Bible, 'poor' often has a distinctively religious connotation. The Psalms, in particular, frequently refer to a group of people described by various Hebrew terms – 'helpless, wretched, oppressed, small, weak, poor' – but they all designate the same entity and 'poor' is an adequate blanket term. Probably some of those thus designated were poor in a material sense but that is not the primary emphasis here: for example, in Psalm 86:1–2 the speaker describes himself as 'downtrodden and poor' but also as 'constant and true' and as putting his trust in the Lord. All the expressions are clearly synonymous nor is there anything in this, and similar psalms, to suggest material poverty. What is meant is a group which represented the faithful members of the religious community of Israel, the centre of whose existence was a living relationship with God and whose trust was not ultimately in political schemes or high position or wealth. After the return from exile, it is this sense of the term 'poor' which becomes most significant as denoting the central division in Judaism, that between the 'poor' or 'righteous', who adhered to worship, to the Law and to the regulations governing devout conduct, and the 'wicked' who no longer adhered to these things.[8] Above all, these 'poor' looked to

---

[7] *Ibid.*, pp. 49f.

[8] For these two groups, see C. Westermann, *The Living Psalms* (1989), pp. 144f, and the discussion by Sue Gillingham, 'The Poor in the Psalms', *Expository Times*, vol. 100 (1988), pp. 15–19.

God for redemption, for his intervention to usher in a new age to be marked by perfect justice and righteousness in contrast to the evils of the present world.

It would now be generally agreed that this situation, and the group of the 'poor' in the sense described, constituted a vital element in the emergence of Christianity. But before turning to the New Testament, it is perhaps worth saying something briefly in answer to the objections which might be raised today by many powerful voices against the description so far attempted of the Old Testament view of wealth and poverty. The 'Liberation' theologians of Latin America and those influenced by them would say that the Old Testament is far more revolutionary and radical than we have pictured it and that its central message is a call to the poor to struggle for their freedom from the oppression of the rich and powerful and that God is seen to be on their side and as the enemy of wealth and authority. In particular, such thinkers give a central place to the experience of the Exodus which, they would claim, 'always carried powerful connotations of liberation' and is 'used as a model for later events and experiences'.[9] But, whatever truth there may be in this, it ignores the caveat uttered at the beginning of this essay in that it is one-sided and fails to take into account so much of the biblical evidence, in particular the concept of a divine commonwealth and a holy community which is so prominent there. The Exodus is not the only, or even the predominant, strand in the Bible as we have it.[10] It is preceded by, and set in the context of, the primaeval history of creation and the patriarchal narratives with their ideal of land and family, and the Exodus itself is not God's supreme achievement for Israel, but rather, as we have already noted, his settling of them in the abundance of Canaan. Though there is a clear awareness of the danger of

---

[9] Richard Bauckham, *The Bible in Politics* (1989), p. 104. See also Emmette Weir, 'The Poor are Powerless', *Expository Times*, vol. 100 (1988), pp. 13–15.

[10] See J. Barr, 'The Bible as a Political Document', *Bulletin of the John Rylands University Library of Manchester* 62 (1980), p. 286.

riches, there is no glorification of the economically poor and, as one scholar has put it: 'There is little sense of the Old Testament as witnessing to the demands of the poor for their rights within their own society. It is rather the expression of the conscience of those who have sufficiency.'[11] Its message is to rich and poor alike and both have their place (Proverbs 22:2, 29:13).

Jesus and the Poor

This essay has concentrated on the Old Testament and that for two reasons. First, the Old Testament is concerned with those who have a direct responsibility for the society in which they are set and who can influence what happens in it. By contrast, the early Christians were a small and mar- ginalised sect who could exercise virtually no control upon public life. Thus we should not expect to find much guidance for those occupied today with political, social and economic questions in the New Testament as compared with the Old. Secondly, the first Christians did not greatly concern themselves with the existing social order because they expected a speedy end to the world age in which they were living and while it may be going too far to describe their social understanding merely as an *Interimsethik* – there are indications in some of the later New Testament docu- ments that the hope of an imminent *parousia* was beginning to fade – it was inevitably limited. Thus the New Testament's relevance to the subject under discussion can be treated more briefly.

The politically radical and revolutionary understanding of the Old Testament has been considered in this essay because similar claims have been made about the message of Jesus – that Jesus taught that the economically poor are specially favoured by God and that the rich are the enemies of the kingdom he came to inaugurate. Attempts to portray

---

[11]R. J. Coggins, 'The Old Testament and the Poor', *Expository Times*, vol. 99 (1988), p. 14.

Jesus as one among a number of political revolutionaries in the troubled climate of first-century Palestine have not proved very convincing and the texts adduced to prove this 'bias to the materially poor' will not bear that interpretation. It would seem that, when Jesus speaks of the 'poor', he is using the term in the religious sense which, as we have seen, had become characteristic of the Judaism of his day, that is, the voluntary poor who were willing to be poor even though they were still in possession of wealth. Significantly, it is in this sense that the members of the Qumran community described themselves as 'poor', a group contemporary with Jesus and with which his own movement had many similarities. It is the poor with this meaning of whom the gospels speak: in the Beatitudes, Matthew's 'poor in spirit' gives the correct understanding of Luke's 'poor' and we should understand in the same way the 'poor' in Jesus's quotation of Isaiah 61:1 at the beginning of his ministry at Luke 4:18, which has often been taken simply to show his identification with the economically deprived. The Isaiah passage also shows clearly that his message for the poor is a sign of the breaking in of the new age: the poor are those whose hope is only in God and his kingdom, who do not put their trust in wealth and secular power, and those who would embrace the kingdom wholeheartedly 'cannot serve God and mammon' (Matthew 6:24).

But this does not mean that as long as they are in the world as it is, Jesus's followers are not to enjoy its benefits or to neglect their social obligations. One is often given the impression that the early Christian communities consisted very largely of the economically poor and socially deprived. However, recent thorough sociological studies have shown that in fact most of their members were reasonably well-to-do, pursuing gainful occupations; in modern terms, they could fairly be described as 'middle-class'.[12] And Paul can

---

[12] Cf. Robert H. Smith, 'Were the Early Christians Middle-Class?' in *The Bible and liberation*, ed. Norman K. Gottwald (1983), pp. 441–57.

say bluntly: 'the man who will not work shall not eat' and he rebukes the idle who will not 'work quietly for their living' (2 Thessalonians 3:10–12) – remarks which are wholly in accord with the outlook of the Old Testament Wisdom literature. Certainly, the New Testament teaches that wealth has very great dangers, that greed is an ever-present temptation and that 'even when a man has more than enough, his wealth does not give him life' (Luke 12:15), while the Letter of James fulminates, exactly as do the Old Testament prophets, against those who use their riches to oppress and exploit the less fortunate (James 5:1–6). But, again as with the prophets, it is reliance on wealth and the lack of responsibility in its employment which is being condemned, not possessions as such, and the remedy is a change of heart, to become 'poor in spirit' by putting one's whole trust in God and accepting that our possessions are only his gift to be used, certainly for ourselves as a mark of his gracious blessing, but also for the good of others. The Christian must always be governed above all by this faith and trust to guide him in any participation in the inevitable imperfections and limitations of secular political, economic and social action.

7

Conservatism before Conservatism: Political Theology in an Anglican Confessional State

J. C. D. Clark

IN the long relationship of Christianity to the political realm, the last century-and-a-half of British history has no privileged status. We have no reasons, theological or historical, for treating the pattern observed in these islands during that period as particularly normative. It is no special case: it underwrites no values; it validates no categories. In Christian history if in no other, we are obliged to regard all ages as equidistant from eternity. The history of Christianity is in this respect unlike the history of the British constitution: the forms and precedents of religion do not become more relevant to us the nearer they are to us in time.

This is not to diminish our recent experience; it is merely to observe that the history of the Church is of more central importance to the argument than the present-minded will allow. Indeed, the liberal who wishes to exalt the claims of reason (that is, of recent opinion) over Scripture and tradition can only do so by a strategy which systematically marginalises the significance of the longer historical record. Only by suppressing the evidence of past forms of life is the rationalist truly free. Only by attenuating our historical vision can he persuade us that the logic of revelation or of social development is unfolding in his direction.

If we seek to discover the theological foundations of political commitment on the territory of British history, a long perspective is of peculiar importance. An historical vision which extended back little more than a century would conceal from us an important fact: the very terms in which sociological reasons alleged to explain Anglicanism's decline were identified changed in fundamental ways in the early part of the nineteenth century. The adjective 'radical' has been traced to 1786, but 'radicalism' did not appear until 1820, closely following 'liberalism' (1819). 'Socialist' as a noun has been traced only to 1827, and 'socialism' did not follow until 1837. 'Industrialism' (1831) was followed by the modern sense of 'exploitation' (1841), but 'industrial revolution' only arrived in the 1880s. 'Individualism' was imported by translation from the French in 1840 and taken up as an antithesis to 'socialism'; 'communist' and 'communism' equally date from 1840, but 'collectivism' waited until 1880 and 'egalitarian' until 1885.[1] What of 'conservatism'?

It, too, was a response to circumstance, those crucial party-political changes which came in 1828–32. The repeal of the Test and Corporation Acts in 1828, and Catholic Emancipation in 1829, shattered the coalition which had been in office for most of the previous half century. 'Tory', by this period, implied the old Anglican political theology, the exclusive link of Church and State, defended at Westminster by a loose and unstructured governing coalition assembled by the crown. Now the old ideology had been made irrelevant by the final, sweeping, victory of the Whigs; party discipline and an official party name suddenly became a necessity for a group newly out of office. A new,

---

[1] Anna Bezanson, 'The Early Use of the Term Industrial Revolution', *Quarterly Journal of Economics* 36 (1922), pp. 343–9; Arthur E. Bestor, 'The Evolution of the Socialist Vocabulary', *Journal of the History of Ideas* 9 (1948), pp. 259–302. Bestor illustrates the brief lives of many other new terms, since deceased: guarantism, pantisocracy, serigermy, phalanstery. Equally with liberalism, radicalism and conservatism, these terms do not identify timeless dispositions.

more neutral, more pragmatic title was felt by some to be appropriate for a new organisation. Was it generically similar or not? Either view seemed possible. In 1830 the Church-and-King enthusiast John Wilson Croker famously sought to argue for continuity in declaring his loyalty to 'what is called the Tory, and which might with more propriety be called the Conservative, party'. Others, like Robert Peel, the Gradgrind of English politics, intended a clearer break from old Anglican commitments; he sought to ground political action on secular expediency. 'Conservatism' was a deliberate invention in this new world, and can be traced only from its use by Thomas Arnold in 1835.[2] It quickly gained currency as the name of the creed of the newly-organised Conservative party. By 1844, the Tory sympathiser Benjamin Disraeli could condemn the short-comings of the new doctrine in *Coningsby*: Peel's Tamworth Manifesto of 1834 'was an attempt to construct a party without principles . . . Conservatism discards Prescription, shrinks from Principle, disavows Progress; having rejected all respect for Antiquity, it offers no redress for the Present, and makes no preparation for the Future'.[3] In his 1849 Preface to the fifth edition, Disraeli made his intention clear: 'In considering the Tory scheme, the author recognised in the CHURCH the most powerful agent in the previous development of England, and the most efficient means of that renovation of the national spirit at which he aimed.' But Anglican hegemony had been destroyed. Despite this critique, the term 'conservatism' took on the appearance of self-evidence, as if it were a timeless temperament, an unchanging attitude to politics. Yet it was as much a specific formation as any of the others, and in Disraeli's formulation it would have seemed unfamiliar and unappealing to the ruling elite of the old world. Such men

---

[2] *Oxford English Dictionary; Quarterly Review* (January 1830), p. 276; Robert Stewart, *The Foundation of the Conservative Party 1830–1867* (London, 1978), p. 69.
[3] *Coningsby*, Book 2, Chapter 5.

neither discarded prescription, nor shrank from principle, nor disavowed progress. Their problems were differently defined.

If the relation of Christianity to politics is to be discerned it can only be by seeing past the terms in which secular society has come to describe itself, since the formulation in the early nineteenth century of the building blocks of our own intellectual world (liberalism and radicalism, class and socialism) contained from the outset, within the categories themselves, a teleology which has locked English Christianity into its subsequent decline.[4] Far from there being something especially relevant for us in 'modern' Christian thought (by which is usually meant twentieth-century Christian Socialism), that tradition is only one among many, and its historical premises – the premises of its claims to timelessness – have come under increasing critical scrutiny. In recent years it has been highlighted as an historical formation rather than as abstract truth: a school of thought with a trajectory from inception through prevalence to bitter decline. We can appreciate its provisional and relative nature only by adopting a longer historical perspective.

Yet all schools of thought demand a similar analysis. The challenge of Roman Catholics to Anglicans, 'where was your Church before Luther?', could be reformulated for present-day Conservatives: 'where were your politics before Conservatism?' For we face the paradox that the subject of this essay – that most conservative era of British history between the Reformation and the Reform Bill of 1832 – lacked an abstract noun to express its attention to tradition, hierarchy and authority. What, then, did structure its reverence for these things? We might reasonably

---

[4] For the emergence of the first three of these terms as part of the assault on the old order, see J. C. D. Clark, *English Society 1688–1832: Ideology, Social Structure and Political Practice during the Ancien Regime* (Cambridge, 1985). The centrality of Karl Marx's critique of orthodox religion to the origins of socialism is a commonplace of scholarship.

seek an answer in society's then-hegemonic system of ideas, Christian theology.

Partly, it was the minimal role of the state in public provision which left its moral function in prominence (in the 1980s, a state which again sought to diminish its public role again found that the sensitive political issues were increasingly moral ones). Largely, however, it was the wide prevalence of Christian practice which made theology the ground on which public issues were automatically debated. Should clergymen pronounce on matters of public policy? Are the spheres of religion and politics distinct? Is party politics, or national identity, ultimately based on moral insights? Is it possible or legitimate to embody Christian doctrines in the traditions, laws and customs of a people? Or does Christian doctrine stand as a set of abstract truths, accessible by reason, but with only an ambiguous application to social forms? Are our values ultimately grounded on tradition or reason? Does Christianity dictate, or specially sanction, any particular forms of government? Is an established Church an essential aspect of the state, or a temporary and dispensable adjunct?

Modern theorising on these issues shares a characteristic which in a longer historical perspective is distinctive: it appears to be conducted *de novo*, from first principles. It is as if a Christian political theology now has to be devised afresh, Anglican tradition on these matters having been wiped away in an act of collective amnesia. That tradition of thought, however, was both great in its extent and distinguished in its intellectual quality.[5] The Church, before its experience of radical reform, was a body of great intellectual power. Its bishops and higher clergy were often men of considerable scholarly distinction, and often willing polemicists in defence of orthodoxy. In the twentieth cen-

---

[5] For a fuller exploration of that tradition, see Clark, *English Society 1688–1832*; Robert Hole, *Pulpits, Politics and Public Order in England, 1760–1832* (Cambridge, 1989). For the damage done to that tradition in 1688, see J. P. Kenyon, *Revolution Principles: The Politics of Party 1689–1720* (Cambridge, 1977).

tury, after the average calibre of its clergy had collapsed, the Church was open to the charge of being merely responsive to secular currents of thought. But before the 1830s, the pattern was strikingly different: churchmen took the lead in developing scholarly disciplines which were later to be appropriated by materialists.[6] Moreover, the more closely the Church approximated to the nation, the more orthodox was its doctrine and powerful its intellectual rationale: Anglicanism's most influential body of social and political teaching was a derivative from the great flowering of patristic and biblical scholarship in the sixteenth and seventeenth centuries.[7] This chapter offers a brief reminder of some themes in a tradition of discourse.

The Nature of Government

The question of the legal status and function of Christianity has, historically, been intimately linked to another question: how was the state assembled, and what was its self-image? The question of national identity in Protestant England, Wales, Scotland, Ireland and North America was determined first by contrast with the Catholic alternatives and, second, by the formative role of Protestantism, especially Anglicanism. Not only England but her American colonies had access to a doctrine of identity, origins, purpose and destiny as a new Israel, a chosen people defined by religious allegiance and practice.[8] It was a religious identity which, in 1642, 1688, 1715 and 1745, even overrode

---

[6] Boyd Hilton, *The Age of Atonement: the Influence of Evangelicalism on Social and Economic Thought, 1795–1865* (Oxford, 1988); A. M. C. Waterman, *Revolution, Economics and Religion: Christian Political Economy, 1798–1833* (Cambridge, 1990).

[7] For which, see especially Paul Elmer More and Frank Leslie Cross (eds), *Anglicanism: The Thought and Practice of the Church of England, Illustrated from the Religious Literature of the Seventeenth Century* (London, 1935), a full anthology, and H. R. McAdoo, *The Spirit of Anglicanism: A Survey of Anglican Theological Method in the Seventeenth Century* (London, 1965).

[8] Ruth Bloch, *Visionary Republic: Millennial Themes in American Thought, 1756–1800* (Cambridge, 1985).

the claims of dynastic allegiance for many Englishmen; the American Revolution in turn merely directed these religious sensibilities against the mother country. These self-images were seldom in our sense pluralist: they were fragmented, each rival vision competing for monopoly.

These contests began close to home. Edward I's conquest of Wales was not conclusive, and many Welsh clergy supported the rebellion of Owain Glyn Dwr against Henry IV; the subordination of the province was finally ensured by Elizabeth I's imposition of the 1559 Church Settlement. Welsh-speaking bishops using a Welsh Bible, and services in Welsh, pre-empted most of the potential sources of cultural nationalism. It was the recrudescence of Dissent in the nineteenth century, leading to disestablishment in 1920, which was a necessary precondition for modern Welsh radicalism and, in the twentieth century, nationalism.

In Ireland Protestantism was more clearly, if less successfully, an agency of English rule. English influence over the Irish Church dated from the conquest of 1172. Henrician and Elizabethan legislation in the Dublin parliament then imposed a liturgy and relationship of Church and State similar to England's, staffed with clergy, and provided with an intellectual rationale, by Trinity College, Dublin (founded 1591). But with the translation of the Prayer Book into Irish forbidden,[9] and successive polarising conflicts between Catholic and Protestant, the Church of Ireland was steadily locked into its role as a pillar of English ascendancy. From 1688, Irish Catholic loyalty to the exiled dynasty was the occasion for a legal code, the Penal Laws, which expressed the religious basis of political power with lasting clarity. But it was not Catholics alone who disputed Anglican ascendancy. From the early seventeenth century, Scots Presbyterian settlers in Ulster produced a second unassimilable bloc, and the disestablishment of the Church

---

[9] The Bible was not translated into Irish until 1658; English remained the overwhelmingly dominant language of the Church of Ireland.

of Ireland in 1871 was similarly a milestone in the process of English retreat. The emergence of a Catholic Irish Republic, and the numerical collapse of Protestantism in the south, were part of the same process.

In Scotland, the Reformation had already produced a Presbyterian settlement before the union of crowns in 1603. The mediaeval Scots Church had maintained its independence of York and Canterbury; under the Stuarts, equally, Scots resistance to the imposition of episcopalianism and an English liturgy led to rebellion, the 'Bishops' Wars' (1639–40), the recall of the Long Parliament at Westminster, and the collapse of the English monarchy. After 1660 the sanguinary conflict between Presbyterian and Episcopalian resumed; but the political significance of the conflict was reversed by the flight of James II in 1688. Henceforth the Episcopalians stood condemned by their disaffection from the exiled dynasty: William III imposed Presbyterianism on the Church of Scotland, and Episcopalians were legally proscribed until the 1790s. As in Ireland and Wales, England's hold on Scotland was effected through the imposition of a religious settlement; of the three cases, the Scots proved the most durable.

Beyond its immediate neighbours, England's astonishingly successful imperial drive was fuelled not least by a desire to win the world for Protestantism and to reclaim the heathen from barbarism. Here too, the weakening of the self-confident missionary instinct within Anglicanism marched in step with England's weakening political hold on her colonies; the collapse of domestic Anglican confidence in the 1960s[10] was matched by a major reversal of the population movements on which the empire had been built, and the arrival in Britain (but especially in England) of large numbers of people of other faiths.

Anglicanism, then, was a central theme in the creation of the nation state out of its component parts – England,

---

[10] For which, see S. W. Sykes, 'Theology, Toleration and Conflict' in J. C. D. Clark (ed.), *Ideas and Politics in Modern Britain* (London, 1990).

Scotland, Ireland and Wales. Was it associated with any particular form of government *within* the state? Did the Church of England lend any special sanction to representative democracy?

No such assumptions surrounded its Henrician origins. On the contrary, Anglican divines praised the *via media* of their Church as one between the extremes of Rome and Geneva, each of which taught a right of rebellion against unjust princes. Civil war in the 1640s emphasised this threat with brutal clarity. In response the Church of England, by taking as its earthly head the monarch, committed itself to an increasing endorsement of the institution of monarchy as such. This naturally reached its apogee after the Restoration of 1660. Robert South gave famous and succinct expression to the doctrine in a sermon:

> The church of *England* glories in nothing more than that she is the truest friend to kings, and to kingly government, of any other church in the world; that they were the same hands and principles that took the crown from the king's head, and the mitre from the bishops. It is indeed the happiness of some professions and callings, they can equally square themselves to and thrive under all revolutions of government: But the clergy of *England* neither know nor affect that happiness, and are willing to be despised for not doing so.[11]

Like the great majority of his fellow clergy, he believed that 'monarchy, or kingly government is the most excellent, and best adapted to the ends of governments, and the benefit of society'.[12] The Church of England was

---

[11] Robert South, 'The Duties of the Episcopal Function: A Sermon Preach'd at Lambeth-Chapel, On the 25th of November, 1666. Upon the Consecration of the Right Revd Father in God John Dolben, Lord Bishop of Rochester' in South, *Sermons Preached Upon Several Occasions* (6 vols, London, 1737), vol. 1, p. 190.

[12] 'The Peculiar Care and Concern of Providence for the Protection and Defence of Kings. A Sermon Preached at Westminster-Abbey, Nov. 5, 1675', *ibid.*, vol. 3, p. 476; cf. 'Ecclesiastical Policy the best Policy: Or, Religion the best Reason of State: A Sermon Preach'd before the Honourable Society of Lincoln's-Inn', *ibid.*, vol. 1, p. 117.

the only church in Christendom we read of, whose avowed
principles and practices disown all resistance of the civil
power; and which the saddest experience, and the truest
policy and reason will evince to be the only one, that is
durably consistent with the *English* monarchy. Let men look
both into its doctrine, and into its history, and they will find
neither the *Calvins*, the *Knoxes*, the *Junius Brutus's*, the
Synods, nor the holy Commonwealths of one side, nor yet
the *Bellarmines*, the *Escobars*, nor the *Mariana's* of the other.[13]

The Anglican theory of kingship came to rest on inter-
linked components: divine, indefeasible, hereditary right.
If obedience to lawful commands was an aspect of Christian
duty, resistance and rebellion became sinful as well as
unlawful. What were the limits of obedience? The doctrine
of passive obedience taught that unjust commands were
not to be obeyed, but that the subject should accept the
penalties for non-compliance rather than rise in rebellion
and involve the nation in the greater evils of civil war.
What, then, were unjust commands? They proved, in the
reign of James II, to be commands which conflicted with
established Anglicanism. The Revolution of 1688 was a step
which involved damage to both Church and monarchy.
The Church lost its power to compel regular mass attend-
ance at its services; the monarchy was restricted by a new
libertarian rhetoric, even though the ideas of an original
contract and of natural rights were not entrenched in
English law. If a minority of republicans and Jacobites
believed that the changes had been fundamental, however,
the mainstream Anglican position denied this. Of the
components of late-Stuart kingship – divine, hereditary,
indefeasible right – most men sought to argue that 1688 had
modified only 'indefeasible'. Into the early nineteenth century, the Church of England therefore continued to insist

---

[13] 'Pretence of Conscience, no Excuse for Rebellion. A Sermon Preach'd before
King Charles II. At his Chapel in Whitehall, on the Thirtieth Day of Jan. 1662/3',
ibid., vol. 5, pp. 97–8.

that the state in general and the existing form of government in particular had received divine sanction.

By comparison with these older conflicts, the gentle decline of the ideologies of Socialism and Whig constitutionalism has left political culture since the 1950s in an ideologically tranquil state. It is too easy to deduce from this that English politics has always been marked by a gentle pragmatism which renders present vacuousness as unproblematic as it is unoriginal. Such a situation is, however, exceptional by the standard of England before 1832, for the classic and momentous issues of political theory were then worked out in a native English context. The period from the Reformation to the Reform Bill witnessed essential and fundamental differences about the nature of the constitution; but they tended to derive from divergent theologies rather than from subscription to secular ideologies.

Recent debate on these issues has been marked less by a failure on the part of clergy to endorse parliamentary democracy (though they may have been unwilling to recognise the legitimacy of its results when these proved uncongenial) than by their failure to give expression to a long tradition of Anglican political theology: far from undervaluing democracy, Anglican clergy have tended to elevate it to the status of unquestionable truth. The idolatry which surrounds this particular (and temporary) form of government is not well grounded in Anglican tradition. For a precedent, we need to go back to those late-seventeenth-century divines who insisted that the throne was indefeasibly attached to a particular dynasty, the Stuarts. The intellectual claims of that theory were widely acknowledged to be considerable. Yet, finally, their rejection allowed Anglicans to reunite behind the perception that *all* forms of legitimate government were divinely ordained. Without a right of rebellion, such a view gave divine sanction to the actually-existing relation of Church and State established by law and theologically grounded by Richard Hooker. Recent Anglican experience has explored the unfolding implications of the partial destruction of that relationship in the 1830s. Far from Anglicanism containing a special endorsement of particular state forms, it has historically worked with and through many political regimes – with most, indeed, more successfully than with modern liberal democracy.

The Establishment

For whom is the Church of England? For the whole nation? For all English Christians? For all who attend any of its services? For its communicant members? The Church's conception of its legitimate sphere has steadily contracted, with more marked downward steps in 1688–9 and 1828–32; but even recently many would have ascribed to it the most extensive scope, a lasting reminder of the official position before 1828. It was a claim grounded both in English law and in the Bible's clear references to the accountability of *nations*, making no allowance for divisions within them on grounds of ethnic pluralism, schism or religious in-difference.

Before the nineteenth century, neither the nation nor the Church was, in its dominant self-image, pictured as a voluntary society. Men were, in law, born members of both. In the Middle Ages, the problem was not complicated by religious diversity. As Archbishop Garbett observed:

> There is no special moment in English history of which it can be said that the Church was established when previously it had no connection with the State. The [mediaeval] con-troversies between the Church and the State were between different sets of officials within the nation, representing respectively ecclesiastical and secular interests.[14]

After the Reformation, this ideal was re-expressed, not abandoned. The Statute of Appeals of 1533 outlined the

---

[14] Cyril Garbett, *The Claims of the Church of England* (London, 1947), pp. 184–5.

Henrician doctrine of England as an independent 'body politick', 'an empire', governed in its spiritual aspect in the Church, in its secular in the State, both under the monarch. This doctrine recognised the Church as what it had always been: it was never 'established', endowed or chosen for a special position from among competitors, by any Act of Parliament. The term first appeared in Canon 3 of 1604: 'the Church of England by Law established under the King's Majesty'; but this recognised the situation as it already was.

Classic expression to this doctrine in the idiom of the Elizabethan settlement was given by Richard Hooker (*c.* 1554–1600). His work, *Of the Laws of Ecclesiastical Polity*, the first and greatest apologia for Anglicanism, was published in instalments (1594, 1597, 1648, 1662); the political Book VIII countered the hostile thesis 'That unto no civil prince or governor there may be given such power of ecclesiastical dominion as by the laws of the land belongeth unto the supreme regent thereof'. It proceeded from the assumption that 'there is not any man of the Church of England but the same man is also a member of the commonwealth; nor any man a member of the commonwealth, which is not also of the Church of England' (ch. 1.2). This, indeed, constituted the political aspect of the Anglican *via media* (ch. 1.7). Hooker argued that

> under dominions of infidels, the Church of Christ, and their commonwealth, were two societies independent. Secondly . . . in those commonwealths where the bishop of Rome beareth sway, one society is both the Church and the commonwealth; but the bishop of Rome doth divide the body into two diverse bodies, and doth not suffer the Church to depend upon the power of any civil prince or potentate. Thirdly . . . within this realm of England the case is neither as in the one, nor as in the other of the former two: but from the state of pagans we differ, in that with us one society is both Church and commonwealth, which with them it was not; as also from the state of those nations which subject themselves to the bishop of Rome, in that our Church hath dependency upon the chief in our common-

wealth, which it hath not under him. In a word, our estate is according to the pattern of God's own ancient elect people, which people was not part of them the commonwealth, and part of them the Church of God, but the selfsame people whole and entire were both under one chief Governor, on whose supreme authority they did all depend.

Political involvement in the life of the Church could not validly be described as Erastianism, it was argued. The monarch was anointed and clothed in priestly vestments at his coronation; parliament was a lay synod. Both were part of the Church, not separate and secular agencies subordinating the Church to their control.[15]

Such views were re-expressed in Bishop Overall's *Convocation Book*, the composition of the Convocation of 1606, published in 1690. It contained a long and careful deduction of political and ecclesiastical authority from Adam and Noah and of the divine sanction of forms of ministry; it argued against the authority of the Pope to depose princes. The Anglican Establishment was thereby set once again in the broadest theological and philosophical setting. Deduction proceeded from an account of the origins of government which became Anglican orthodoxy:

> If any Man shall therefore affirm, that Men at the first, without all good Education, or Civility, ran up and down in Woods, and Fields, as Wild Creatures, resting themselves in Caves, and Dens, and acknowledging no superiority one over another, until they were taught by Experience the necessity of Government; and that thereupon they chose some among themselves to order and rule the rest, giving them power and authority so to do; and that consequently all civil Power, Jurisdiction, and Authority was first derived from the people, and disorder'd multitude; or either is originally still in them, or else is deduced by their consents naturally from them; and is not God's Ordinance originally descending from him, and depending upon him, he doth greatly Erre.

---

[15] G. W. O. Addleshaw, *The High Church Tradition* (London, 1941), ch. 6.

Men were born members of families, and familial authority was affirmed as the model for civil authority. From there it proceeded to argue for the authority of the civil magistrate in ecclesiastical affairs:

> As it is apparent in the Scriptures, that the Israelites general-ly, as well the Priests as the People, were equally bound, as Subjects, personally to honour, reverence, and obey their Kings: So it is there also as manifest, that the Authority of their Soveraigns over them, did not only extend to civil Causes, but in like manner to Causes Ecclesiastical. For as it was then the duty of Parents, so by the Law of Nature, was it of good Kings and Civil Magistrates, to bring up their Children and subjects, in the true service and worship of God; as having a care committed unto them, not only of their Bodies but likewise of their Souls. In which respect the chief charge that all Subjects and inferior Persons, of what con-dition soever, should diligently observe the said Law of Nature (being the very same in substance that God, writing with his own Finger, gave unto *Moses*, and stiled by the name of his *Ten Commandments*) was principally imposed upon Kings and civil Rulers.

Thirdly, it insisted on the special appropriateness of mon-archy. God had indeed instituted monarchy among the Israelites. Other nations had chosen differently:

> Whereupon divers other kinds of Governments, termed according to their Temper, *Aristocratical*, *Political*, *Tyrannical*, *Oligarchical* or *Democratical*, &c. were afterwards settled in many places. The Inconveniences of which Forms of Government being found (upon many occasions often times) to be very great; the People have been driven, of necessity, in sundry Countries, to frame them again, as near as they could, to the *Monarchical* Government . . .[16]

---

[16]William Sancroft (ed.), *Bishop Overall's Convocation-Book, MDCVI. Concerning the Government of God's Catholick Church, and the Kingdoms of the Whole World* (London, 1690), pp. 3–4, 32–3, 56.

Even in Hooker's day, this ideal was challenged by the separate existence of Roman Catholic recusants; increasingly through the seventeenth century, it was challenged by the proliferation of varieties of Protestant Dissent. James II's policies on toleration, and the outcome of the Glorious Revolution, placed permanently beyond reach the project of Archbishops Sheldon (1663–77) and Sancroft (1677–90) for the recreation of a practical identity between the Church of England and the nation. Yet, despite the *de facto* recognition of religious pluralism given by the 'Toleration' Act of 1689, the ideal of the Church as the highest and all-encompassing religious expression of the nation survived. That ideal was given most cogent expression in the defences mounted by Anglicans of the Test Act (1673) and Corporation Act (1661), those lasting monuments of Restoration exclusiveness, in which a militantly Anglican Parliament had sought to restrict office in central and local government to Anglicans.

The three premises of such a view were set out by Edmund Gibson:

> Religion, and the general Practice of it in a Nation, is the surest Establishment of States and Kingdoms. That therefore, in every Nation, it is the proper Business of the Civil Magistrate, as such, to vindicate and maintain the Honour of Religion. That without a serious Regard to the Moral and Spiritual Duties of Religion, the greatest Zeal in other Matters, even tho' it be for the establish'd Worship of God, will not secure the divine Favour and Protection, either to Persons or Nations.

It followed that

> . . . in a Christian Country, every *Civil* Magistrate is obliged to consider himself also as a *Christian* Magistrate; as one, who has not only received a Commission from the Prince, to maintain Peace and Order in the State; but who has also,

thro' the hands of the Prince, received a Commission from God, to maintain the Honour of his Religion upon Earth.[17]

This being so, defence of the Anglican ascendancy could proceed from the Hookerian premise that

> We are obliged to receive the Sacrament in *the Church of Christ* in obedience to an institution of Christ; and consequently we are supposed to be in Communion with that visible part of the Church with which we receive the Sacrament.

The sacramental test was uniquely effective as a test of allegiance; but it was a central tenet of Anglican apologists that this did not misuse a divine ordinance for profane ends:

> That receiving the Sacrament, *according to the Usage of the Church of England*, is not the qualification for an Office, within the intent of the Act, but only the proof of such qualification: The qualification required is, That the Person be well affected to the Ecclesiastical State and Constitution of these Realms; and the receiving the Sacrament according to the Rites of the establish'd Church is the proof or Test required that he is so.[18]

The Church's claim to Apostolic authority was bound up with this mode of defending its position:

> What then shall exclude the Papists, if the Sacramental Test be abolished? Not Oaths, nor Declarations, which it is plain the Legislature at that Time looked upon as dispensable Matters, and such Securities as might be broke thro' for the Good of the Catholick Cause. But their joining with the

---

[17]Edmund Gibson, *Religion, the best Security to Church and State. A Sermon Preach'd at the Assizes Held at Kingston in Surrey, March the 10th 1714/15* (London, 1715), pp. 7, 13.

[18]Thomas Sherlock, *A Vindication of the Corporation and Test Acts. In Answer to the Bishop of Bangor's Reasons For the Repeal of Them* (London, 1718), pp. 9, 72.

Church of *England* in the most solemn Act of Christian Worship, is a Bar of the strongest kind; it is an open and publick Acknowledgement, that our Church is a true Church, and our Ministry a true Ministry, and We true Members of the Catholick Church of Christ; notwithstanding our Separation from the Church of *Rome*.

It was a system premised, therefore, on divine rights rather than on natural rights:

In the Books which have been written upon this Subject, in Favour of the Dissenters, we have heard much of *Natural Rights*, and the unjust Invasion of those Rights by the Corporation and Test Acts. But is not Society and Government itself founded in an *Abridgement* of Natural Rights, in such Instances and such Degrees, as in the Judgement of the Legislature the Safety and Welfare of the *whole* requires?[19]

If such an abridgement of natural rights were legitimate, then a distinction could be sustained between toleration of Dissenters' private worship, and their admission to political power:

In framing the Test Act, both Houses of Parliament put a just Distinction between the relieving of *Conscience*, and the entitling to Power; the same Distinction that was afterwards made in framing the Act of Toleration, which gives Relief to Conscience, but expressly debars from Temporal Power.[20]

Thus expressed, the case for Anglican ascendancy became a well-rehearsed orthodoxy, readily and ably expounded, often in the same terms. Apologetics such as these were reprinted on the occasion of later attempts to repeal the

---

[19] [Edmund Gibson], *The Dispute Adjusted, about the Proper Time Of Applying for a Repeal of the Corporation and Test Acts: By Shewing, That No Time is Proper* (London 1732), pp. 10–11.

[20] [Thomas Sherlock], *The History of the Test Act: In which the Mistakes in some late Writings against it are rectified, and the Importance of it to the Church explain'd* (London, 1732), p. 9.

Acts: Sherlock's *Vindication* in 1787, 1790 and 1827, his *History of the Test Act* in 1790, and Gibson's *Dispute Adjusted* in the same year. Samuel Horsley, the ablest Anglican apologist of the latter part of the century, endorsed and restated the same case in 1790, looking equally to the efficacy of legislation. If repeal passed, he predicted,

> Government will have thrown down the best barrier it had to oppose to innovation; and the work of reformation will go on, without obstruction, till one stone will not be left standing upon another of the admired fabrick of the BRITISH CONSTITUTION.[21]

By 1828, when the final and successful application for repeal was made, the ancient doctrine was still current. 'It is not that the Christian Religion is patronized by the State; but that the Christian religion is the ground and basis of the State,' wrote one clergyman, Edward Irving.[22] Another, Stephen Hyde Cassan, agreed:

> The question of the Repeal of the Corporation and Test Acts is, as was well incidentally observed by Lord Redesdale in the House of Lords, one of a *political* and not a religious nature: and, indeed, Dissenters themselves are conscious that their aim and object is exclusively political aggrandisement – they neither can, nor do in reality, consider it a religious question; for they know full well that they already have ample liberty of conscience – liberty enough and more than enough – for every *good* purpose: they know they are uninterrupted in their own modes of worship, however fanatical, and however unscriptural.[23]

---

[21] [Samuel Horsley], *A Review of the Case of the Protestant Dissenters; with reference to the Corporation and Test Acts* (London, 1790), p. 59.

[22] Edward Irving, *A Letter to the King, on the Repeal of the Test and Corporation Laws, as it affects Our Christian Monarchy* (London, 1828), p. 24.

[23] Stephen Hyde Cassan, *Considerations on the Danger of any Legislative Alteration respecting the Corporation and Test Acts; and of any Concession to Dissenters or Papists* (London, 1828), pp. 4–5.

Such apologists shared an analysis of the sources of discontent:

> The Unitarians, and Deists, and Infidels, who are now multiplied to a mighty host within the realm, taking to themselves the name and banner of liberality, in order to entrap the unwary, are the disaffected unto Christ the King, whose Lieutenant your Majesty is.[24]

Cassan added:

> The very *'principium et fons'* of all dissent, where the communion that is left is not sinful, (and no one ever could assert that ours is sinful,) is nothing else than a satanic impatience of godly discipline – a hatred of, and rebellion against, constituted authorities. He who impugns the hierarchy of the Church of England, and contends for the equality of all ministers of religion, recognized and distinctly defined as the three orders are in Scripture – he who advocates the right of the people to follow spiritual teachers with no ostensible commission, at the same time that they forsake those who are sent forth by Christ, cannot but be considered as deeply imbued with principles in their very nature and essence democratical. The principle is a principle of rebellion: and dissent or schism may not inaptly be termed spiritual republicanism. Now, allegiance to God is higher than allegiance to man, and *he*, whose mind is so weak that he can see no sin in resisting the spiritual government established by the Deity, cannot be expected to see any sin in resisting civil government, and more especially as such an one fancies that civil government is an institution of man, forgetting *'whose* authority he hath' who is at the head of civil government.[25]

They shared a view of the likely outcome:

> . . . if the Bill, as it now stands, should pass into a law, integrant and essential parts of the constitution of the king-

---

[24] Irving, *Letter*, p. 8.
[25] Cassan, *Considerations*, pp. 28–9.

dom do straightway become unchristian, from having been Christian; and there is no let, nor hindrance, why the whole body political should not in like manner renounce Christ, and turn to infidelity.

Such a Bill could not be passed

unless we are from henceforth to constitute your Majesty independent of Christ, Lord in your proper right, and not by vicegerency from God, which would destroy the ground of all Christian government; or, upon the other hand, to allege, as some most unconstitutionally do allege, that your Majesty deriveth your right from the people, and is responsible to the people.[26]

Cassan concluded:

All applications of this nature, whether from Papists or Dissenters, I fear, are 'but the beginning of sorrows' – the prelude to the development of that system which appears to be ripening in this country for the subversion of both the civil and religious constitution, in order that the system of one or other of those sturdy claimants may eventually become dominant and established.[27]

It cannot be argued that Christianity was an agreed, accepted common denominator of political action for all parties until a great secularisation set in during the twentieth century.[28] Theological disagreements inevitably had implications for the connection of Church and State, that is, for the dependence of collective public action on moral premises. Anglican ascendancy was continually contested. Equally, however, it was ably and successfully defended until the third decade of the nineteenth century. The campaign of those years to break the Anglican

---

[26] Irving, *Letter*, pp. 4, 11.

[27] Cassan, *Considerations*, p. 6.

[28] Theological controversies can best be followed in John Hunt, *Religious Thought in England from the Reformation to the End of the Last Century* (3 vols, London, 1870–3).

monopoly was not undertaken in a spirit of neutral libertarianism, religion being merely another arena for the freedom
of the individual. It was essentially religious in its impetus –
part Dissenter, part Catholic, part atheist.[29] Whatever the
situation in the twentieth century, there are no grounds for
arguing of the world before 1832 that the issues of the
connection of Church and State were incidental details
rather than aspects of fundamental differences of principle.

From a twentieth-century perspective, the problem of
Church and State could still be posed within a moral
framework. On the eve of the Second World War, Bishop
Henson was still teaching that

> from the Christian point of view, the convenient and con-
> ventional distinction between the secular and the spiritual
> spheres has no inherent validity. Both spheres lie within
> the empire of the Moral Law . . . Both Church and State
> are divinely appointed instruments through which the
> Kingdom of God shall be set up on earth.

Yet it seemed clear to Henson that Hooker's model was
based on premises which no longer obtained: 'when the
State is frankly non-Christian, and the Church is notori-
ously divided into sections, it is obvious that such a scheme
of harmonious co-operation is altogether impracticable'.[30]

After 1828–9, the Church of England was committed to a
legal setting which entailed a steady contraction of its
understanding of its proper sphere, at the same time as the
Tractarian movement encouraged it to distance itself from
purely local loyalties. But an extensive understanding of
the Church's role was surprisingly resilient: it did not
quickly or totally disappear in the nineteenth century. The
Archbishops' Commission on Church and State of 1935
rejected the image of the Church as 'a devotional club
which those who are so disposed are at liberty to join'. It
could not

---

[29] For this thesis at length, see Clark, *English Society 1688–1832*, chs. 5–6.
[30] Herbert Hensley Henson, *The Church of England* (Cambridge, 1939), pp. 35,
38, 40.

acquiesce in such a view of its nature and function without repudiating its trust. For it believes that it is more than a voluntary society. It is the Body of Christ, the organ and will of the divine Lord. And though in a sense it is true to say that to become a member of the Church requires a volitional act both from the individual or his sponsors and from the society which receives and welcomes him, in another and deeper sense no one can be incorporated in the supernatural society except by the activity of the Holy Spirit and through the sacrament of Baptism. Yet in the eyes of the State, and as viewed from its standpoint, the Church is bound to appear as a voluntary society, because for the State all that is not done by legal compulsion or by force of nature is voluntary.[31]

By the late 1960s, this Catholic vision had faded among Anglican clergy. The next Commission, meeting first in 1966 and reporting in 1970, expressed very different doctrine. They avoided using the term 'establishment' because, they claimed, it had 'an overtone of privilege, reaction, apathy and self-satisfaction'. While professing balance, the Commission was influenced by those who wished 'to see things as they are, to strip off the sentiment or the ritual of another age, and to make the Church relevant to the age in which it works even at the cost of demolishing traditions which in the past have elicited affection and loyalty'. Such men 'suspect that the inheritance of history can be a dead hand, heavy upon the present'. By contrast, the Church must 'take account of the general questioning of authority and so learn to make its way in the modern world'.

Imbued with such beliefs, the Commission was horrified to make an unwelcome discovery:

Some of our laws descend from a time when Church and State were identified, when the Church was believed to be society in its religious aspect, and when to call the Church of

---

[31] *Church & State: Report of the Archbishops' Commission on the Relations between Church and State 1935* (2 vols, Westminster, 1935), vol. 1, p. 7.

England the 'national' church meant that it was the Church of the nation. We used to doubt whether any of our laws today would suggest this to anyone. But we have been surprised to find that they do; that some suppose the Church of England to claim, not only to be the Church of its members, but to be the Church of all Englishmen; and that some imagine us never to have reconciled ourselves to the Toleration Act, the emancipation of Roman Catholics, the freeing of Nonconformists and later Jews from their civil disabilities, or the admission of atheists to Parliament.

We want to make it clear (while we blush to assert something so obvious) that we are not blind to the plural nature of English society. The Church of England is one church among several. So far as it is called a 'national' Church, it professes a mission to all the nation. It does not claim to cast its shadow over men or women who repudiate it. The Church of England does not suppose that it is an 'expression of society', 'the religious aspect of society'.

The concept of the 'plural society' was devised during these years. It lacked a theoretical defence or a democratic endorsement, and the Commission could point to neither in support of its views. While professing its disbelief in the doctrine of historical necessity, the Commission nevertheless propagated the view that the trends towards pluralism of the previous 120 years would 'continue, until the Church of England is autonomous and the intervention of the State will vanish'.[32] Whether this would promote or diminish Christianity itself was not a question on which the historical record was allowed to bear.

The Rule of Law

The Church of England was, from its outset, governed by its own system of law. From 1534 to 1833 the supreme

---

[32] *Church and State: Report of the Archbishops' Commission* (London, 1970), pp. 1, 6–7, 10, 15.

ecclesiastical court of appeal, replacing appeals to Rome, was the High Court of Delegates; it was served by ecclesiastical lawyers gathered in Doctors Commons, their equivalent of an Inn of Court.

> Professional honour made them preserve the ecclesiastical law as a separate, and independent system . . . They naturally tended to interpret the ecclesiastical law in agreement with the *jus commune* of the western Church and to treat it as a part of western canonical jurisprudence . . . an independent ecclesiastical judicature and a body of professional ecclesiastical lawyers, like Doctors Commons, were the corner stones in the High Church conception of the oneness of Church and State; they ensured that the community had a legal system suited to its nature as a Church. The substitution of the Privy Council in 1833 for the High Court of Delegates, as the supreme ecclesiastical court of appeal, meant that a temporal court with temporal judges tried ecclesiastical cases and interpreted the ecclesiastical law according to rules and maxims alien to its ethos. The doctrine of binding precedents, a doctrine alien to the ecclesiastical law, compelled the diocesan and provincial courts to follow the opinions of the Privy Council, and administer a law, which was nothing but a secular law attempting to deal with spiritual things.[33]

The rejection both of absolutely binding precedent and of unconstrained reason had been given classic expression by the Laudian bishop Robert Sanderson (1587–1663) in his Preface to the 1662 Prayer Book:

> It hath been the wisdom of the Church of *England*, ever since the first compiling of her Public Liturgy, to keep the mean between the two extremes, of too much stiffness in refusing, and of too much easiness in admitting any variation from it . . . Yet so, as that the main Body and Essentials of it (as well in the chiefest materials, as in the frame and order thereof) have still continued the same unto this day, and do yet stand

---

[33] Addleshaw, *High Church Tradition*, pp. 172–5.

firm and unshaken, notwithstanding all the vain attempts and impetuous assaults made against it, by such men as are given to change, and have always discovered a greater regard to their own private fancies and interests, than to that duty they owe to the publick.

Sound doctrine as identified by living tradition, rather than formal precedent or a historical reason, identified the Anglican *via media*: its existence encouraged the development of the law of equity to soften the formal rigours of the common law.

Richard Hooker had similarly avoided the scriptural literalism of the Puritans by positing in its place an overarching natural law, conceived as the expression of God's reason: Scripture was to be interpreted, and civil laws framed, in the light of this natural law. In place of a rigid and mechanical adherence to the text of Scripture, Hooker posited the Church of England as an organic and developing institution, possessing an essential continuity with the mediaeval church. Scriptural literalism and abstract natural rights were both replaced by Anglican tradition as the yardstick to which the content of legislation was referred.

Anglican tradition was, initially and centrally, a theological one. The state therefore embodied and enacted specific and positive views on what counted as acceptable religious doctrine. The Act of 1 W & M, c. 18 was inappropriately nicknamed the 'Toleration Act': toleration was not mentioned either in its title or its text, which consisted of a mere suspension of penalties incurred under still-unrepealed legislation.[34] Moreover, its benefits were confined to Trinitarian Protestant Dissenters: Roman Catholics and anti-Trinitarians were still held to be beyond the pale. This interpretation of the 'Toleration Act' makes intelligible the Blasphemy Act of 1698, which provided penalties for those who 'deny any one of the persons in the Holy Trinity to be God, or shall assert or maintain there are more gods than

---

[34] Especially the Acts of 5 Eliz. I, c. 1 and 13 Car II. st. II, c. 1.

one, or shall deny the Christian religion to be true, or the holy scriptures of the old and new testament to be of divine authority'.[35] Socinians, Deists and their publishers therefore found themselves the subject of legal proceedings into the early nineteenth century.

Anglicans regarded their exclusiveness as fully consistent with their praise of the constitution. William Blackstone merely reflected widespread opinion in announcing that 'the idea and practice of this political or civil liberty flourish in their highest vigour in these kingdoms, where it falls little short of perfection'.[36] He modified the common law doctrine of binding precedent by Hooker's doctrine of law as a reflection of natural law, and natural law as (in Blackstone's words) 'dictated by God himself'. Man 'must necessarily be subject to the laws of his creator, for he is entirely a dependent being'.[37] Revelation, revealed law, was a reiteration of natural law. 'Upon these two foundations, the law of nature and the law of revelation, depend all human laws; that is to say, no human laws should be suffered to contradict these'. Divine law ultimately overrode even precedent itself.[38]

This was the theological context for Blackstone's account of the criminal law relating to religion. 'Of Offences against God and Religion', chapter 4 of the fourth volume of the *Commentaries*, was the first of his categories of specific crimes, even taking precedence over High Treason. Blackstone professed that 'the preservation of Christianity, as a national religion, is, abstracted from its own intrinsic truth, of the utmost consequence to the civil state': the law protected religion because of its social utility. Nevertheless, the forms which that protection took were hardly distinguishable from a defence of Anglican Christianity as a body of dogmatic truth. First of the offences against religion was,

---

[35] Danby Pickering (ed.), *The Statutes at Large*, vol. 10 (Cambridge, 1764), p. 177.
[36] William Blackstone, *Commentaries on the Laws of England* (4 vols, Oxford, 1765–9), vol. 1, pp. 122–3.
[37] *Ibid.*, vol. 1, pp. 38–41, 69–70.
[38] *Ibid.*, vol. 1, pp. 42, 70.

therefore, apostasy, an offence once cognisable in the ecclesiastical courts, which had grown 'obsolete' there, but which had been (argued Blackstone) implicitly re-enacted as a criminal offence in the Blasphemy Act of 1692. Blackstone paraphrased it:

> that if any person educated in, or having made profession of, the Christian religion, shall by writing, printing, teaching, or advised speaking, deny the Christian religion to be true, or the holy scriptures to be of divine authority, he shall upon the first offence be rendered incapable to hold any office of place or trust; and, for the second, to be rendered incapable of bringing any action, being guardian, executor, legatee, or purchaser of lands, and shall suffer three years imprisonment without bail.

Apostasy was a total rejection of Christianity; a partial denial constituted heresy, left as an offence at common law alone by the Act of Supremacy of 1559, which repealed all former statutes, and subjected to lesser penalties by the Heresy Act of 1678, which abolished the ancient writ *de haeretico comburendo*.[39] With these limitations, believed Blackstone, 'it seems necessary for the support of the national religion, that the officers of the church should have the power to censure heretics, but not to exterminate or destroy them'. Hence, he claimed, the propagation of anti-Trinitarian doctrines were made subject to the same offences as apostasy by the Blasphemy Act.

Offences against the established Church took two forms. Reviling its ordinances was the first:[40] such laws had been necessary, suggested Blackstone, to defend the English liturgy against the 'utmost bitterness' of Rome and Geneva. They

---

[39] 1 Eliz. I, c. 1; 29 Car. II, c. 9.

[40] Reviling Holy Communion was punishable by fine and imprisonment under 1 Edw. VI, c. 1 and 1 Eliz. I, c. 1; 1 Eliz. I, c. 2 defended the Prayer Book from criticism by the penalties, in the last resort, of forfeiture of goods and life imprisonment.

proved a principal means, under providence, of preserving the purity as well as the decency of our national worship. Nor can their continuance to this time be thought too severe and intolerant; when we consider, that they are levelled at an offence, to which men cannot now be prompted by any laudable motive; not even by a mistaken zeal for reformation: since from political reasons . . . it would now be extremely unadvisable to make any alterations in the service of the church; unless it could be shewn that some manifest impiety or shocking absurdity would follow from continuing it in its present form. And therefore the virulent declamations of peevish or opinionated men on topics so often refuted, and of which the preface to the liturgy is itself a perpetual refutation, can be calculated for no other purpose, than merely to disturb the consciences, and poison the minds of the people.

The second type of offence against the established Church was nonconformity. Those who 'absent themselves from the divine worship in the established church, through total irreligion, and attend the service of no other persuasion' were liable to heavy fines.[41] He explained:

The second species of non-conformists are those who offend through a mistaken or perverse zeal. Such were esteemed by our laws, enacted since the time of the reformation, to be papists and protestant dissenters: both of which were supposed to be equally schismatics in departing from the national church; with this difference, that the papists divide from us upon material, though erroneous, reasons; but many of the dissenters upon matters of indifference, or, in other words, upon no reason at all. However the laws against the former are much more severe than against the latter; the principles of the papists being deservedly looked upon to be subversive of the civil government, but not those of the protestant dissenters. As to the papists, their tenets are undoubtedly calculated for the introduction of all slavery, both civil and religious: but it may with justice be questioned, whether the spirit, the doctrines, and the prac-

---

[41] By the Acts of 1 Eliz. I c. 2, 23 Eliz. I, c. 1 and 3 Jac. I, c. 4.

tice of the sectaries are better calculated to make men good subjects. One thing is obvious to observe, that these have once within the compass of the last century, effected the ruin of our church and monarchy; which the papists have attempted indeed, but have not yet been able to execute.

The sin of schism, in itself, was beyond the scope of the civil magistrate:

> If through weakness of intellect, through misdirected piety, through perverseness and acerbity of temper, or (which is often the case) through a prospect of secular advantage in herding with a party, men quarrel with the ecclesiastical establishment, the civil magistrate has nothing to do with it; unless their tenets and practice are such as threaten ruin or disturbance to the state. He is bound indeed to protect the established church, by admitting none but its genuine members to offices of trust and emolument: for, if every sect was to be indulged in a free communion of civil employments, the idea of a national establishment would at once be destroyed, and the episcopal church would no longer be the church of England.

Hence the penalties imposed on Protestant Dissenters by sixteenth- and seventeenth-century Acts;[42] hence, too, the mere suspension of these statutes by the Toleration Act. Hence the sixteenth- and seventeenth-century legislation against Papists, still current when Blackstone suggested that

> If once they could be brought to renounce the supremacy of the pope, they might quietly enjoy their seven sacraments, their purgatory, and auricular confession; their worship of reliques and images; nay even their transubstantiation. But while they acknowledge a foreign power, superior to the sovereignty of the kingdom, they cannot complain if the laws of that kingdom will not treat them upon the footing of good subjects.

---

[42] 31 Eliz. I, c. 1; 17 Car. II, c. 2 and 22 Car. II, c. 1.

Meanwhile, the Test and Corporation Acts were fully justified. Given the interdependence of civil and spiritual jurisdiction which they underpinned, both the civil and ecclesiastical courts were able to punish a range of 'general immoralities' including swearing, cursing, witchcraft, simony, sabbath-breaking, drunkenness, lewdness and, most notably,

> *blasphemy* against the Almighty, by denying his being or providence; or by contumelious reproaches of our Saviour Christ. Whither also may be referred all profane scoffing at the holy scripture, or exposing it to contempt and ridicule. These are offences punishable at common law by fine and imprisonment, or other infamous corporal punishment: for Christianity is part of the laws of England.[43]

Blackstone echoed a maxim of Lord Chief Justice Coke (1552–1634), which became a truism of the common law. In a case of 1676 in the Court of King's Bench, Chief Justice Sir Matthew Hale said that

> such Kind of wicked blasphemous words were not only an Offence to God and Religion, but a Crime against the Laws, State and Government, and therefore punishable in this Court. For to say, Religion is a Cheat, is to dissolve all those Obligations whereby the Civil Societies are preserved, and that Christianity is Parcel of the Laws of England; and therefore to reproach the Christian Religion is to speak in Subversion of the Law.[44]

In the trial of the Deist Thomas Woolston in 1729, Chief Justice Robert Raymond repeated the same doctrine:

> Christianity in general is Parcel of the Common Law of England, and therefore to be protected by it; now whatever strikes at the very Root of Christianity, tends manifestly to a

---

[43] Blackstone, *Commentaries*, vol. 4, ch 4.
[44] *The Reports of Sir Peyton Ventris Kt.* (2 vols, London, 1726), vol. 1, p. 293.

> Dissolution of the Civil Government . . . so that to say, an Attempt to subvert the establish'd Religion is not punishable by those Laws upon which it is establish'd, is an Absurdity.

Blasphemy remained an offence at common law, Raymond insisted, despite the more specific additional provisions of the Blasphemy Act.[45] Even its repeal in 1813, at the instigation of Dissenters, left in place the common-law offence of blasphemous libel, and prosecutions for this offence reached a peak during the tenure of Lord Eldon as Lord Chancellor. Only from the 1830s did the Church progressively lose this power to enforce its doctrine.[46]

In a society in which Christianity was displaced from its hegemonic position, the ideal of the rule of law was reformulated. Previously, law was primarily conceived as the embodiment of morality. Henceforth, law and the rule of law was increasingly praised for its equity between individuals, its certainty, its uncorruptibility, its effectiveness. English society from the nineteenth century has phrased the conservative version of its self-image as 'freedom under law', freedom being negatively defined as freedom *from*. In earlier centuries a different formulation was current: people praised or questioned their enjoyment of 'the rights of Englishmen', their positive freedoms *to* do the things which, together, constituted Englishness.

From our perspective, 'freedom *to*' is alleged to have unacceptably totalitarian overtones. This is understandable, given the most lurid exponents of that view in the twentieth century. But this apparent distinction between 'freedom *from*' and 'freedom *to*' is the effect of historical circumstances, not of analytical separateness. The implied distinction is, indeed, untenable: a longer perspective shows how freedom *from* and freedom *to* are sides of the

---

[45] John Fitz-Gibbons, *The Reports Of Several Cases Argued and Adjudged in the Court of King's Bench* (London, 1732), pp. 61–65.

[46] William H. Wickwar, *The Struggle for the Freedom of the Press 1819–1832* (London, 1928).

same coin, ways of describing a society's practice. English law itself, by protecting the individual, also historically confronted the individual with a set of duties as well as rights. As we have seen, English law until 1828–9 affirmed a link between political power and Anglican allegiance. Full participation in civic life was largely reserved for members of the Established Church. Moreover, such an arrangement was defended as a bulwark of moderation against fanaticism, of 'liberty and property' against 'Popery and wooden shoes'.

This re-expression of national ideals is understandable against the background of the advance of democracy. Beginning in 1832, and progressively with the Reform Acts of 1867, 1884 and 1918, Anglicans lost their electoral dominance. From being the expression of Anglican ascendancy, the rule of law became valued as a defence against majoritarian tyranny. So, too, society's myriad organisations – clubs, societies, firms, families, towns, regions, Burke's 'little platoons' – took on a different role. In Burke's polity they were pictured as acting to integrate the individual fully into the life of the nation. Henceforth they were praised as intermediate agencies, defending the individual *from* the state and its laws. By the 1980s, the Church of England had contracted in the opinions of many both within and beyond its communion so that it increasingly took on the role of an intermediate agency, its clergy defending their private conception of the national interest (often itself drawn from the secular consensus of the previous decade) against governments with a new conception of the national interest, a conception ostensibly grounded in the Christian teaching of an earlier age.

Social Teaching

Whatever Anglicanism's doctrines of universal redemption and benign providence, its social theory before the nineteenth century can seldom be characterised as optimistic.[47] Seldom, perhaps never, did its *social* teaching align it in opposition to the government of the day. Even in its Latitudinarian forms, that teaching did not look to economic growth or social reconstruction to effect any major change for the better in the human condition. Poverty, disease, and early death were too widespread not to pre-empt moral naivety.[48] War too was a recurrent experience (British casualties in the wars of 1793–1815 were higher in proportion to population than in the war of 1914–18), and re-emphasised not only the collective dependence of the state on divine providence, but the personal responsibility of the individual to conform to those national standards of piety and morality which, alone, would be rewarded by national military victory.[49]

The collapsing of religion into morality was regularly resisted. Even James Woodforde, whose diaries are regularly cited as archetypal proof of the amiable, worldly optimism of the Georgian Church, preached a quite different message in his sermons. Life was 'not a place of reward but of trial'; it was 'one incessant struggle, one scene of toil, of suffering, of cruel fate . . . its instability will never bear the weight of the most slender dependence; our expectations are infinitely larger than our enjoyments, and our supposed happiness seldom within our reach and seldom a single minute assured to us'. How 'guileful and detestable are the ways of Man, formed in the image of God but transformed into that of Satan!' Man's 'provocations every

---

[47] Synoptic studies of this question are rare. See, however, three distinguished works: Richard B. Schlatter, *The Social Ideas of Religious Leaders 1660–1688* (London, 1940), written from a Marxist standpoint; R. A. Soloway, *Prelates and People: Ecclesiastical Social Thought in England 1783–1852* (London, 1969); E. R. Norman, *Church and Society in England 1770–1970* (Oxford, 1976). For a longer perspective, Ernst Troeltsch, *The Social Teaching of the Christian Churches* (2 vols, London, 1931).

[48] The classic formulation of such assumptions is contained in the writings on population of the Rev. Thomas Malthus (1766–1834). E. A. Wrigley, in the introduction to his edition of Malthus's *Works* (8 vols, London, 1986) argues that he was correct in identifying the demographic constraints which continued to apply to English society.

[49] Cf. Soloway, *Prelates and People*, pp. 26–33.

day are so heinous, our offences so great, and our rebellion so obstinate, that we every moment deserve to be cut off and doomed to eternal death'. Religion was the only civilising principle:

> The true cultivation of this principle is of such consequences to the peace, order, and happiness of the community, that without it the laws of the land lend but feeble aid to prevent and restrain personal injuries. Religion is the strongest bulwark to any nation, and the best security to the legislature. The most religious man, from inward conviction, without the fear of penal sanctions of the law, will always prove the most peaceable subject.[50]

Within a post-Calvinist Christian mental universe, determinist patterns of social explanation were largely absent. Neither psychological nor historical theories purporting to explain individual conduct as responses to environmental pressures had yet achieved significant currency in Britain. The author of *The New Whole Duty of Man* (1744), placing 'The Necessity of Caring for the Soul' first among Christian duties, insisted that the individual had the freedom and power, despite his sinful inclinations, to hear and obey divine injunctions. Social theory was, consequently, strongly ethical in its content and individualist in its focus. Paternalism, an ideal often expressed in that society, was an ethical and ultimately religious relationship: it expressed the Anglican model of social structure as a 'great chain of being', an ordered hierarchy of finely differentiated and providentially disposed parts rather than an economically structured antagonism of classes or interest groups.[51] Inequality was widely accepted: to Anglicans it did not necessarily define, or give evidence of, exploitation. (Only

---

[50] James Woodforde, manuscript sermons of 1793, quoted in Norman Sykes, *Church and State in England in the XVIIIth Century* (Cambridge, 1934), pp. 262–7.

[51] Arthur O. Lovejoy, *The Great Chain of Being: A Study of the History of an Idea* (Cambridge, Mass., 1936), p. 183, pointed out that it was in the eighteenth century that these ideas 'attained their widest diffusion and acceptance'.

in more recent years did the advance of economic doctrines antagonistic to Anglican teaching generate a picture of society, structured by ideas of class and exploitation, which locked Christianity into a pattern of institutional decline.)

Differences of degree were conventionally pictured as differences of quality: status was described as inherent. As George Horne, the new Bishop of Norwich, pointed out to his diocese in 1791, 'A natural equality amongst mankind is contradictory to the actual condition of human nature . . . Equal liberty is another idea which cannot take place in society, because men are not equal in virtue.' Bishop Richard Watson, though from a different political standpoint, echoed the same doctrine in 1796: 'Personal distinctions, arising from superior probity, learning, eloquence, skill, courage, and from every other excellency of talents, are the very blood and nerves of the body politic.'[52]

In that picture, the poverty of individuals was pictured as a hazard like disease rather than as the predicament of an economically-defined stratum. Before David Ricardo (1772–1823), economic theory did not conventionally blame poverty on exploitation. The general rewards of labourers were ascribed instead to their low productivity. In Gregory King's analysis of 1688, more than half of the population were held to be diminishing the wealth of the nation, consuming more than they produced. The rich, by contrast, were conventionally regarded as a source of wealth, a cornucopia from which affluence flowed to the rest of the community. Archdeacon Paley drew the moral: 'To abolish riches would not be to abolish poverty; but, on the contrary, to leave it without protection or resource.'[53] Long into the nineteenth century, despite the invention of economic theories of exploitation, the same attitudes prevailed at local level: according to one historian,

---

[52] George Horne, *A Charge, Intended to have been Delivered to the Clergy of Norwich at the Primary Visitation* (Norwich, 1791), p. 28; Richard Watson, *An Apology for the Bible*, p. 378; quoted Norman, *Church and Society*, p. 36.

[53] William Paley, *Reasons for Contentment. Addressed to the Labouring Part of the British Public* (London, 1793), p. 5.

What the poor *saw* the rich do, was give and spend, rather than take. The poverty of the poor arose, often very noticeably, from the unproductiveness of their labours, and it was understandable that the poor should regard the rich as a national resource like coal, a bonus given by nature which radiated benefits without taking anything back . . . the general feeling of the country was that it was the rich who maintained, and whose duty it was to maintain the poor, not the poor who maintained the rich. Still less did any argue that the richness of the rich created the poverty of the poor. The experience of working class life was all against such doctrine.[54]

Such a world view was resiliently hierarchical. Anglicans attended to the low material standard of living of labourers as a whole, regarding it as the norm rather than as an exception which called for a special explanation. As in the Bible, 'the poor' was often merely synonymous with 'most people'. The facts of disease, deprivation and dirt were commonplace: they did not shock the genteel observer, coming on them unawares. Before the general rise in agricultural (and therefore clerical) incomes at the very end of the eighteenth and the early nineteenth century, the Church of England was overwhelmingly a Church of, and among, the poor: its accounts of crime and exceptional individual poverty were based on detailed knowledge of individual failings.[55] Until the disastrous rise in food prices in the wartime 1790s plunged large numbers below a conventional subsistence level (and even, in many minds, thereafter), the extreme poverty of some individuals was normally ascribed to special circumstances, whether of age and disease, or idleness and wastefulness. Clergy often gave expressions to these assumptions. In 1816 J. B. Sumner distinguished between 'indigence', the plight of

---

[54] John Vincent, *The Formation of the Liberal Party 1857–1868* (London, 1966), pp. 79–80.

[55] Cf. the diaries of Anglican clergymen discussed in J. C. D. Clark, 'England's Ancien Regime as a Confessional State', *Albion*, 21, no. 3 (1989).

individuals, and 'poverty', 'the natural lot of many, in a well constituted society'.[56] The poverty of mankind in general was part of the divine order: 'Poverty, with every other evil, came in, upon man's transgression,' explained George Horne in 1788.[57]

The theoretical premises of public welfare were therefore distinctive, and can be summed up in the term 'charity'. They entailed personal benefits targeted at the most needy individuals and carrying with them strong moral, even religious, overtones (patients cured in charity hospitals, for example, were required to attend divine service to mark their gratitude). Those premises contrast sharply with early- and mid-twentieth-century ones, which issued in morally neutral assumptions of universal entitlement as the result of an underlying economic theory of exploitation, and took their place within a wider policy of redistribution.

As yet it was hierarchy, not exploitation, which was seen to entail inequality. A pre-romantic sensibility did not romanticise poverty: only at the end of the eighteenth century did the popular art of men like George Morland begin to retail images of innocent, well-fed labourers in picture-postcard cottages. Furthermore, a pre-liberal age did not, in general, treat inequalities of power, status or privilege as aberrations: the social hierarchy was to come under most bitter attack from those heterodox religious minority groups which identified squire with parson, peer with bishop. Is a social policy which omits equality as an explicitly-avowed goal 'wicked'? The attitudes of English churchmen to poverty and inequality before the nineteenth century contrast markedly with those of their colleagues in later decades.[58] According to Bishop Richard Watson,

[56] Norman, *Church and Society*, p. 64.

[57] Cf. Schlatter, *Social Ideas*, pp. 142–3; Soloway, *Prelates and People*, pp. 21–2, 64–84.

[58] Cf. especially J. R. Poynter, *Society and Pauperism: English Ideas on Poor Relief, 1795–1834* (London, 1969). Gertrude Himmelfarb, *The Idea of Poverty: England in the Early Industrial Age* (London, 1984) focuses on a slightly later period.

> God . . . never meaned that the idle should live upon the labour of the industrious, or that the flagitious should eat the bread of the righteous: he hath therefore permitted a state of property to be everywhere introduced; that the industrious might enjoy the rewards of their diligence; and that those who would not work, might feel the punishment of their laziness.[59]

Anglicans possessed few economic or historical theories to inhibit them from preaching to the poor the duties of 'submissiveness, work, and patience',[60] or stressing 'the solid reasons they have for contentment in their stations'. These could be justified on utilitarian grounds; but 'If in comparing the different conditions of social life, we bring religion into the account, the argument is still easier. Religion smooths all inequalities, because it unfolds a prospect which makes all earthly distinctions nothing.'[61]

Within this mental world, societies were not classified into types ('feudal', 'absolutist', 'industrial') presumed to be inherently appropriate or inappropriate to certain forms of Christian social teaching: moral and pastoral theology still owed more to patristics and church history than to sociology and economic history. Was the 'old society' collectivist? In the relative absence of acknowledged 'rights' for the individual, in the analogies drawn between political and familial authority, and in the non-contractual nature of many social ties, the 'old society' is likely to seem so. Yet one characteristic distinguished the 'old society' from the new more sharply than those apparent similarities identified it: the weakness of those institutions which, in a later age, were to be redefined as intermediate agencies. Here again, language provides a clue to a quite different understanding of the world. Readers of Alexander Cruden's definitive *Concordance* (1738, and many later editions)

---

[59] Richard Watson, 'A Sermon . . . 1785' in *Miscellaneous Tracts on Religious, Political and Agricultural Subjects* (2 vols, London, 1815), vol. 1, p. 450.

[60] Schlatter, *Social Ideas*, pp. 146–57.

[61] Paley, *Reasons for Contentment*, pp. 6, 15.

would find no biblical anticipations of the twentieth-century usages of 'community', 'class', or 'society'. Instead of 'classes' or 'communities', the basic units of Anglican thought were families. It was a commonplace of Anglican teaching that men were not born as autonomous individuals, free to form all social and political relations via contracts, but as members of families, churches and nations, possessing loyalties, faiths and allegiances which were indefeasible. Since the Church was pictured in its ideal form as co-extensive with the nation, however, Anglican social teaching did not sanction or dignify any important intermediate agencies between the family and the state. In this sense, that teaching was not corporatist. Intermediate corporatist fictions like 'communities' and 'classes' did not yet exist to provide a yardstick against which the economic activities of individuals could be identified as selfish.

Instead, Anglican theorists gave an exalted role to the family,[62] both as the pattern and the building block of the state. As Richard Baxter (1615–91) expressed it, in sentiments still common to Anglicans and Nonconformists, 'A *holy well-governed family* is the preparative to a *holy and well-governed Church* . . . *Well-governed Families* tend to make a happy State and Commonwealth.'[63] If theologians could trace the family to divine revelation, philosophers were equally certain that it could be defended in the complementary realm of natural law. Richard Cumberland (1632–1718), later Bishop of Peterborough, so argued in his classic *De Legibus Naturae Disquisitio Philosophica* (London, 1672: translated in 1727 as *A Treatise of the Laws of Nature*). So did Jeremy Taylor, Bishop of Down and Connor, in his

---

[62] See especially Schlatter, *Social Ideas*, pp. 1–86.
[63] Richard Baxter, *A Christian Directory: Or, a Summ of Practical Theologie, and Cases of Conscience* (London, 1673), pp. 512–14. The four parts of Baxter's massive work indicate the scope of Anglican social teaching: *I. Christian Ethicks (or Private Duties) II. Christian Oeconomicks (or Family Duties) III. Christian Ecclesiasticks (or Church Duties) IV. Christian Politicks (or Duties to our Rulers and Neighbours).*

classic *Ductor Dubitantium, or The Rule of Conscience* (2 vols., London, 1660). In such works, Anglican divines designed the ideal of marriage which is held to have become dominant in the nineteenth century: the monogamous nuclear family founded on the mutual love of husband and wife, the discountenancing of adultery, divorce and abortion, and the cherishing of legitimate children.[64]

Moreover, much Anglican teaching on business ethics was still subsumed under the heading of 'the family', since the relation of master and servant was interpreted as including employers and the majority of wage labourers.[65] This teaching did not attempt to establish wage levels and was reticent about 'whether or not the state had the power to make important changes in the system of ownership' of property; but it assimilated the questions of the discipline of and care for workers to the father's relations with his wife and children. Within these assumptions, 'such matters as wages were a minor consideration beside the problems of moral discipline and government . . . Servants' duties were summed up in obedience, faithfulness, and contentedness' in return for just and fatherly care.[66]

'Industry' before about the 1840s still meant the virtue of hard work rather than a particular form of manufacturing (the term 'capitalism' has similarly been dated only from 1854). Its status as a duty towards one's neighbour was underlined by the 1662 Prayer Book's Catechism, in which confirmation candidates promised 'not to covet nor desire other men's goods; but to learn and labour truly to get mine own living, and to do my duty in that state of life, unto which it shall please God to call me'.[67] The thirty-eighth Article of Religion had already established that 'the Riches and Goods of Christians are not common, as touching the

---

[64] Schlatter, *Social Ideas*, pp. 29–30.

[65] *Ibid.*, pp. 60–86.

[66] *Ibid.*, pp. 61, 81–2, 102; Norman, *Church and Society*, p. 38.

[67] Cf. Gilbert Burnet, *An Exposition of the Church Catechism for the Use of the Diocese of Sarum* (London, 1710).

right, title, and possession of the same'.[68] To most Anglicans, it was 'evident that private property is essential to the very existence of civil society'; here was 'a principle which is the foundation of every social comfort'.[69] Individual effort was, consequently, the only route to advancement. Parents had a duty to teach their children:

> to be diligent and industrious, to close application, and attention to what they are employed in. For that must be the best provision for children, which will stand them in best stead in all conditions; which will help them to rise from meanness to sufficiency, and to improve a good estate to a better, and to prevent a fall, or to bear it well, and to recover what has been lost.[70]

Moral discipline was exercised partly through church courts administering canon law, increasingly by civil courts and by clerical JPs administering a Christian common law, but at all times by reference to a body of Anglican moral teaching which emphasised duties over rights. Christians owed a duty of obedience not only to their civil but to their 'spiritual governors',

> not only in whatsoever they out of scripture declare to us to be God's commands, either by publick preaching, or by private exhortations; because they are the messengers of the Lord of hosts, so long as their doctrines are agreeable to the word of God; but likewise in submitting to that discipline they shall inflict . . . from a pure sense of that right they have to command, intrusted to them by our Saviour Jesus Christ.[71]

---

[68] For Anglican arguments against property in common, drawn from both revealed and natural law, cf. Schlatter, *Social Ideas*, pp. 96–7; for the relation of this teaching to the duty of personal charity, *ibid.*, pp. 124–45.

[69] George Pretyman, *Elements of Christian Theology* (2 vols, London, 1799), vol. 2, p. 560.

[70] *The New Whole Duty of Man* (22nd edn., n.d.), Sunday VIII, p. 212.

[71] *Ibid.*, p. 192.

The two centuries before the 1830s were marked by the extreme longevity of Anglican works of devotion and social teaching.[72] Richard Allestree's *The Whole Duty of Man* (1658), the spiritual best-seller of the period, was continually reprinted, and echoed by works with titles like *The Whole Duty of Woman* (1753) and *The Whole Concern of a Christian* (1703). Allestree's later titles, *The Ladies Calling* (1673) and *The Gentleman's Calling* (1660), were equally in demand, and different emphases were given to this teaching in the orthodox *New Whole Duty of Man* (1744) and the Evangelical Henry Venn's *The Compleat Whole Duty of Man* (1763). Equal currency was enjoyed by such texts as *A Week's Preparation towards a Worthy Receiving of the Lord's Supper* (1678; 52nd edn., 1764); Robert Nelson, *A Companion for the Festivals and Fasts of the Church of England* (1704; 36th edn., 1826); Jeremy Taylor's *Holy Living* (1650) and *Holy Dying* (1651; 30th combined edn., 1820); and William Law's *A Serious Call to a Devout and Holy Life* (1729; 20th edn., 1816).

The long currency of Anglican social teaching marked the stability and success of a certain social order. To the social theorists of the *ancien régime*, one proposition could be taken as central:

> For a state to exist without a religion of some sort being united to it, is a solecism in the world; the new revolutionary democracy of America being the first that ever attempted it: so that the experience of four thousand years in every corner of the globe, might have taught some diffidence to those who fondly dream that the Christian religion would thrive equally well if the king were an atheist, and if it had no more protection or encouragement from him than Mahometan-

---

[72] On the long currency of devotional works, see J. Wickham Legg, *English Church Life from the Restoration to the Tractarian Movement* (London, 1914), ch XI. The same conclusion emerges from the publication dates of the titles listed in the Bishop of Chester's bibliography: William Cleaver, *A List of Books Intended for the Use of the Younger Clergy, and other Students in Divinity, within the Diocese of Chester* (Oxford, 1791; 3rd edn., 1808).

ism, Judaism, or Deism. Woe be to that king and to that nation in which such maxims shall ever prevail.[73]

Partially and ambiguously, the principles of an agnostic state came to prevail in England during the nineteenth century.

The Current Problem

The predominant attitude of the defenders of the Anglican establishment before 1828–32 was that principles could be embodied in institutions with usable clarity and with trustable permanence. The destruction of the legal forms of this achievement, especially after 1828, was paralleled (unfortunately for its subsequent reputation) by the development of relativist, evolutionist ideas in historiography[74] and in theology. Progressive revelation meant that change, not establishment, was henceforth to be the yardstick of truth. The invocation of precedents before the 1830s could now be condemned as nostalgia, as attempts to 'put the clock back'. This vivid metaphor begged a number of historical questions of the first importance; but the privileged position of Whig teleologies meant that the metaphor was, until recently, seldom challenged.

Pragmatism and relativism could now seem allies. Yet a fuller understanding of the role of religion in early-modern political ideologies destroys the comfortable notion that Britain has long characteristically exemplified either pragmatism or relativism in its attitude to religion or politics.

---

[73] Henry Drummond, *Social Duties on Christian Principles* (London, 1830), pp. 155–6. For similar insights expressed in an academic rather than a polemical idiom, cf. Troeltsch, *Social Teaching of the Christian Churches*, vol. 2, pp. 991–3.

[74] T. P. Peardon, *The Transition in English Historical Writing 1760–1830* (New York, 1933); Duncan Forbes, *The Liberal Anglican View of History* (Cambridge, 1952); John Burrow, *Evolution and Society: A Study in Victorian Social Theory* (Cambridge, 1970); P. B. M. Blaas, *Continuity and Anachronism: Parliamentary and Constitutional Development in Whig Historiography and in the Anti-Whig Reaction between 1890 and 1930* (The Hague, 1978).

Rather, as students of the nineteenth century have shown, Britain is distinctive in and from that century in the rise of an historiographical tradition which elided the determinative crises and marginalised the spokesmen of informed commitment, leaving only a story of bland, sensible progressivism.

Progress was defined as the collapse of orthodoxy, and proved by historicism in one of its two forms:

> Ernst Troeltsch in 1913 . . . sees in 'historicism' the dominant attitude of the nineteenth and twentieth centuries. The core of historicism consists in the recognition that all human ideas and ideals are subject to change. This attitude, Karl Mannheim suggests about ten years later, has led to the rejection of the stable, transcendent norms to which medieval Christianity had clung and which in a secularized form the rationalist philosophers of the Enlightenment had maintained. Historicism is now identified with cultural relativism. In the course of the nineteenth century, Troeltsch observes, historical scholarship showed how all institutions and ideas were historically related and thus destroyed all points of reference . . . Karl Popper gave the term 'historicism' a meaning, which has not been generally accepted, as a theory of historical predictability and determinism in contrast with the usual meaning of the term which denotes the opposite, individuality, spontaneity, and the avoidance of generalizations.[75]

In Troeltsch's sense, modern Conservatism has been shaped not least by the advance of heterodoxy and the triumph of historicism. Such a belief that 'progress' was right to destroy the older order was congruent with populist Protestantism; but neither conservatism nor historicism effectively stood in the way of either Liberalism or Socialism. Conservatism at its more theoretically convincing could remain as an attitude of patrician, even Olympian detachment, a scepticism of worldly engagements which

---

[75] Georg G. Iggers, in Philip P. Wiener (ed.), *Dictionary of the History of Ideas* (5 vols, New York, 1973), vol. 2, pp. 456–64.

allowed its practitioners to remain afloat yet retain a com-mitment to Christian otherworldliness while the turbulent current of events hurried them ever further down a stream the nature and dynamic of which their ideology was less and less able to explain.

Conservatives, it is now supposed, are those who are sceptical about the possibility of embodying ultimate values in transient political forms. If no political party can provide a coherent account of the moral bases of its policies, it is held to follow that moral pluralism in the state is the most prudent course. At the end of all other roads, some argue, lie fanaticism and intolerance. England's experience before the 1830s contrasts sharply with this position. Indeed, it suggests that a weary scepticism is an aspect of defeat rather than of otherworldliness. Can Christians use the power of the state to promote Christianity, or is a plural society inevitable? For the first three centuries of their Church's post-Reformation history, most Anglicans assumed that the first of these two alternatives was both practicable and legitimate. In the next century and a half, they increasingly persuaded themselves of the truth of the second.

The decline of the Church of England was, historically, not uniform: brief and traumatic episodes of downward adjustment were normally followed by long periods of relative stability and slow erosion in which certain positive features could be greeted as evidence of regeneration. One such seismic shift may have been imposed in and around the 1960s by the nexus of ideas and values loosely charac-terised as 'the plural society'. It was not a formula for stability, and was soon itself subject to damaging tensions. From the governments of the 1980s came a call for the restoration of an organic moral community expressing family values, the work ethic and moral discipline within an English Christian tradition. Senior Anglican clergy often replied that society was irredeemably multi-cultural; that Anglican tradition had always been a chance collection of historically determined commitments; that that tradition was in flux, proceeding by dynamic evolution; that all simple, timeless moral teaching was merely naive in respect of these realities of cultural relativism.

Yet, despite this anxious Anglican unwillingness to question the assumptions of the plural society,

> there persists the assumption, true or false but certainly deep-seated, that any society, liberal or illiberal, rests for its preservation on its submission to common values. In the late nineteenth and earlier twentieth century men asked whether the tolerance which the Victorians had achieved could survive the drift into materialism, and whether a State which had distanced itself from the Church could retain its moral authority. Now . . . we wonder what values can hold a multi-cultural society together, and confront the question how far a tolerant society can tolerate intolerance.[76]

Because of the historical vicissitudes discussed in this paper, few Anglican theorists were able to offer an effective response. If the law of England has been deprived of its basis first in Anglican exclusiveness, then in a wider Christian morality, its content can be defended only on the lesser ground of a secularised concept of natural law. This position is essentially a defensive one: it represents a phase in the long retreat of English Christianity. We arrive in that position largely because of political contingency: the result of early-nineteenth-century political conflicts left England with an established Church, but one less and less able to embody its teaching in positive law. Reason rather than tradition became its yardstick; and, finally, reason to the exclusion of tradition.

If Conservatism is not a stable doctrine of successful resistance to historical or economic change, lastingly embodied in a genealogically continuous party, then theorists wishing to explain it might have recourse to the particular agenda of things which are, or were, to be conserved. In

---

[76] Blair Worden, 'Uncommon Rights of Man', *The Times Literary Supplement*, 2–8 June 1989, p. 621.

Britain, the single largest source of public morality has been Christianity, and, in England, Anglican Christianity. It was Anglican theology (rather than secular political theory) which first carried within it an understanding of doctrinal authority and of the way in which ideas can be embodied in, and promoted by, institutions. The further the Conservative Party moved from its Anglican heritage, therefore, the less precommitted it was among the pragmatic policy options which present themselves in daily affairs (and are often mistaken for ideologies); the same was true of the Labour Party, as it finally lost touch with its Nonconformist roots. For that reason, all parties until recently have been almost equally willing to countenance, and co-operate in, that pragmatic reconstruction of national life which has issued, ironically without democratic sanction, in an atheist, multi-racial, high-divorce, high-crime society.

Many Anglicans, while stopping short of the idolatry of particular state forms, will nevertheless wish to endorse Britain's institutions of parliamentary democracy as the most appropriate for the present time and place. But, if so, how are they to be defended, justified and safeguarded against rival claims, whether of European supra-national organisations or of ethnic or religious exclusiveness from Britain's minorities? Have our present political practices been more securely grounded in recent decades on natural rights doctrines than they once were on Anglican tradition? Historical precedent would suggest that they have not.

8

Do British Parties Need Philosophies?

Edward Norman

THE idea that political parties should be organised around policies was a nineteenth-century development in Britain. It reflected the decline of the immediate powers of the crown to constitute or reconstitute governing elites, and the decline, also, of patronage as a means of consolidating government. It reflected, in addition, the growing existence of an independent educated body of opinion – the fruit of the reforms of education and the first consciousness of the implications of mass education. Before those changes political parties had been the coherence of series of interest-groups, or family and territorial connections, all of whom, it is true, owed some kind of allegiance to a tradition of political loyalties which they associated with events of the past. They differed, not about the nature of the constitution, but about the means of its management and the extent to which – this was especially a feature of the reign of George III – it could be adapted to circumstance without injury to its basic integrity.

The preservation of religion, of Christianity, was regarded as one of the highest duties of government: high, that is to say, on the rather short agenda of pre-collectivist government. This preservation was effected by an obligation to maintain the union of throne and altar, of Church and State. As political parties came to redefine themselves around policies, which they did in the middle years of the nineteenth century, the maintenance of a Christian note in the purposes of government remained. Only a handful of 'Philosophical Radicals' – and certainly not the popular radicalism of the provinces and the countryside – were hostile to a connection between the organisation of society and the sanction which Christianity supplied as the basis of the obligation to recognise the moral nature of law.

Political parties, in their new guise as purveyors of a systematic scheme of policy, simply left the Christian note as posited; it was assumed as part of the sacral texture of public life. They allowed themselves to differ about certain actual arrangements for religion and, most importantly of all, they came to differ about the desirability of maintaining a formal union of Church and State. At the end of the century the Liberal Party adhered itself to a policy of disestablishment all round, though its application to England and Scotland (unlike Ireland and Wales, where the policy was carried out) was allowed to remain, as it has contrived to remain, one of latency. The Conservative Party, almost by negative deduction, became the party of support for the Anglican Establishment, as an establishment. The centre of the political divergence became the question of state support for denominational education. Yet both the major parties saw themselves as maintaining an agreed understanding of Christianity as the basis of public life – it was simply that the Nonconformist wing of the Liberal Party had shifted so that the state would no longer support one denomination over another as the official recognised guardian of the general public profession of Christian belief. In the United States, with its constitutional separation of Church and State, and in some of the British colonial territories and dominions where separations had also occurred, it was quite usual for political groups of all shades to profess a Christian basis to public life, and to the legislative process, while at the same time declining to subscribe to a formal connection of the state with a particular Church.

As British political parties emerged into the twentieth

century, therefore, and as they began to clothe themselves, however reluctantly, with collectivist powers and responsibilities, it can hardly be said that differences over religion related to anything other than particular policies in relation to practice, rather than differing attitudes to Christianity as such. The broadening of the basis of the constitution, as a result of pragmatic nineteenth-century adaptations, had not only incorporated new social classes; it had also brought in first Dissenters and Catholics, and then Jews and Freethinkers. These reforms were only made, however, in a general context of civil liberties and with no intention of weakening the Christian basis of law. Experience elsewhere could be very different. In some European countries, and in South and Central America, modern political parties emerged which were actually hostile to religion as such. These developments occurred in countries which lacked the pragmatic basis so characteristic of Britain. For it is one of the most extraordinary features of development here that the political change, from parties organised around interests to parties organised around policies, should have occurred in a political context of pragmatism. There was an almost complete suspicion of 'philosophy' as germane to the make-up of a party, and when Robert Peel, for example, wanted to commend an extension of policy he would do so, as many of his contemporaries did, on what he called 'the high grounds of expediency'.

The beginnings of the decline of the Liberal Party, and the rise of Labour politics, did not alter this arrangement of things. The Labour Party, if anything, reinforced the assumption of a Christian political basis, since it was, as is well known, more indebted at its real foundations of support to the Nonconformist conscience than it was to the secular ethicism of left-wing members of the intelligentsia. As they have delivered themselves to modern times, therefore, the British political parties can scarcely be said to have any radically differing attitudes to Christianity, and there is actually very little real sense in which any one of them can be claimed as a more authentic guardian of religion than any other. The modern Conservative Party may certainly still see itself as the traditional party of the maintenance of a union of throne and altar – but that is, in this widest perspective, a detail of application rather than a fundamental commitment to Christianity as such which marks it off from other political groups.

Political parties, like all human institutions – and like Churches themselves, indeed – are greatly given to emphasising their community with a particular tradition, or to seeing themselves as the present embodiment of a continuing tradition which has a discernible pedigree. In reality, of course, almost everything has changed over time, and within the deceptive walls of institutional apparatus, and the surviving symbolism of apparent timelessness, there is a permanently evolving content. All life is change, Cardinal Newman observed, and to be perfect is to have changed often. The truth of this is evidenced with some clarity within both the Conservative Party and the Christian Churches. In reality, the divisions within such bodies represent different degrees of responsiveness to external ideas and situations, and actually tend to produce a closer proximity between the educated leadership of seemingly quite rival bodies than exists between the leadership and the rank-and-file following of each internally. Thus in the first decades of the nineteenth century educated opinion at the top of political and ecclesiastical society was attracted to the ideas and practices of Political Economy – the enlightened science of society, as it seemed, of the day. Leading Tories and leading Whigs were equally won over to its allure, and it united them, at least in this particular, with the Philosophical Radicals. The effective division, in ideas terms, was then not between Whigs and Tories, but between the educated leadership of each party and their own backwoodsmen – who were in a substantial majority. Leading bishops in the Church were just the same. Some of the most articulate and successful advocates of Political Economy were to be found in the front ranks of the episcopate of the established Church, and included Sumner, Archbishop of Canterbury. The result was a sharp division between these bishops and the lower clergy. Popular opinion in the country, like the rank-and-file of the political parties and the clergy, regarded Political Economy as an insensitive assault upon hallowed traditional relationships, and looked, still, to a continuation and even a restoration of a paternalistic set of social obligations as the foundation of the social nexus.

That will seem a long way from the position as it is today. But in reality there are many points of similarity. The basic divisions in contemporary political and ecclesiastical society persist in being between the 'educated' leadership – those in touch and in sympathy with the shifting values of the intelligentsia and its following in the media – and those whose consciousness is formed and maintained by adhesion to ideas derived more immediately from local sources or family-inherited wisdom. Let those who suppose otherwise behold the range of issues, and especially those relating to law and order and to education, in which the governing classes have for long been out of touch with opinion in general. The gap, when it is sufficiently wide to prove a difficulty, gets discussed in terms of the doctrine of parliamentary duty to lead opinion and not to follow it. The issue of capital punishment has illustrated it in a stark form for many years. When all the heat of the debate, and the consequent polemics, are laid aside for the purposes of analysis, it becomes clear that – in terms of ideology, whatever may be said – leading political opinion in this country agrees, across the party division, much more than it disagrees. Were this not the case the practice of parliamentary democracy, in which the competing elements politely agree to accept the general, constitutional terms of reference, and the rules of the game, would probably not work at all. The world of values that is maintained at the top of political society by this arrangement of things, however, is very different from the values of the *demos*. The leadership of the Church shows the same sort of accommodation by the ruling elites. The bishops at the top belong to the value inheritance of the intelligentsia, whose idealism, and whose very agenda of 'moral' concern, is faithfully reflected in their own understanding of fundamental Christianity. It is ethicist and, in the strictest sense, worldly – its pre-occupation, that is to say, is with the right ordering of human society and its needs rather than with the preparation of souls for another world of values altogether.

What is called 'Thatcherism' is a disposition to question the effect on individuals, and on the well-being of society generally, of 'excessive' collectivism. It is not a radical, but a moderate departure from the previous consensus of the 'educated' leadership. Contemporary Conservatism shows how, even in doing this, the leaders of 'Thatcherite' politics continue to accept the moral value of *most* of the machinery of collectivism: ministers have been very emphatic that they are *not* about to dismantle the welfare state, but are produc-ing a series of reforms which will make it work more effectively and in a fashion which will encourage parallel personal initiative. The programme of 'privatisation' in the economy is also about the enhancement of individual exer-tion, but it is centred in a doctrine of cheap government: that state enterprise in the economic area has been costly and has involved governments with a machinery of control which has added dangerously to its powers. In reality, of course, the legislative regulations that accompany pri-vatisation, to secure the fair operation of the various enter-prises and the rights of citizens to services, maintains a high level of state involvement. Yet the general picture is clear. The contemporary Conservative leadership has moved nearer to the national rank-and-file, and in some things has made a moderate and controlled departure from the values of the 'educated' elites. The 'educated' elites, both in State and in Church, have noticed this, and hence the degree of their hostility to 'Thatcherism'. The move, furthermore, illustrates the permanence of the internal divisions within public bodies. The present Conservative leadership, in siding with the prejudices and expectations of the rank-

and-file (at least before the imposition of the poll tax in 1990), has elicited the dislike of traditional Conservatives: in this case this means the consensus-seeking Conservatives of the Macmillan era. And because 'Thatcherism' represents the successful emergence of a radical bourgeoisie it has encountered the hostility of traditional Tories – and of what is left (which is quite a lot) of the marginated remnants of the former landed ruling class.

Critics within the Conservative Party suspect that the present leadership does not represent authentic Conservatism at all. They are correct in this. But neither do they. For there is, in truth, no continuing organic tradition of ideas, only a set of symbols and a shared institutional sense. The Labour Party is in a not dissimilar position, with its own Socialist custodians thrashing around in a frustrated and sterile attempt to make its leadership, too, correspond to the ideological symbols of the past. In religious terms, both parties, like the other political associations in Britain, have no particular or distinctive attitudes or policies. Religion has simply faded from consciousness, with the progressive but (in Britain) benign secularisation of the intelligentsia. Even on issues of policy which have the most obvious religious associations – legislation over marriage and divorce, for example – Parliament no longer acts as if there was a distinct Christian presence in the life of the state, and the public ideology upon which such legislative adjustment proceeds issues from a kind of anonymous agreed ethicism rather than from any resort to religious doctrine. Controversy about the 'moral high ground' in politics has been a slight rippling of the surface of the waters, no more. When the controversy with the bishops occurred over the Government's educational legislation (an issue which, in every country, produces classic confrontations of Church and State, and always has done) no basic issues of policy were allowed to obtrude. No great debate opened up about the relationship of the state to religious truth or whether there should be such a relationship at all.

If the present Conservative Government expresses ideals

which have any distinct historical pedigree they are not exactly Conservative ones. Its doctrines of individual initiative, relative freedom from excessive collectivist controls by the state, retrenchment, and respect for the rights of small nations (the Falklands) are actually those of classic Gladstonian Liberalism, and represent a critique of traditional society. The Liberal Party itself, in the decades between Lloyd George's leadership and its own recent self-dissolution, had abandoned Gladstone's suspicions of collectivism and had espoused a kind of social democracy. At the heart of 'Thatcherism', however, there may well exist a *social* critique which is very different from Gladstonianism.

Gladstone's opposition to the growth of the machinery of the state was because he feared for the freedom of the individual. His doctrine of cheap government was a form of protecting liberty: a state with a large income used it to extend its capacity to interfere in relationships in a fashion which diminished the general area of freedom. Thus far 'Thatcherism'. But Gladstone had a pretty monolithic view of society as such. For the purposes of political management, it was true, there was a need to respect localism – his own party was a coalition of local interests, and in the case of Irish Home Rule he came to see the need for a very large measure of local autonomy. Society as such, however, had unitary qualities; it was knit together by a community of religious and cultural values which needed freedom to develop but whose development in freedom would always, it was supposed, exhibit a great deal in common. Now the Britain of today is very different. Although it is not always as diverse in its value-assumptions as intellectual analysis would assert, the fact remains that it is becoming a 'plural' society. This is the form in which we now tend to define 'freedom'. It is a matter of allowing the legitimate expression of differing values, ethnic traditions, religious beliefs, and so forth, to flourish without state interference, while at the same time creating a machinery of state control to guarantee each component in the continuation of its witness to diversity. It is about allowing individual choice in some basic moral areas because there is no longer any agreement about the pedigree of the moral basis. All the political parties – and, amazingly, all the Churches – accept the legitimate existence of the plural society and are prepared to sacralise it.

The Conservative Party, which traditionally has regarded itself as the guarantor of an organic conception of national self-consciousness, is now second to none in its acceptance of social and moral diversity. It is a very good thing that it does so – but for a reason other than the factual acceptance of existing realities. It fits in well with the 'Thatcherite' critique of excessive collectivism. If the state can no longer determine the nature of philosophical truth, if it can no longer, in any realistic or effective sense, employ religion as the sanction at the heart of its operations, if its own moral incoherence is such that few in public life would care to define the moral basis of government which has come in to replace the now largely discarded Christian confessionalism, then plainly the fewer powers such a state has, the better from the point of view of personal freedom. In practice, the whole of the welfare state, and the still accumulating weight of collectivist agencies and controls, exist for 'moral' purposes – as Labour Party critics of government policy are quick to declaim. This moral basis is left undefined, however, even by the Labour Party. 'Thatcherism' seems to be saying that the aim of government, in conditions of social pluralism, should be to govern as little as it has need to, since that will prevent the creation of a secular colossus with a huge range of powers ready to fall into the hands of whoever or whatever may be its eventual successor. That is a profoundly wise thing to be saying. Conservatives should be, in this light, the party of political scepticism – the party whose opposition to other parties is because those parties are prepared to employ high levels of state power in the furtherance of blue-prints for a better society. Conservatives, however, because they too lack a coherent philosophical or ethical basis – something that can be held up to an electorate for periodic inspection –

and are not even prepared to acknowledge scepticism as their philosophy, agree only on the doctrine that government is safest when it governs least. This is an old theme in Western political thinking. But it is now set in a new way – in a context provided by a general acceptance of pluralism within the intelligentsia and those fashioned by them.

Pluralism, itself, it should be noticed, is an approved ideal of 'educated opinion', and has been much promoted by educational and religious reformers. In this sense, therefore, 'Thatcherism' is not so far removed from the older distinction between the 'educated' and the rank-and-file as at first appears. The bishops, too, have been warm in their endorsement of the concept of social pluralism, but their understanding of it has been extremely narrow. Pluralism is really a phenomenon which exists where those who determine the values of a society cannot agree among themselves about the moral and other bases of human association. The bishops have reduced it to a matter of ethnic minorities. This is because they are eager to exude goodwill in racial issues, but are hardly well-placed to promote moral relativism in the social sphere since their own adhesion to a dogmatically 'progressive' social morality is usually very precise. They are quite unwilling, because of ordinary political prejudice, to regard the diminished role of the state in contemporary Conservative thinking as an obvious accompaniment of the acceptance of pluralism. And their objections to 'Thatcherism' are usually expressed in high moral language. This involves them in a dilemma which they have not yet appeared to recognise. The national popularity of 'Thatcherism', tested in appeals to the electorate, now has the seal of the democratic process upon it. If the bishops saw the state and politics as a mere affair of nuts-and-bolts management then the option of the voters, on so large and consistent a scale, would just represent a series of technical wrong choices by them. But the bishops regard the political organisation of society in high moral terms, and the option of the people for 'Thatcherism' must logically imply the capability of the masses to act on immoral premises – if 'Thatcherism' is immoral as some have contended. There are implications here for the episcopate's subscription to democratic theory which they do not care to pursue.

For all its acceptance of pluralism, and for a doctrine of the state which emphasises the area of choice left to individuals, the existing Conservative leadership is persistently looking for ideological bases: for some sort of coherent systematic 'Tory Philosophy' within which to render the practice of present policy. It is as if the recognition of political scepticism is not somehow respectable. This is the context which the Conservative Party, stung by accusations from moralists of the political left and from the Churches of lacking 'compassion', and so forth, have sought to reestablish a Christian basis – or, in the Prime Minister's words, a 'Judaeo-Christian' basis. But it is very difficult to see why modern Conservatism should be thought to be more or less Christian than modern British Socialism, since none of the political parties in this country have a coherent moral foundation and there is considerable agreement in public life about the sort of provisions which government should make to provide social services, popular education, defence, and so on. The differences, in reality, are over style and management rather than morality. If the British Labour movement had ever gone over to Marxism, to an organisation of society which attempted to express social reality in terms of philosophical materialism, then there would indeed be a difference. As it is, the few genuine Socialists within the Labour movement are a major embarrassment to it, and the Labour Party, under existing management, is a classic bourgeois reformist party, whose moral resort, for all its declared importance, is actually left nameless. There is no doubt that for most of those who vote for the Labour Party its moral view of social needs is thought to be established in Christianity – as popularly understood (and as understood by some leading Anglicans) as a kind of hedonistic ethicism. Most of those who vote Conservative probably have a very comparable moral end in view, but for them the Conservative management of the state is more calculated to furnish the means by which creative social amelioration is possible. In the gentle pragmatism of British political experience the major questions about the purposes of human association, which have troubled political and moral theorists since the time of the Sophists in ancient Greece, are left unasked.

Christianity, for its part, is compatible with a wide range of political organisations. Since most of its time in the world has been spent before the invention of the collectivist state in the later nineteenth century, there can be no sense in which an advanced level of welfare collectivism is an essential expression of Christianity. Suggestions to the contrary arise because there is in Britain, and especially in England, a very long-standing disposition to reduce the Christian religion to an affair of moral concern. It is as if love of neighbour was its sole purpose, and as if its primary teachings can be exhausted in the cultivation of a sense of concern for human material needs. This interpretation, so frequently offered by Anglican luminaries, is a very unsatisfactory understanding of Christianity. It is to depict it, indeed, not as a *religion*, but as an ethical blue-print for society. Contemporary Conservatives, seeking to show how their political applications can be as 'caring' as those of their opponents, easily fall into the habit of expressing Christianity in this inadequate manner.

Christianity, however, is addressed to the *spiritual* capacities of men and women, and describes their relationship to the divine. It sees mankind as transcending the material preoccupations of society, and, in present circumstances, it should recognise that the real danger to human life does not come through mass poverty, or the threat of nuclear extinction, or an ecological catastrophe, or issues of 'justice', or the 'uncaring' imposition of some new level of charges for social services, but from the subtle acceptance of men and women as products of material phenomena. Christianity teaches that men and women are children of God, citizens of an unseen world whose truths are known by the mysterious operation of celestial forces which are not analysed or understood by the methods doubtless adequate to provide information about social trends or the exact chemical composition of a bit of matter. A great advance has been made in modern times to an understanding of revealed religious truth by testing some of its data with intellectual instruments originally fashioned for other areas of intellectual enquiry, but to reduce religious phenomena themselves to merely *moral* phenomena, which is what happens in so much contemporary understanding of Christianity, is to destroy its essential genius.

It therefore causes real spiritual pain to witness the frequency with which even the most serious of Christian clergy themselves speak of the 'moral' when in reality they are trying to speak of the 'spiritual'. But this is also what happens when politicians seek to compete with one another, on a party basis, to establish who has the most likely chance to qualify as the purveyor of Christian values within their policies. If the English political parties were organised around genuinely divergent philosophical positions – as between Marxist and liberal systems, or those systems which have deified the state and seen the functions of human society as exhausted within its service – then there would be a real obligation to sort out the political sheep from the goats. Contemporary Conservatism, in these circumstances, will be as Christian as its custodians and advocates themselves are. In recognising the incompetence of the state to involve itself with many of the most deeply-felt values of its citizens, the philosophical scepticism of Conservative politics has the prospect of performing a real service for the preservation of the truth, existing alongside all the error, in the competing fabric of society. The danger comes from those who, with partial understanding, seek to embody what they think of as ultimate truth in the transient forms of contemporary politics.

There is a long tradition within Christian understanding of distinguishing general social principles, which it is the duty of the Church to define for its members, from particular applications, which it is the duty of the laity to seek out and to employ. In our century it was Archbishop William Temple who articulated this distinction with the greatest influence. Those members of the laity who participate in civil government thus have the clear duty to make their pursuit of policy correspond to their profession of Christianity. This is not an easy or a very coherent undertaking. For the object is not the creation of a 'Christian' state – of a kind of neo-Byzantium. That would destroy the existence of social, moral, and religious pluralism; and with its destruction would vanish some of our basic conceptions of individual liberty. In an imperfect human society the preservation of error is the price to pay for the maintenance of truth: humanity is the habitation of both, mixed together, inseparably united in even the highest aspirations. Christians in the political realm are not seeking to use the coercive power of the state to make other people Christian. They are there as witnesses to their own understanding of the faith, achieving the service of others in the only way they know as authentically expressing the love of neighbour. They are there because the management of society has to be undertaken by somebody, and there is no reason why they should stand aside and see it done by their ideological opponents. They are there, also, because the extended realm of modern collectivism has moved the competence of the state progressively into areas of life that once were the exclusive responsibility of religion. And they are there, finally, because God ordained government as a remedy for men's evil – or, to express the matter less traditionally, because without government the order in which the moral life can be pursued would not exist. Yet government itself, in existing conditions, has necessarily to be 'secular', at least in the sense that it should not invade the capacity of the citizens to cultivate the diversities of what we now call 'pluralism'. In the light of all this, and as at present indeed happens, individual Conservatives are right to express their political obligations in terms of their understanding of Christian teaching, just as, for example,

Jewish Conservatives should express theirs in terms of the Jewish religious tradition.

British pragmatism may still come to the rescue over another implication of this view of things. If the maintenance of 'pluralism' is a desired end of government, then the continued existence of a union of Church and State is plainly an anomaly. It is actually an anomaly for another reason, too. Democratic practice among a moralistic electorate suggests that ultimate values may be decided on a majority basis. That is plainly unacceptable as a condition for determining religious truth. One solution is to reduce the level of the state's competence, so that ultimate values are no longer its concern, but where that is suggested as a dimension of 'Thatcherism' a howl of objection goes up from the other political groups. The other solution is disestablishment. But England, happily, is not logical about such matters, and there is no popular call for a severance of the connection of Church and State. In public sentiment there is no agreed alternative basis ready to fill the gap left by a withdrawal of Christianity from the centre of the state's identity. But this all only works because it is left undefined and largely undiscussed. It is doubtless best that it is so, and that the establishment of the Church is left undisturbed. The Conservative Party, as the purveyor of scepticism rather than ideology in the political sphere, will surely agree.

9

Poverty and Wealth Creation

Lord Harris of High Cross

WHEN I went with a scholarship from my grammar school in Tottenham to Cambridge University in 1945, the Economics Faculty included outstanding teachers of contrasting political and philosophical dispositions ranging from Conservative, through Liberal to outright Communist. My good fortune was to have escaped the proselytising attentions of Maurice Dobb and to be grounded in the broad Liberal–Socialist sympathies of Alfred Marshall who had been Professor from 1885 to 1908 and of whom his successor, Pigou, said that 'alone among English economists he stands the companion and the equal of Adam Smith and of Ricardo'.

Marshall was no desiccated academic economist. Having graduated in mathematics as an unorthodox prelude to ordination, he switched to ethics as a stepping-stone to his life-long dedication to the study of economics. His inspiration, in the words of Keynes, was the solution of economic problems as 'a prior condition of the exercise of man's higher faculties'. In his own words, the problem was 'how to get rid of such evils in society as arise from a lack of material wealth'. More positively, he described his aim as freeing man from destitution so that he could become 'the noble being he might be . . . if we might so say, what God intended him to be'. To this elevated end Marshall studied contemporary life and labour at first hand and got to know the leading trade unionists and consumer co-operators. In the words again of Keynes, 'he sympathised with the labour movement and with socialism in every way, except intellectually'.

Towards the end of his life, Marshall summed up his reason for withholding support from Socialists:

> I do not doubt that the paths on which they would lead us might probably be strewn with roses for some distance. But I am convinced that as soon as collectivist control had spread so far as to narrow considerably the field left for free enterprise, the pressure of bureaucratic methods would impair not only the springs of material wealth, but also many of the higher qualities of human nature, the strengthening of which should be the chief aim of social endeavour.

In the same essay (entitled 'Social Possibilities of Economic Chivalry' and reprinted in *Memorials of Alfred Marshall*) he mildly reproved people who delight in 'vehement indictments of existing social conditions'. Their efforts, he observed, may arouse 'a passing enthusiasm' but 'they nearly always divert energies from sober work for the public good and are thus mischievous in the long run'. As evidence that his contemporary age was not as selfish as was often claimed, he adduced the extent to which government expenditure chiefly benefited women and children who could not 'enforce their will at the polling booth'. At the same time, 'young people's wages have risen faster than those of women, and those of women have risen faster than those of men'. From the vantage point of 1990, we may take encouragement that these beneficent trends have broadly continued in the intervening decades.

To restore a sense of proportion, he then turned to consider Booth's survey of the London poor in the 1880s, which estimated that a million people, amounting to a third of the population, were in poverty with an income below twenty-one shillings a week. Marshall pointed out that this sum would buy more than four times the amount of wheat than could be bought by the average wage of English labour from the Middle Ages until quite recent times. Poverty was exaggerated, not only on historical standards, but also by comparison with other similar countries. Thus, Marshall suggested, Germans who heard that a million people in London were living in poverty would

> open their eyes when they learn that under this misleading title are included all members of families with a less aggregate income than 21 marks . . . For 21 marks will buy much less food than 21 shillings will, and 70%, if not more, of the German working-class families have an annual income less than 1,100 marks.

I have perhaps laboured this measured, scrupulous approach to poverty by a scholar whose sympathies are without question on the right side, in order to draw the contrast with the 'vehement indictments' of Thatcherism by the academic and theological spokesmen for such lobbies as the Child Poverty Action Group. In a recent CPAG publication, tendentiously entitled *Poverty: The Facts*, it is claimed that in 1985 twenty-nine per cent of the population were living 'in or on the margins of poverty'. Closer inspection reveals the *fact* that only five per cent (2.4 million) were living *below* the level of Supplementary Benefits which, rechristened Income Support, is the payment from public funds intended to keep people out of poverty. Another twelve per cent (7 million) are shown to be *on* the Supplementary Benefits level, that is to be out of poverty, and a further twelve per cent to have up to forty per cent *more* than the SB level of income, which tautologically the CPAG define as 'on the margins of poverty'.

Comparisons over time are distorted by the habit of regarding poverty as a relative, rather than an absolute, standard. Successive increases in the real level of SB payments will therefore show 'poverty' continuing, if not rising, for ever. This optical illusion is exploited in another CPAG publication, *The Growing Divide*. After acknowledging that SB payment *rose* between 1978 and 1987 by five per cent more than prices, one author complains that average personal disposable income rose by fourteen per cent more than inflation and concludes that by comparison 'benefit levels have *fallen* considerably'. In this way, *more* can be advertised for party political purposes as *less*. Yet it is on the basis of such confused and misleading comparative calculations that CPAG authors hurl vehement indictments at the Thatcher Government for 'grotesque inequalities' which prove that Britain is 'rapidly losing its claim to be a civilised society'.

What passes for the contemporary debate on poverty in Britain is informed by no historical or international perspective, such as Marshall brought to the problem. It is not cheered by any sense of the progress already achieved in transforming the luxuries of yesterday's privileged minorities into the conventional necessaries of today's masses. Above all, the bitter, barren debate on poverty is not illuminated, least of all from the pulpit, by any shaft of understanding about the nature of the competitive market economy which has contributed more than any alternative system in history to the annihilation of disease, squalor, hunger, ignorance, destitution and other manifestations of poverty.

Instead of gratefully fostering and strengthening the market economy as an unrivalled machine for the creation of wealth, today's poverty lobbyists can think of nothing better than calling for the progressive extension of state action. From his wide historical study, Marshall offered the following assessment of the scale of sacrifice risked by reliance on such socialist expediencies:

> Government creates scarcely anything. If government control had supplanted that of private enterprise 100 years ago, there is good reason to suppose that our methods of manufacture now would be about as effective as they were 50 years ago, instead of being perhaps four or even six times as efficient as they were then.

But there was no complacency in his concluding magisterial warning:

> The world under free enterprise will fall far short of the finest ideals until economic chivalry is developed. But until it is developed, every great step in the direction of collectivism is a grave menace to the maintenance even of our present moderate rate of progress.

Why should this be so?

The Creation of Wealth

It is only one of the wonders of God's creation that individuals, even in the same family, differ so widely in their physical, psychological, intellectual, temperamental and other endowments. Such differences are further multiplied by variations in education, training, experience and personal preferences. The central question for social philosophers in a free society is: how can millions of people with such diverse talents be brought together in voluntary co-operation to supply most effectively their own and one another's requirements?

In his crowning work, *The Fatal Conceit* (1989), F. A. Hayek argues that the case for market economy does not depend on value judgments or ideology, as was commonly supposed in the pre-Gorbachev era. Instead, it rests on the firm *fact* that man's finite knowledge falls short of the infinite complexity of the physical creation. The extent of human ignorance and uncertainty is compounded by ceaseless changes in production, techniques, resources, invention and consumer preference. Accordingly, if society is to make the fullest use of scarce and changing human and material resources, we need to draw as much as possible on detailed, fragmentary, even contradictory, information which is dispersed among millions of people. This assorted knowledge cannot be fully known to any group of central planners, let alone a bench of bishops. The miracle of the market is that, without a directing intelligence, it shapes an extensive international division of labour and brings about a spontaneous order which is, in a favourite phrase of Hayek's, 'the result of human action but not of human design'.

The paradox that markets yield order while, as Gorbachev acknowledges, central planning leads ultimately to chaos, follows from the role of market prices as signals that guide the actions of producers and consumers so as to bring supply and demand everywhere towards equilibrium. Even Gorbachev has now come round to the view that output will not match demand unless wage and salary differentials are more closely related to productive performance. But if rewards for work are to be determined by unequal payment through markets for labour, how can we measure this productive performance? Again, Gorbachev has mocked output that fulfils the plan but does not supply even the meat, bread, clothes and homes that people want, let alone their more sophisticated preferences. Indeed, he is increasingly sounding like Adam Smith who declared in *The Wealth of Nations* (1776) that 'consumption is the sole end and purpose of all production'.

From such elementary requirements for an effective economic system follows the logic of market pricing for competitive production to meet consumer choice. It would take volumes to deck out that skeleton in full raiment. We would have to expound the indispensable role of government, not least in protecting private property rights, imposing the rule of law against force and fraud, and providing other services which markets cannot (economically) supply.

But Gorbachev's confessions have made it easier to assert that the system variously described as liberal capitalism, economic freedom, market economy or private (competitive) enterprise has no rival in the multiplication and spreading of wealth. It is fashionable for the poverty lobby to mock the 'trickle down' effect of prosperity in elevating the poor. Yet how otherwise can they explain why their chosen standard of poverty is above the average earnings of such well-endowed socialist regimes as the USSR? The transformation of standards of living, conditions of work and prospects for leisure over the past century or more has sprung from the process of innovation, investment and competitive production of which dispersed initiative has proved, without doubt, the most powerful stimulus known to man. For nostalgic readers who long to retain their belief in public services, Marshall delivered the briefest reprimand back in the early years of this century: 'The carcass of municipal electric works belongs to the officials; the genius belongs to free enterprise.' He did not rule out all municipal undertakings but had no doubt about the general rule:

> I am only urging that every new extension of Governmental work in branches of production which needs ceaseless creation and initiative is to be regarded as *prima facie* anti-social, because it retards the growth of that knowledge and those ideas which are incomparably the most important form of collective wealth.

Writing as one who has increasingly come to believe in the primacy of moral values over 'economic salvation', I take comfort that competitive markets which help us resolve the central economic conundrum of how and what to produce, are consistent with maximum freedom for individuals to make their own choices and keep the reins of their own mortal and immortal destinies so far as possible in their own hands. Christian critics have too easily taken for granted the twin boons of material progress and freedom conferred by liberal capitalism. They ignore the lesson that religious freedom has historically been most severely curtailed in countries that lack the *dispersed* initiative and *private* property rights which are the cornerstone of a market economy. They are too ready to appeal for state intervention, and ignore that government necessarily involves coercion. Hayek's ideal set out in *The Constitution of Liberty* is the limitation of state power so as to minimise that coercion which occurs where 'one man's actions are made to serve another man's will, not for his own but for the other's purpose'.

Despite the rhetoric of party politicians, the choice for government is not between collectivism and *laissez faire*. The strongest adherents of market economy acknowledge an indisputable role for strong (not big) government. Markets cannot work in a vacuum. It cannot be too often repeated that they require a framework of law to protect person and property, specify standards, enforce contracts, police monopoly and check pollution. Competing producers catering for consumer choice are not appropriate for the supply of 'public goods' like national defence, street lighting or a social safety net. There is a growing 'market' in charity, despite the 'crowding out' effect of the providential state. Thus people still supply personal services or cash (encouraged by tax concessions) to satisfy the needs of others who cannot help themselves. But until private philanthropy is stronger, few economic liberals deny an essential role for state finance to support social services so long as they are administered in ways that will do least damage to the incentive for able-bodied recipients to support themselves and their families.

Anyone attending a debate in the House of Commons, or more sedately even in the House of Lords, could be forgiven for believing that since 1979 the Conservatives under Mrs Thatcher have been fully engaged in dismantling state services. A sharply contrasting picture is presented by the audited national accounts for 1988, the last as I write. The figures show that what is blandly called 'public expenditure', which I would describe more graphically as politically-controlled spending, amounted to £175,000 million, which was forty-four per cent of a total national income of around £400,000 million. This outlay was equal to more than £3,000 a year for every man, woman and child in the United Kingdom or, on a more homely scale, an average of £240 *a week* for a family of four. Social services alone accounted for £100,000 million (averaging £140 a week), made up of over £22,000 million on state education, £23,000 million on the health service and a massive £54,000 million on social security. Since 1979 each of these lines of spending has increased significantly in real terms after generous allowance for the inflation of prices.

Is it not remarkable that this massive and mounting outlay under the sacred banner of the welfare state, absorbing one quarter of the total value of rising national output, appears to satisfy no one, neither teachers, parents, doctors, patients, ancillaries, pensioners, nor poverty lobbies? The most obvious explanation is that social spending is not efficiently managed. Instead of being directed scrupulously and selectively at the declining minority in need, this largesse is sprayed indiscriminately in 'free' services or social benefits for everyone in the name of universalism. It was a bishop in the House of Lords who most vividly expressed the fallacy which this wasteful policy embodies:

> The image of strong, independent citizens who do not need help from the resources of others is feasible for only a very few privileged people . . . Today the great majority of people, and I include myself, depend upon the social wage to maintain the quality of life.

Here is the most naive expression of the fantasy of a universal free lunch. A question I have asked before is whether it is forgivable, even for an unworldly bishop, to confuse counsels by preaching the self-evident falsehood that the welfare state could enable (nearly) everyone to live better at someone else's expense? The plain truth is that the cost of universal benefits is so high that they require finance by taxes falling on millions of people with incomes well below CPAG's poverty line. Most people pay their own way in welfare through general taxation which allows them no consumer sovereignty over the suppliers of education and health care.

Economic textbooks have much to say about theoretical imperfections of the market. But the practical failures of government are far more pervasive and less corrigible. Books have been written about the inefficiency and outright waste of resources inseparable from government provision of monopoly services like education or medical care without charge or choice for the conscripted consumer. If politicians defer to elitist sentiment in perpetuating this economic abomination of zero pricing, literally a free-for-all, they must not be surprised that large additional expenditures continue to fall short of unpriced expectations. More recently, American and British students of social policy have pointed to accumulating evidence that today's more generous social benefits have the perverse effect of undermining self-help by prolonging, deepening and extending dependency and voluntary unemployment. For able-bodied claimants, including heads of 'single-parent' families, the social benefits intended to keep them out of poverty at the same time exert an *unintended* disincentive to striving harder for training, mobility and employment as more fulfilling routes to self-support, self-respect and self-fulfilment.

Economic analysis can point to dozens of similar examples where well-intentioned government policies have perversely led to deplorable results. As with welfare, the reason is that politicians take a narrow and short-term view which overlooks the full effects on human action of distorting prices or incomes. The classic example has long been rent control which protected sitting tenants only by excluding others, often more deserving, and (unintentionally) destroying the incentive for landlords to keep property in good repair, much less build additional houses to rent at a loss. Equally disastrous has been the effect under the Common Agricultural Policy of raising food prices in the interests of less efficient farmers which (unintentionally) induces higher production, costly surpluses and the closing of markets to cheaper produce from poorer farmers in Africa and the West Indies, as well as to the abundant supplies of wheat, meat and dairy produce from Australia and New Zealand. The opposite policy by many African governments of fixing farm prices too low, in the short-term interests of urban consumers, has everywhere had the (unintended) consequence of discouraging peasant production and condemning millions to chronic deprivation, periodic starvation and lingering death. No less malignant have been government and trade union policies to raise minimum wages which have (unintentionally) increased unemployment and then provoked monetary expansion which, in turn, has unleashed inflation. In all such cases, governments of both advanced and backward countries have sought to win short-term support by expediencies that work through suppressing market forces, distorting production, destroying wealth and retarding the benign processes of increasing and spreading economic welfare.

The explanation of so much misdirected political travail is not simply the widespread misunderstanding and mistrust of market pricing. The economic analysis of democratic politics teaches us that politicians are subject to the 'vote motive' which leads to corrupting pressures from sectional interests that offer to trade their electoral support in exchange for special favours. Competition in the electoral market cannot be presumed to promote the elusive 'public interest'. So long as political parties can promise people more than they could earn in a competitive market, farmers, trade unions, professions, owner-occupiers, tenants, pensioners and other lobbies are not slow to push their claims.

The chief novelty of Thatcherism has been to confront such pressures by resisting union and professional special pleading, by reducing subsidies, deregulating markets and sharpening competition. The success of such policies can be measured by the reversal of economic decline and the record increases in productivity, output and incomes since 1979. But ten years have not proved long enough to reverse over half a century of creeping collectivism. There is still a long way to go in removing restrictions on competitive markets that continue to hamper mobility and adjustment in response to new opportunities, for example in the

European market, and to meet the growing challenge from Japan and the newly industrialised economies of the East. Yet all the opposition parties confronting Mrs Thatcher's radical, reforming Government are already back at the old game of promising less bracing routes to easier times for (almost) everyone. Against this sombre background, I conclude that the priestly disposition to join in calling upon the 'state' to promise short-term soft options for deep-seated economic problems is one of the most dispiriting forms of idolatry in my lifetime.

It is commonplace that people sharing similar if not identical aims, whether in social policy or other spheres of human action, may conscientiously differ sharply about the best way of achieving their shared purposes. From some acquaintance with church spokesmen and Labour as well as Conservative leaders, I have no doubt that most serious disagreements on policy are about means rather than ends. Would it not anyway be more charitable, especially for Christians, to assume that people on both sides of the argument are equally concerned to eradicate such scourges as poverty, homelessness and unemployment? On social issues where sentiment often prevails over disciplined reason, it would hardly be remarkable for bishops among others to adopt a preference for the socialist ideal, even if collectivism has not invariably worked very well in practice. What is surely inadmissible is for them to proclaim their chosen method blessed and to denounce the way of the market, which is conscientiously preferred by other Christians and which has proved the chief engine of economic and social progress.

In Defence of the Market

To judge by the tendency of Socialists to boast of superior compassion, a large part of the explanation is that they persist in assessing the merits of alternative approaches by their professed motives rather than their practical outcomes. At the heart of this widespread emotional distaste for the competitive market is its reliance on the supposedly narrow motive of individual self-interest, which in political debate is too easily equated with greed and single-minded selfishness. The case for the prosecution is too well-known to require further elaboration. In the space that remains I shall offer ten reasons why this charge should be earnestly reconsidered, if not rejected outright, by those who conscientiously wish to understand the case for the defence. At the outset we must dig deeper into the setting in which self-interest is assumed to operate.

As founder of modern political economy in *An Enquiry into the Nature and Causes of the Wealth of Nations*, Adam Smith asserts that 'the principle from which public and national as well as private opulence is originally derived' is nothing more nor less than 'the uniform, constant and uninterrupted effort of every man to better his condition'. As though anticipating the poor performance of our post-war dalliance with collectivism, he declared that this principle, which might be described in more homely terms as self-improvement,

> is frequently powerful enough to maintain the natural progress of things towards improvement, in spite both of extravagance of government and of the greatest errors of administration. Like the unknown principle of animal life, it frequently restores health and vigour to the constitution, in spite not only of the disease, but of the absurd prescriptions of the doctor.

My first plea is that the classical economists never denied that most people are capable of acting from compassion or altruism, which Adam Smith calls 'benevolence' and Alfred Marshall 'chivalry'. We may thank the Lord that, despite the undoubted strength of original sin, most of us do not exclusively seek to maximise our incomes or wealth. But might not bishops acknowledge that they also act from mixed motives? Or would they blame their own falls from grace on the market, like the fat man in the restaurant who curses the waiter for his own obesity?

Before his famous *Wealth of Nations* Smith wrote the little-known *Theory of Moral Sentiments* (1759) in which he denounces as sternly as any bishop the man who 'devotes himself for ever to the pursuit of wealth and greatness'. More positively, he emphasises our need for 'love, friendship and gratitude' and dwells on the promptings of conscience as the 'impartial spectator' or 'the great inmate of the breast, the great judge and arbiter of conduct'. For Smith as moral philosopher, 'the perfection of human nature' would require us 'to restrain our selfish, and to indulge our benevolent, affections'. As a practical Scot, however, he concludes, not without reverence, that

> the care of the universal happiness of all rational and sensible beings is the business of God and not of man. To man is allotted a much humbler department, but one much more suitable to the weakness of his powers and the narrowness of his comprehension – the care of his own happiness, of that of his family, his friends, his country: that he is occupied in contemplating the more sublime can never be an excuse for neglecting the more humble department . . .

My second witness for the market is Hayek whose extensive writings have demonstrated the indispensable role of the incentives of price and profit (and loss) as key signals to guide consumers, workers, investors and entrepreneurs in the daily process of economising scarce resources. The nice bishop who complained that firms closed down factories only because 'the market has shifted away' later excused his part in 'the painful processes of making some churches redundant in areas where the population has drastically reduced'. Bishops, like entrepreneurs and ordinary families, have to be guided by financial calculations in deciding the most effective disposition of limited resources.

Likewise, prices in the form of income differentials which the Left find so offensive are necessary to guide the local, national and international division of labour. In 1947 when

British planning was suffering a periodic crisis, Mr Clement Attlee as Prime Minister appealed to the nation in a radio broadcast as follows:

> Ask yourself whether you are doing the kind of work which the nation needs in view of the shortage of labour. Your job may bring you in more money but be quite useless to the community.

That incomparable economic jester, George Schwartz, pictured the chaos that would result if people had tried to act on that advice, with every worker unilaterally deciding what job was more useful to his fellows. He hinted that the resignation might best start with the civil servants responsible for economic planning!

A third affidavit for the market can be stated in seven words: *voluntary exchange yields benefits to both parties*. Buyer and seller both derive what economists call 'gains from trade'. So long as competition prevails, we can only 'better our condition' by serving others through supplying something for which they choose to pay. In short, as Milton Friedman has said: you have to do good to do well. Henry Ford may have sought riches, but he ended up enriching society far more. Let critics ponder the concept of a cheap millionaire.

My fourth claim emerges when we contemplate the opposite to voluntary exchange. The distinctive feature of collectivism is that it coerces others to behave in ways the government decrees. We cannot avoid overriding individual choice for public goods, including national defence, law enforcement and standards of purity, environment safety and weights and measures. But pushed beyond such essential services, consumer choice is frustrated with no guarantee of countervailing public benefit. If individual self-advancement is transmuted by Adam Smith's 'invisible hand' of competition into increased output, state coercion of production, consumption and exchange is often perverted into decreased supplies, as we have argued in respect of nationalisation, rent control, agricultural price-fixing and other policies, where results mock the best intentions.

A fifth argument against involving government in activities better left to the market is that it diverts over-worked politicians from tasks only they can discharge but so often neglect, like avoiding inflation, enforcing the law, policing competition and helping people who through physical or mental handicap cannot unaided 'better their own condition'. The familiar result is that the most persistent difficulties arise in the over-extended public sector where a wag has complained that political 'solutions' are the cause of most of the problems.

A sixth argument is that the processes of democratic government are far from immune to the worst manifestations of self-interest by politicians bidding for power, and special interest groups seeking sectional privileges. Since concentrated producers, whether capital or labour, can be organised more effectively than scattered customers, policies are likely to favour the producer interest in higher prices and restricted output over the consumer interest in cheapness and plenty.

The seventh consideration is that by calling on government, we do nothing to transform human conduct or to subdue self-interest. We simply transfer the same self-seeking propensities in human nature to the political plane where their scope for abuse is far more corrupting of public morality as well as damaging to freedom and economic progress. At every election I have observed since 1945, the Labour Party has certainly not shunned the most blatant, calculating appeal to naked, short-term self-interest of pensioners, parents, tenants, trade unionists, welfare beneficiaries and most other sizeable lobbies, with the bill to be paid by a conveniently small minority of higher-rate taxpayers with 'the broadest backs' and not too many votes.

An eighth argument for the market based on dispersed initiative and power is that it sets narrow limits to the evil that bad men can perpetrate. Keynes, who was no uncriti-

cal champion of the free economy, said almost the last word
with his warning:

> . . . dangerous human proclivities can be canalised into
> comparatively harmless channels by the existence of oppor-
> tunities for money-making and private wealth, which if they
> cannot be satisfied in this way may find their outlet in
> cruelty, the reckless pursuit of personal power and auth-
> ority, and other forms of self-aggrandisement . . . It is better
> that a man should tyrannise over his bank balance than over
> his fellow citizens . . .

My post-script would be that people who tyrannise over
their fellow citizens seldom neglect to attend to their personal bank balances, as so many African socialist leaders
have demonstrated.

A ninth argument is that socialist policies, which purport
to protect the poor from the insecurity of the market,
disable them from doing what they could to help themselves and their families. It must have taken rare courage
for Frank Field, as a Labour MP, to agree that the plight of
single-parent families has been intensified by the incentives
which social benefits and housing priority now give for
abandoned or unmarried mothers to continue depending
on state support. A market solution would seek to
strengthen the positive incentives for responsible parenthood and self-support by requiring contributions from the
fathers of abandoned children, developing child-minding
facilities and making it easier and more accepted for
mothers to take suitable employment. A truly compassionate policy towards the able-bodied poor would rely less on
doling out unconditional benefits and more in tackling the
personal handicaps and deficiencies, including education,
training and motivation, which inhibit self-support.

My final testimony for the market is that it provides our
best, if not our only, hope of eradicating the causes of
poverty in Britain and around the world, without risk to
freedom and other values. Whatever lip-service collectivist
bishops pay to the necessity for wealth creation, there is

little dispute that their dominant obsession is with the redistribution of existing wealth; such policies, Marshall argued, would be likely to reduce wealth. If we look back in history, or around the contemporary world of Eastern Europe, Africa and South America, we may more easily conclude that the most effective war against poverty is being fought not from the pulpits, but on the advancing frontiers of modern technology powered by dispersed initiative, competitive innovation, bold risk-taking and high enterprise.

So let the debate continue with less intimidatory de-nunciation of the market and its upholders. Perhaps one or two bishops might even break ranks and give a lead in celebrating next Rogation Sunday the remarkable social advance which economic freedom has enabled frail, fallen men to achieve in fulfilling God's command in Genesis (1:28): 'Be fruitful, and multiply, and replenish the earth, and subdue it . . .' Bishops may even take heart from the increasing acceptance that the pollution of our natural environment can most quickly be remedied by deploying part of the wealth that man's enterprise has multiplied and by shaping market incentives to reward the kind of produc-tion that sustains our natural environment; also to penalise both public and private enterprise that does it harm.

10

The Feeding of the Billions

Michael Alison, MP

'NUMBERS,' wrote E. H. Carr in his 1961 Trevelyan Lectures, 'count in history,' and there can be few if any better examples of this generalisation than that of the staggering growth in the numbers of the human race since about 1830.

It is worth focusing on the actual figures because, like some gigantic tidal movement, this population growth is curiously imperceptible and unobserved in its full historical sweep by those living in its midst. The figures show that the growth in numbers of the human species was a slow and halting affair until the nineteenth century AD, but that then they exploded. Thus it took some ten thousand years of human history before a global population of 1,000 million was reached, in about 1830. But it then took only *one hundred* years – 1830 to 1930 – for the world to double its population to 2 billion. It then took just thirty years – 1930 to 1960 – for the third billion to be added; and fifteen years – 1960 to 1975 – for the fourth billion. Since that date a fifth billion, approximately, has come into existence. So: 10,000 years to reach one billion; 150 years to reach 5 billion.

This veritable revolution in numbers is one of the few in human history at once both cataclysmic and benign. In the historical perspective, indeed, the sudden growth in numbers seems miraculous, like the miracle in Ezekiel's valley of dry bones where the ingredients and potential for human life lay inert and unrealised until one day 'breath entered them; they came to life and stood up on their feet – a vast army' (Ezekiel 37:10, NIV). What new spirit, if any, breathed over the human race to multiply its numbers so vastly and rapidly after 1830?

The limitations upon population growth before 1830 were, of course, material. Disease and famine were the twin blades continuously scything through budding human life. (War helped to cut down numbers too, though not on the same scale.) History records at least 750 famines in earlier times, spanning some six millenniums. In the period 501 BC to AD 500, Mediterranean Europe, the crucible of Western civilisation, was the region where famine was most endemic. The first century of the Christian era was, indeed, noted for disastrous famines, with thousands dying of hunger in the famine of AD 6. European famines continued down to modern times, and in Eastern Europe particularly the period AD 1501 to 1700 was a notably bad one. But even in Western Europe on the eve of the Industrial Revolution, in relatively modern times, Michael Novak, the Catholic economist and historian, records that '. . . a permanent condition of poverty was taken as given. Indeed in the 1780s in France, four-fifths of all French families spent 90 per cent of their incomes simply on buying bread – only bread – to stay alive.' The rich fared little better than the poor in terms of life expectancy, with disease still acting as the great leveller: it had robbed Europe of at least a fifth of its population through the Black Death after 1350. And Professor Fernand Braudel wrote in *Capitalism and Material Life* (1967): 'In the Beauvais in the middle of the seventeenth century over a third of the children died every twelve months; only 58 per cent reached their fifteenth year; people died on average at about the age of twenty.' Yet France at this time was one of the world's most advanced and developed nations.

It is this sombre background which makes the total transformation in human life and fortunes in the last 150 years so astounding. The age-long universal struggle for survival against the elemental forces of famine and disease suddenly ceased. It is as if an exhausted swimmer had suddenly felt the firm beach under his feet, and had walked up out of the sea. Billions of human beings now live and breathe with an average individual life expectation world-wide of sixty years, where for ages past relatively paltry numbers survived and then only for a third of that life span. Viewed historically (and perhaps romantically) this population explosion represents the first great universal emancipation, liberation or exodus from elemental thraldom in human history.

For Christians, in particular, this vast increase in human numbers living and surviving must be seen as an absolute good in itself. For every live human birth embodies potentially not only a consciousness of the creation, but a chance of knowing the Creator. Not only life but immortality was brought to light through the Gospel. Our Lord lived at a time when the combination of hunger, disease, material scarcities and political disabilities was incomparably more oppressive than in most parts of the world, certainly in the West, today. Yet of only one class or category of human beings in his own day did he say that 'it would be better for him if he had not been born', and that was of one 'who betrayed the Son of Man'. So Christians can unreservedly welcome the growth in human numbers in modern times.

Of course, disease, hunger and poverty have not been universally eliminated. Figures from the 1970s suggest that over 500 million of the world's inhabitants may be suffering from severe malnutrition. More recently, Pope John Paul II said that there were 800 million hungry persons on this planet. And between one-third and one-half of mankind probably still have no access to well-organised and sophisticated health services. Against this background, it would be odiously complacent for any relatively prosperous Western Christian to applaud the growth in world population on religious grounds, whilst ignoring the human plight of those, even if they represent a minority, who barely survive in conditions of absolute poverty. Many living in sub-Saharan Africa provide only too vivid an example of growing populations in growing poverty. The World Bank report on this region (of November 1989) spoke of 100 million people facing chronic food shortages, rising malnutrition, and relatively astronomic maternal mortality rates (500 deaths for each 100,000 live births, compared with forty-four in China and ten in Western Europe).

Yet what makes the sub-Saharan (and other comparable) scenes so shocking is that, in global terms, they are now so exceptional. And the fact that they *are* exceptional means that there is manifestly hope for bringing relief, as the World Bank report and its recommendations make clear. As Professor F. A. Hayek has written in *Capitalism and the Historians* (1954):

> The very increase of wealth and well-being which had been achieved raised standards and aspirations. What for ages had seemed a natural and inevitable situation . . . came to be regarded as incongruous . . . Economic suffering both became more conspicuous and seemed less justified, because the general wealth was increasing faster than ever before.

Thus the sheer scale of recent human growth, in numbers and life expectation, still remains the dominant indicator of a revolutionary change for the better. The starving or severely under-nourished represent perhaps one-tenth of the world's current population. One eminent authority, Professor Simon Kuznets of Harvard, wrote in *The Gap between Rich and Poor Nations* (1972) that

> in many 'poor' Less Developed Countries . . . the ratio of calorie consumption to requirements is close to 100 per cent (e.g. Pakistan 98%, Ceylon 99%, Ethiopia 95%, Uganda 97%) and in many LDCs the net protein intake is at or above the required level.

Clearly he wrote before political and tribal disputes later disturbed economic and social progress in some of the countries he mentioned. Yet the fact remains that the technology of the 'green revolution' – the development of more productive strains of wheat and rice – resulted in erstwhile poor countries like Mexico and India becoming self-sufficient in cereals during the 1970s. Meanwhile more advanced countries like the United States produce a vast surplus of foodstuffs available for distribution in food aid to countries or regions afflicted by localised famines. And if well-organised health services remain comparatively scarce, the pharmaceutical revolution – the giant strides taken in the creation and distribution of modern drugs and vaccines – has spread throughout the world and underpinned the growth in population which agricultural and industrial advances first set in train.

The Rise of Democratic Capitalism

How do we account for this great transformation of the material conditions of human life? It is vital to recall that, historically, the origins were localised, not generalised. Christian Europe was the nuclear family, Britain the first individual womb, to give birth to the world revolution in numbers. In the hundred years between 1750 and 1850 the population of Great Britain grew from 7.5 million to 18 million, and industrial output rose five times in the fifty years between 1800 and 1850 alone. Real wages quadrupled, then quadrupled again between 1850 and 1900. The proximate causes of this transformation are more or less agreed amongst historians; in the bald summary of the *Encyclopaedia Britannica*'s article on population in the fifteenth edition:

> the super-death rate from acute famine and epidemics virtually disappeared during the 18th century in Western Europe because of agricultural advances, international trade that improved the availability of all resources, and better hygienic defences (the famine of 1847 in Ireland was atypical).

But that is not the whole story. It must be stressed first that Britain's transformation after 1780 was a revolution in productiveness not in acquisitiveness. We are not talking of a 'zero-sum' game in which the wealth of one nation – in this case Britain – was increased merely by the diversion of the equivalent wealth from another, as with the sixteenth-century Spanish shipment of silver from the Americas. Nor are we talking of such an equivalent transfer between classes, from masses of toiling poor to a handful of rich capitalists. On the contrary, it was essentially capitalism which gave rise to the numbers, not the other way round: the revolution in productivity, initially agricultural productivity, was the key to Britain's nineteenth-century explosion in population.

Nor are we talking of British economic and military strength suddenly surpassing that of her neighbours and rivals, as if that were the sufficient explanation of her extraordinary relative growth in wealth and numbers under George IV and Queen Victoria. On the contrary, France's population was 27 million in 1800, Spain's 10.5 million, whilst Britain's was nearer 9 million than 10. Indeed, British governments and politicians played hardly any significant part in the national economic transformation. Lord North himself, as Paul Johnson has observed, although Prime Minister in the 1770s and 1780s, 'went to his grave quite unaware that he had presided over an economic miracle'. Paul Johnson elaborates this point in an essay on 'A World without Politics'. He writes that 'so far as government was concerned it is impossible to point to any political decision which had a critical effect in promoting (or indeed retarding)' the momentous economic changes of the period. He then describes what actually went on. The changes were

> generated by mysterious and anonymous interactions within the areas of technology, production and marketing. They took place, as it were, within the hidden bowels of the industrial capitalist process, as a result of hundreds of innovations, and thousands of initiatives, and millions of decisions. In each phase, there were outstanding inventors and pre-eminent entrepreneurs. But in none of them was there a plan, let alone a mastermind.

Here is a vivid description, amongst other things, of Adam Smith's famous 'invisible hand' of market forces at work. And yet even this falls short of a fully adequate explanation of what occurred. For we cannot be content to rest upon the notion of some kind of blind automaticity, flowing naturally and inevitably – like fermentation in grapes – from the interaction of certain conditions and ingredients in eighteenth-century Britain. Thus the natural 'ingredients' of Britain's capitalist transformation in economic terms – private property, markets, profits, and incentives – had existed in the world since time immemorial; they were indeed all discernible in the background social fabric of Old and New Testament times. But these old ingredients all evidently failed, over huge stretches of time, to deliver any great revolution in human well-being or life-expectation comparable to the modern one we are discussing.

It might be tempting, again, to think of the Industrial Revolution as being sparked off by the chance attainment of some sort of a 'critical state' in the global, and local, economic environment, analogous to and as impersonal as the global climatic changes of prehistoric times which suddenly abolished the dinosaurs and promoted the reptiles. Propitious climatic conditions did assist in the take-off of the Industrial Revolution, but such an explanation again would fail to do justice to the human factors and faculties involved in the British, and later Western, economic miracles.

The real causes of the great transformation were neither random, nor impersonal, nor accidental. Fundamentally, they were Christian and biblical. They relate to the specific evolution, above all in Christian Europe, of forms of human consciousness and aspiration which, developing over long periods of time, finally matured and crystallised in what Michael Novak defines as 'democratic capitalism'. His analysis, indeed, is the essential input for much of what follows. In an article in *Policy Review* (No. 13, 1980), he wrote that

> by *democratic capitalism*, one means a society no longer structured like a traditional society . . . but rather a society differentiated into three social systems: a political system, an economic system, and a moral–cultural system. As the Church is separated from the State, so also the economic system has a certain independence from the political system.

He notes that the modern conception of democracy 'springs from centuries of meditation upon the biblical vision of humankind'. And the tripartite structure he cited reflects three important Christian social insights. First, the notion of human sinfulness is an essential part of that biblical vision. Bishop Richard Holloway, writing in *The Times* in 1975, noted in a refreshing refinement of Lord Acton's well-worn dictum that, 'it is not power which corrupts man. It is man's original corruption which leads to the inevitable misuse of power.' And C. S. Lewis expressed the same idea with typical incisiveness in his essay on Equality in the *Spectator* (27 August 1943):

> I am a democrat because I believe in the Fall of Man. I think most people are democrats for the opposite reason. A great deal of democratic enthusiasm descends from the ideas of people like Rousseau, who believed in democracy because they thought mankind so wise and good that everyone deserved a share in the government. The danger of defending democracy on those grounds is that they're not true. And whenever their weakness is exposed, the people who prefer tyranny make capital out of the exposure. I find that they're not true without looking further than myself. I don't deserve a share in governing a hen-roost, much less a nation. Nor do most people – all the people who believe advertisements, and think in catchwords and spread rumours. The real reason for democracy is just the reverse. Mankind is so fallen that no man can be trusted with unchecked power over his fellows. Aristotle said that some people were only fit to be slaves. I do not contradict him. But I reject slavery because I see no men fit to be masters.

Next, the principle of the separation of powers, particularly as between the economic and political sectors in a state, is inherent in a truly democratic social framework, though the idea itself of course ante-dates modern democracies. The rise of the free cities and free republics of fifteenth-century Europe were early examples of economic independence evolving within the then still feudal framework of Christendom. But the primitive society of Old Testament Israel provides an even earlier model: here there was not only a separation of powers under a form of the rule of law, but economic independence was provided for in the shape of a general freeholding of agricultural land, involving two of the most important factors of production.

The third fundamental Christian input to the idea of democratic capitalism flows from the biblical ideal of harmony and balance between an individual body and a body corporate. The parable of the Lost Sheep expresses the harmony perfectly, with the overriding value it places upon the life of the individual one lost, whose greatest good and need can only be provided for in restoration to membership of the flock with the other ninety-nine. In his article already cited, Novak points out that, 'the basis institution of capitalism is the corporation – a social organism'. He goes on to observe that

> the origins of the corporation lie in ancient religious communities, whose purpose transcended the life of individuals. These communities incorporated for 'profit', in the sense that they needed to be sufficiently productive to have time for other things (prayer, honouring the dead) than mere subsistence, and to maintain independent continuity over time.

In this connection it may be recalled that the agricultural skills which mediaeval monasteries developed, and which succeeded in yielding the required surplus in output, were the precursors of those later improvements which in due time facilitated the migration from field to factory in Britain and sustained the early phases of the Industrial Revolution.

Even the dissolution of the monasteries yielded a dividend. As Weber pointed out in *The Protestant Ethic and the Spirit of Capitalism*, 'those passionately spiritual natures which had formerly supplied the highest type of monk were now forced to pursue their ascetic ideals within mundane occupations'.

But if the corporation is paramount in capitalism, its vitality and fruitfulness has reflected the biblical insight about individuals, above all their freedom and independence. Again Novak:

> The most distinctive contribution of Judaism and Christianity to social theory is the identification of the individual conscience as a major source of social energy. Not all energy comes from authority, as the ancients held; nor from social structures as the Marxists hold; nor from historical necessity; nor from 'class struggle', etc. The individual is an originating source of insight, decision and action.

In *Will It Liberate?* (1986) he insisted that

> The cause of wealth is creativity. Not natural resources. Not labour. Not planning. Rather, human wit, intelligence, inquiry, invention – in a word the old *caput* [Latin: head] from which the name for the system, 'capitalism', is appropriately derived.

Incidentally, nothing could more grossly caricature or misrepresent democratic capitalism than to describe it as a system which panders inordinately to the claims of the individual in isolation – in a word, to individualism. Magnification and glorification of the individual was, rather, a feature of pre-capitalist, aristocratic, forms of society. And the isolation of the individual is an essential feature of Marxist social engineering, where the individual must be confronted and isolated at every turn by the monolithic state and thus disbarred from finding security or refuge in the mediating structures of non-statist voluntary associations. In contrast, the essential feature of democratic capitalist societies is precisely the emergence on a huge scale of diversified, differentiated forms of voluntary association, greatly extending and elaborating the primitive norms and forms of sociality, whether of clan, family, or tribe.

Is too much here being claimed for Christianity, as the ultimate source – the long-hidden leaven – for what has finally burgeoned in the form of the modern, prosperous, open societies of the West? What about the closed world of mediaeval Christendom, regulated, restricted, even policed by the institutional Church? Was not the growing influence of radical secular thinkers, often atheists, aided and abetted by the growing technology of printing and publishing, the real cause of the break-up of the old closed order of the Middle Ages? I do not think so. The pioneers of printing and more widespread publishing were certainly key figures, but they were largely Christian pioneers – for example, Gutenberg and Tyndale – and it was the Word of God in Old and New Testament which they sought to propagate. It was this same Word which had earlier lodged and borne fruit in the heart and mind of Luther. And it was from Luther, from within the very kernel of institutional Christendom, that the seed of a new movement of liberation first fought its way to the light. Printing aided its wider propagation. Many new autonomies, for example in art and literature, were later claimed by Luther's intellectual heirs and successors, often moving away from the Church. But his defiant act of 'private judgment' was first in the field. Hence so distinguished an authority as Christopher Hill can write in his *Essays in the Economic and Social History of Tudor and Stuart England* that most 'historians would now accept the existence of some connection between Protestantism and the rise of capitalism, though Professor Trevor-Roper is a conspicuous exception'.

The Liberation of Humanity

It was inescapable, given the specific and local origins of the Industrial Revolution, that sharp disparities of material prosperity and human well-being should initially emerge from that Revolution, as numbers grew across the world. But should these disparities have persisted down to modern times? Critics of the persistence of these disparities, of the manifestly unequal shares of the world's material resources enjoyed by different nations and peoples, often approach the issue along the line of maldistribution. Novak described it thus:

> The classic moralist's principle for the economic order is distributive justice. This principle was a first principle in traditional societies which had no decision to make about growth. Traditional societies were, on the whole, static. When the sum of worldly goods is finite, limited, and already known, traditional ethicists properly concentrate attention upon how the known store of goods ought to be distributed.

But the rise of democratic capitalism has introduced a new ethical obligation. The fact and the possibility of economic growth, the basis for the huge expansion in human numbers and human freedom, has, Novak suggests,

> introduced an ethical principle prior to distributive justice. Moral decisions about growth and productivity are prior, both in logic and in the real world, to questions of distribution. What is not produced cannot be distributed, and choices about production condition choices about distribution.

Moreover questions of distribution, at least internationally, are profoundly complicated by the fact that immaterial, rather than material, resources have held the key to the revolutionary growth in productivity and output of modern states, as we have seen from our consideration of the rise of democratic capitalism. Professor Bauer has observed, laconically, that: 'the vast natural resources of the United States were *in situ* for many centuries, but that did not enable the American Indians to pass beyond a most primitive level of economic achievement'. And Professor Kuznets makes the point even more explicitly:

> This reformulation of the gap [between rich and poor] is important because it emphasises the association between the disparity in *per capita* product and those in economic structures and in social ideology (i.e. views on man and nature prevalent in various societies). The gap is not merely between rich and poor, but between the industrialised, urbanised, mechanised, modernised countries with distinctive economic institutions, demographic processes, political characteristics and ideological patterns, on the one hand; and the largely rural, agricultural, traditional countries, with only small nuclei of modern industry, modern firms, modern government and modern views, on the other. Difficult as it may be to establish the specific connection between economic development, as measured by some index of aggregate product, and economic and social structures, institutions and ideological notions, the evidence on such historical association is too weighty to be denied or neglected. And the association provides a basis for interpreting and analysing the aggregative gap.

Professor Kuznets' analysis is far from being merely academic. It is vividly substantiated and illustrated by the paradox that, for example, Latin America has done so much worse with its own vast natural resources in terms of economic advance than such diverse yet brilliant performers, all markedly deficient in natural resources, as Belgium, Holland, Japan, South Korea, Taiwan, Singapore and Hong Kong. The Asian contingent of this cohort have indeed increased their national wealth *ten times over* in the last twenty years, with dramatically beneficial material effects upon their teeming populations, not excluding their poor. And the World Bank report on sub-Saharan Africa, referred to earlier, produced the staggering statistic that this region of Africa, with a population of 450 million people, has an annual gross domestic product, at $135 billion, which is the same as Belgium with a population of 10 million.

The explanation for the imbalance in performance between Latin American and African countries and the other countries cited lies in the failure of the former to modernise themselves upon democratic, pluralistic, capitalist lines. This is not, of course, a socio-economic structure compatible exclusively with modern Conservatism. Modern social democratic parties are broadly 'within the family' of those who endorse the political and economic pluralism of democratic capitalism. But as early as 1776 Adam Smith predicted that Latin America would end in poverty and tyranny unless it reformed its economic and social structure along the lines then already taking shape in Europe, and Michael Novak's more recent diagnosis in *Will It Liberate?* echoes that of Adam Smith:

> Liberation theology says that Latin America is capitalist and needs a socialist revolution. Latin America does need a revolution. But its present system is mercantilist and quasi-feudal, not capitalist, and the revolution it needs is both liberal and Catholic. The present order is not free but statist, not mind-centered but privilege-centered, not open to the poor but protective of the rich. Large majorities of the poor are propertyless. The poor are prevented by law from founding and incorporating their own enterprises. They are denied access to credit. They are held back by an ancient legal structure, designed to protect the ancient privileges of a pre-capitalist elite.

The misreading of economic and social realities with which Novak indicts some Latin American theologians needs to be further spelt out. Typically these theologians argue that the United States and Western Europe are rich not only because they are privileged possessors of bountiful natural resources (which they should share more equitably) but because, by their economic strength and dominance, they drain away natural resources from other weaker and more backward countries. A standard accusation indicts the countries of the North Atlantic community for controlling and exploiting some eighty per cent of the world's natural resources whilst themselves accounting for only twenty per cent of the world population. Central to the processes of this maldistribution, liberation theologians allege, are the investment policies of big multinational business corporations based in north America and Western Europe but operating overseas. These multinationals, like parasites, drain away the resources of the host nations on whose territory they operate.

But neither of these indictments will bear factual examination. First, so far as the consumption of material resources is concerned, a number of the allegedly 'exploiting' countries are in reality massive exporters. For example, Canada and the US have become far larger exporters of raw materials – grain, lumber, coal, etc. – than the whole of Latin America put together. J. K. Galbraith has observed that 'if to be a part of the Third World is to be a hewer of wood and a producer of food and natural produce, the US and Canada are by a wide margin, the first of the Third World countries'. And so far as the allegedly debilitating effect of the United States' multi-national investment is concerned, it is significant that the fraction of such investment overseas that goes to Latin America is about sixteen per cent. By contrast, about seventy per cent of such investment goes to Western Europe, Canada and Japan, and scarcely seems to damage them much in the process. This does not mean, of course, that multinational corporations are invariably faultless in their local policies and actions, particularly in their more backward host countries. The US business corporation, United Fruit, has been sharply indicted, for example, for cultural arrogance, high-handedness, corruption and insensitivity to the values of democracy, in its activities in Guatemala. Yet in mitigation it must be recorded that a dilemma often faces such multinational corporations, where certain traditional practices in some host countries are regarded as locally acceptable, but would amount to corrupt practices in Western societies.

Kuznets' comments on the connection between material economic progress or the lack of it, and non-material social attitudes and ideologies, offer a far more convincing explanation of the poverty and backwardness of some countries – not all in the Third World – than notions of 'capitalist exploitation'. And this conclusion is borne out by the World Bank report of 1989. Commenting in the *Independent* of 22 November 1989, Michael Prest wrote that 'the Bank has . . . addressed directly issues which are central to development . . . the need for good government, for accountability, for serious pursuit of objectives, for lower military spending, and above all, for liberalisation'. The report also concluded that adverse terms of trade, so often relied upon as an explanation for African economic decline, could no longer be cited in this context. The World Bank estimated that over the last thirty years Africa had gained from the terms of trade.

A Christian Vision

This essay has focused on the phenomenon of the vast increase in human numbers and life expectancy in modern times, and has sought to view it in a Christian perspective. I have suggested that this increase is, in and of itself, one of the great blessings and advances in history, since every living human being is made in the image of God, and potentially immortal. Human life is a quality independent of its environment, and an absolute good in itself.

It might at first sight seem naive, if not artificial, to lay deliberate emphasis on the notion of life as a quality, and to distinguish it from 'quality of life', since the two in the real world seem to be inextricably mixed. But our Lord himself did no less: 'Is not the life more than meat, and the body than raiment?' (Matthew 6:25, KJV). Indeed Jesus went further: his advice about an enhanced 'quality of life' was that, though it was admittedly desirable – indeed needful – it was in truth subordinate and derivative, flowing from attention to other priorities:

> Therefore take no thought saying, What shall we eat? or,
> What shall we drink? Or, Wherewithal shall we be clothed?
> (For after all these things do the Gentiles seek:) for your
> heavenly Father knoweth that ye have need of all these
> things. But seek ye first the kingdom of God and his
> righteousness; and all these things shall be added unto you.
>
> (Matthew 6:31–33)

It is all the more necessary today to maintain this distinction between life and 'quality of life', since the democratic capitalist revolution, in spawning the vast increase in world population, also gave birth to an unimaginable cornucopia of material goods and services, only a proportion of which were (and are) strictly necessary for maintaining the huge new global population in tolerable health. It is easy to be dazzled by the modern world of consumer durables, along with the profusion of other products available for mass consumption, and to regard them as ends, rather than means. These products were, for so many aeons of history and for so many millions of human beings, not available, so their sudden appearance in profusion can easily be viewed as a kind of triumphant historical climax, an end and good in itself. But this approach leads down a blind alley. The consummation and fulfilment of the New Testament miracle of the Feeding of the Five Thousand is, for example, not the modern technological miracle of limitless sliced and packaged bread on a million supermarket shelves. It is rather that 5 billion human souls today, potentially, can hear the message that was originally delivered to the Five Thousand, that bread is good – but not enough.

For in many respects the 'quality of life' enhancement brought about by democratic capitalism is deceptive, and changes nothing in relation to the deepest human needs. Thomas Hobbes, whose life spanned parts of the sixteenth and seventeenth centuries, described human life in its natural and primitive state as 'solitary, poor, nasty, brutish, and short'. However, his own day, viewed from a twentieth-century perspective, might seem to merit the same description; likewise our own day, viewed from the twenty-fifth century, might well appear to be as benighted. Yet the undoubted 'quality of life' advances between these different centuries do not necessarily yield a comparable advance in individual human happiness, contentment, fulfilment, and satisfaction, corresponding to the material progress. The quality of human pains, passions, and pleasures was essentially the same, surely, for the contemporaries of Homer, or Chaucer, or Shakespeare, or Keats as for those of T. S. Eliot.

To be more specific, the contemporary range of annual *per capita* income spread is admittedly gigantic, from at least $12,000 in advanced Western societies, to $120 in some of the least developed Third World countries. But it does not follow that the happiness of a poorer country necessarily depends on reaching the elusive goal of equality in *per capita* income with the richer. What is needed is a reasonable standard of living. The typical accompaniment of life in advanced Western societies today, even for the poorest households, is access to a house or flat, with beds, chairs, tables, a TV set, probably a refrigerator, electric lighting and heating, running hot and cold water and probably a bath, a variety of items of clothing, as well as access to fresh meat, vegetables, canned goods, books, newspapers, magazines, postal services, fire services, schools, doctors, and hospitals. Yet possession of and access to such goods and services is no guarantee of human satisfaction or fulfilment. Thousands of poor inner-city families dispose of all of them, yet remain despairing or dispirited. Others, in the same environment, with the same assets, are buoyant, optimistic, and content. For an individual's consciousness of well-being, or its reverse, surely owes little in its degree of intensity to the particular set of material circumstances which give rise to it. The despair, for example, of a poor family on a corporation estate in Liverpool, in finding it can no longer finance extensive hire-purchase debts incurred in buying a range of desirable consumer durables for the home, and hence faces extensive repossession, is not necessarily any different in quality or intensity – though obviously in causation – from the despair of a smallholder in first-century Palestine when the rains or crops have partly failed, and he wonders from whom he should borrow to tide over the shortfall. This is why our Lord's first-century gospel of hope and encouragement, based upon proper priorities, is as relevant today as it was then.

The point is worth emphasising because a number of prominent voices in Christian leadership in Britain today blur or ignore the distinction between life and 'quality of life'. They readily, and rightly, warn society at large against the illusion or mirage of seeking fulfilment in life through multiplying material goods or possessions. Yet, often simultaneously, they conduct a zealous crusade on behalf of a large but undifferentiated and vaguely defined cohort labelled 'the poor', usually in inner cities, for whom their remedy and prescription is entirely material. At what point in the income scale, one might ask, is it possible for such 'poor' to cross the vital dividing-line, and be considered eligible for Christ's teaching about life, which so often subordinates material to spiritual objectives?

The use by the secular bureaucracy of certain material and impersonal 'indicators of deprivation' as a basis for disbursing public funds is of course perfectly admissible. There can indeed be no acceptable basis for such a distribution other than in terms of broad, undifferentiated categories. But it is surely inappropriate for Christian church leaders likewise to approach the needs of the urban poor in such technical and statistical terms, knowing that these 'poor' are not a mere collective abstraction, but a mass of highly differentiated families of individuals, likely to be hugely varied in their real needs and perceptions, and as often as not beset and preoccupied by problems only remotely connected to their bureaucratic designation in terms of material deprivation.

The book of Proverbs (29:18) records the well-known saying that, 'Where there is no vision, the people perish'. For the Church of England, in *Faith in the City* (1985) – its most prestigious proclamation of a contemporary gospel for the nation – to conclude that 'the background is sombre but the vision of a nation working and living in a land of garden cities remains as an ideal which could be realised through imaginative and determined collective effort . . .' is surely to fall below the level of its calling. Much more convincing is the balance between worship, evangelism and far-reaching social action demonstrated by the group of Pentecostalists in the Wirral whom Frank Field describes in *The Politics of Paradise* (1987). Frank Field is no slouch when it comes to analysing and evaluating contemporary levels of material deprivation. But he writes that, 'if each local church council had the faith to match the witness of this particular group, then the writing of much of this book would have been superfluous'.

There is much to be conserved today: the sustaining and well-being of the new billions enfranchised to life by the material revolution since 1830; the reputation and accessibility of the principles of democratic capitalism, which have unlocked the secret of how to produce sufficient wealth for all; a world environment which has proved to be a dazzling fulfilment of the Old Testament picture of the Promised Land as

> a good land, a land of brooks of water, of fountains and depths that spring out of valleys and hills; a land of wheat and barley, and vines, and fig trees, and pomegranates; a land of olive oil, and honey; a land wherein thou shalt eat bread without scarceness, thou shalt not lack anything in it; a land whose stones are iron, and out of whose hills thou mayest dig brass . . .
>
> (Deuteronomy 8:7–9)

But above all to be treasured is the Christian heritage and revelation. From that source came the early injunction to mankind: 'Be fruitful and multiply'. From that source, I have argued, has come the principal effectual means for multiplying human numbers. And it is from that same source that mankind's greatest hope and vision springs: immortality.

11

The Conservative Quadrilateral

Brian Griffiths

IN an address on 'The Market' at Bristol Cathedral in 1986, the Bishop of Durham summed up Mrs Thatcher's view of society as the Conservative Quadrilateral, namely: the individual – choice – the market – wealth creation. He did so to show its inadequacy as a basis for social policy and to point out its inconsistencies with Christian belief. The Bishop is not alone among churchmen in holding such views. Similar comments are being made regularly in synodical reports and statements by church leaders.

In essence, what the Bishop and others have done is to define modern Conservatism as materialistic, secular and individualistic, and that seems to be the very antithesis of the Gospel. Therefore they have no option but to reject it. Meanwhile the Churches have made their own position very clear: the major goal of social policy should be to reduce inequality which is something that can be achieved only through collective action imposed by government.

The Bishop's Conservative Quadrilateral is said to encourage wealth creation. But even in its view of the economy, modern Conservatism is concerned with much more than the market and wealth creation, although it includes a realistic understanding of both. To understand Conservatism, the Bishop's Quadrilateral needs to be complemented by a second Quadrilateral, namely: community – responsibility – welfare – trusteeship. This would reflect the fact that the individual is the building brick of the community, that choice entails responsibility, that the market cannot be relied on to provide welfare, and that wealth creation is equally if not more concerned about the future renewal of resources than their immediate use.

This is modern Conservatism as I understand it. It is not a narrow ideology based on the survival of the fittest. Neither is it a belief in unregulated *laissez faire* capitalism. Modern Conservatism is firmly rooted in nineteenth-century tradition which always sought to place wealth creation in an effective legal and institutional framework and emphasise our shared responsibility to help others who could not help themselves.

In this essay I shall argue that the Bishop of Durham's interpretation of modern Conservatism is mistaken, and that it is vital to distinguish the approach of the present Government from a completely free market, *laissez faire* form of economic libertarianism, which is thoroughly secular and firmly rooted in the Enlightenment. Modern Conservatism has developed as an alternative to the post-war Keynesian, corporatist and egalitarian 'middle ground', which proved such a treacherous foundation for policy in the 1970s. If we wish to place present Conservative philosophy in a theological context, then it rests firmly within the Judaeo-Christian tradition. It follows that the Churches should respect modern Conservatism as a legitimate political option for Christians.

Individual and Community

Judaism and Christianity have always stressed the importance of the individual. The Old Testament affirms that man is created in the image of a personal God. As Emil Brunner has stated:

> The Christian principle of the dignity of the person is unconditionally personal; the personal God creates the personal and individual human being. Thus the origin of the

dignity shared equally by all mankind is not to be sought in abstract reason, nor in a general order of being, but in the will of a loving God, who addresses every man as 'Thou' and summons him to responsible being.

Hence it comes as no surprise that the commandments in the Old Testament and the Sermon on the Mount in the New Testament are both addressed to individuals. In our Lord's parable of the talents it is individuals who are endowed with talents. The Gospel is an appeal to the individual. Faith is something personal. And it is as individuals that we are held accountable for our actions and called to repentance and salvation. Historically in the West, the value and dignity which people possess as individuals form the basis of human rights and the obligations of the rule of law. It would be very surprising if this left economic life untouched, not least because throughout the Bible a great deal of attention is devoted to economic life. And of course it does not. The reason for the success of the market economy is that it creates room for the individual. It rewards individuals who are enterprising, innovative and hard-working. The engine driving prosperity and employment in the last decade has been the growth of small firms and self-employment. And in almost all cases the success of small firms is associated with the leadership of one or at most a few individuals. This emphasis on the individual was also the basis for recent trade union reform in Britain.

The problem facing anyone who stresses the importance of the individual in economic life (in sharp contrast to anyone who stresses the importance of the individual in cultural affairs) is that he is immediately accused of defending greed, selfishness and individualism. *Faith in the City* stated quite categorically: 'We believe that at present too much emphasis is being given to individualism and not enough to collective obligation.' But defending the individual is very different from defending individualism. Although some versions of individualism are more attractive than others, pressed to extremes individualism is at root a deeply non-Christian, if not anti-Christian, philosophy, in which the individual is considered morally autonomous, in which contractual relationships are emphasised at the expense of natural relationships and in which the impact on personal liberty is made the sole test of legislative change.

It would be difficult for even the most committed opponent of Conservatism to argue that the policy of the present Government is individualistic in this sense. Take for example three Bills which are before Parliament during 1990. *The Food Safety Bill* will better protect the consumer and raise still further safety standards and the quality of food produced and sold in Britain. *The Environment Protection Bill* will improve pollution control, reform the system for dealing with waste disposal, strengthen the law on litter and intensify protection of the countryside. *The Broadcasting Bill* will deregulate commercial television while at the same time preserving quality for Channel 3 in a number of different ways; it will also retain the existing remit for Channel 4 and place the Broadcasting Standards Council on a statutory basis. This is not *laissez faire*! Each of these Bills strikes a balance between encouraging a thriving market, protecting consumers and setting standards. As with so many other examples which could be given, it is quite wrong to suggest that the major, if not the only, test made by the Government in framing new legislation is whether it reduces state intervention.

Individualism also strikes at the heart of the Christian view of society. If the Old and New Testaments affirm one thing, it is that we are not isolated individuals bound together simply by contractual relationships. Israel in the Old Testament was a community. Each of the twelve tribes was a community. And the essential core of each community was the family, which is the archetype of all communities. Many of the Pentateuchal laws, such as those relating to the Jubilee and usury, had as their objective the preservation of the community.

The New Testament also emphasises the importance of communal life – whether through the example set by our

Lord and the disciples, or through use of metaphors to describe the Church, such as the household of faith, the vine, or the building of God. Most powerful of all metaphors is the Body of Christ. Our Lord in the New Testament sums up the laws of the Old Testament as just two precepts: love of God and love of neighbour. Therefore Cain's question 'Am I my brother's keeper?' is answered directly by our Lord's words: 'Love your neighbour as yourself'.

What, however, modern Conservatism refuses to do is to equate this necessary concern for others with the pursuit of equality or corporatism. All too often in the eyes of the Church in recent years the litmus test of compassion has been whether egalitarian policies are being advanced. The presumption is that equality, corporatism and growing state provision are the only authentic expressions of Christian concern in society. Anything else is dismissed as individualism or materialism. To quote one prominent democratic socialist: 'We can only fulfil our obligations to our neighbours when society takes collective decisions about individual rights and individual responsibilities.'

Equality and Justice

It is worth considering why the Churches have come to equate social concern not just with equality of opportunity or equality before the law, both of which are vital to a creative society, but also with equality of result or equality of outcome.

'A liberative gospel must echo the egalitarian torrent which we find in the New Testament.' Those holding this view expressed in the 1989 report *Living Faith in the City* believe that equality is a Christian virtue and argue that metaphors such as the Body of Christ, while originally used as a description of the Church, should not be limited to it. They should become the vision for human society as a whole. If the state is concerned to legislate for the common good, this will mean implementing policies to reduce inequality and to extend state provision of services. Three pieces of evidence are usually advanced to support this idea that equality is a Christian ideal: the fact that all persons are created equal in the sight of God; the various laws in the Pentateuch describing the political economy of Israel (such as those relating to the restoration of land at the Jubilee, the cancellation of debts every Sabbath year or the prohibition of usury) which involve a redistribution of income and wealth, or attempt to prevent inequality developing; and the so-called 'communism' of the early Church.

Using such precedents to justify equalitarian policies gives rise to a great many difficulties. The fact that all people are created equal in the sight of God is an important basis for equal human rights and equality before the law, but this is hardly sufficient in itself to require, for example, after-tax equality of income with all the distinctive effects that must follow. Similarly, in no sense can the laws of the Pentateuch be said to have had *equality* as their purpose. In fact, they neither sought nor achieved equality. Their objective was to ensure that each family retained a permanent minimum stake in the economy, and that economic life did not undermine the cohesion and stability of Israel as a nation. Then again, the sharing of property which characterised the Church at Jerusalem in the early years was entirely voluntary, and cannot be a proper model for state concern. Christians were to meet the needs of the poor within the growing Christian Church through their own personal charity. Such giving was always voluntary, and the basis of St Paul's argument when the church at Jerusalem was in distress was an appeal based on compassion and fairness.

Theologians over the centuries have rarely interpreted the practice of the early Church to mean that governments should legislate for economic equality. With the exception of certain sects and cults, the social concern of Christians has always been social *justice*, conceived as fairness but not equality. In any case, one crucial point which is so often overlooked by those who relate Christianity to equality is the unbridgeable gulf between the two communities of the New Testament – the Church and the world. Lord Hailsham has repeated in this book St Augustine's distinction between the *Civitas Dei* and the *Civitas terrena*. No one can read the New Testament without a profound sense that although the Church is in the world, it is a wholly different community. It was this understanding, and his own personal experience in opposing apartheid, which led the former Archbishop of Cape Town, William Burnett, to say:

> The fact is that to attempt to superimpose a particular spirituality, a teaching on Christian ethics, or social action, as an expression of the love of God upon lives that do not know his love for them in Jesus Christ, and who do not experience the power of his Holy Spirit, is an exercise in futility. It leads to frustration, boredom, irritation and unbelief. To renew society with unrenewed Christians is like a non-swimmer trying to rescue a drowning man.

It is therefore quite invalid to move from the practice of personal generosity based on a voluntary appeal within the early Christian churches to the pursuit of equality in a pluralistic and secular society using the coercive power of the state.

'Little Platoons'

Christian theology reminds us of our obligations to our neighbours, but it offers no justification for compelling others to submit to the pursuit of economic equality by governments.

Participation in the life of modern democracies is not confined to government action or even to the political process. People participate in the life of a community by belonging to or participating in a variety of institutions – family, parish, school, neighbourhood, church, work place, trade unions, charities, professional bodies and so on. They do so because it is only by joining with others that they feel fulfilled as individuals. In this sense the conflict between the individual and the community is more imaginary than real. As Charles Murray has observed, 'The pursuit of individual happiness cannot be an atomistic process: it will naturally and always occur in the context of communities.'

In 1790 Edmund Burke described these communities as 'the little platoons' of our society. More recently they have been referred to as 'mediating structures', namely, those institutions which stand between the individual in his private life and the large institutions of public life, especially the state. It is the absence of such unofficial agencies that helps to explain the horrors of totalitarian states.

These little platoons are important for a number of reasons. They enable us, as Burke so clearly argued, to develop a sense of community:

> To be attached to the subdivision, to love the little platoon we belong to in society, is the first principle (the germ as it were) of public affections. It is the first link in the series by which we proceed towards a love of our country and to mankind.

These little platoons are the cradles of civic responsibility. They provide diverse ways in which individuals are relieved of their isolation. By joining together for limited purposes, but always to do with the common good, people are able to transfer the values of individual life to the larger institutions of society. Hence they are able to identify themselves much more with the greater community.

The little platoons are also a way of empowering people. They help people 'make a difference' by improving the communities in which they live. The Churches are not alone in pointing to the feeling of powerlessness which exists today in the face of large bureaucratic institutions in modern society. Recently a journalist friend (who is most definitely not a Conservative) observed how a recent visit to Liverpool taught him that the options facing local residents in the inner city allowed them little choice because they were all in the public sector: council housing, local education authority schools, public transport, welfare benefits, public sector employment. It is this politicisation and centralisation that explains why the mediating structures that thrived in the nineteenth century have become so weak. Policies which attempt to strengthen these structures hold the key to any lasting regeneration of our inner cities.

Despite the aggrandisement of government the little platoons remain significant providers of welfare. The family which is the archetypal community is also the primary supplier of education, health care, training and other welfare, in addition to food, shelter, moral support and love. Indeed, most of the welfare enjoyed by our society is provided through families. Apart from the family, the many charities and organisations of the voluntary sector are also generous and pioneering providers of welfare. In addition there are schools, community organisations and the welfare provisions of companies and trade unions.

Finally, mediating structures are important as the sources which generate and maintain values in society. The family, the school and the Churches are particularly influential sources of values. When such institutions are suppressed, the state itself becomes the major source of values, almost invariably with disastrous consequences. Totalitarian governments hate mediating structures because they challenge their attempts to exert total control over society. Meanwhile modern democracies require robust independent mediating structures for their health and survival.

These four functions of mediating structures – the development of civic virtues, the empowering of people, the provision of welfare and the generation and maintenance of values – make them of vital significance to a modern democratic society such as ours. That is why Conservatism attempts to strengthen them.

For schools which do not have voluntary status, large local education authorities can seem bureaucratic, impersonal and arbitrary, as can housing estates for tenants, and the NHS for patients. Schools will be strengthened as communities by effective arrangements for parents and independent persons to be appointed as governors, and for them to have greater financial powers, the right to appoint staff and the responsibility to oversee delivery of the curriculum. By enabling tenants who do not wish to buy their council houses to opt out of local authority control through the Tenants' Choice Scheme, the Government is empowering them, and creating the opportunity for power to be exercised at the level of an individual estate rather than at that of the town hall. By allowing hospitals to have trust status, rather than just being one of many 'units' in the regional health authority, the Government is creating conditions in which the local community spirit can flourish. In all cases where the Government has restored former freedoms there is also a transfer of power from local authorities or from the National Health Service; but it is a downwards transfer to a more basic level – the individual school, the individual housing estate, the individual hospital – not an upwards transfer to central government.

It is important to notice two particular implications of mediating structures. First, their growth and their robustness would be severely limited if government attempted to pursue a policy of economic equality. The pursuit of equality can be advanced only by the centralisation of power which must be hostile to the development of the little platoons. Smaller communities are bound to emphasise local differences, easily denounced as 'inequalities' because they produce variety and hold out as centres of excellence against central controls. A state determined to achieve equality of outcome would have to suppress the little platoons. In this context, nothing has been more distorted than the Prime Minister's remark during an interview: 'There is no such thing as society.' It is worth placing it in context:

> I think we've been through a period where too many people have been given to understand that if they have a problem

it's the government's job to cope with it. 'I have a problem; I'll get a grant.' 'I'm homeless; the government must house me.' They're casting their problem on society. And, you know, there is no such thing as society. There are individual men and women, and there are families. And no government can do anything except through people and people must look to themselves first. It's our duty to look after ourselves and then, also, to look after our neighbour. People have got the entitlements too much in mind, without the obligations. There's no such thing as entitlement, unless someone has first met an obligation.

What this passage plainly says is that society does not exist as an abstraction set apart from the people who compose it. Society is us, immanent rather than transcendent. The Prime Minister's words were an affirmation of the importance of personal responsibility and of the need for people to face up to the consequence of their own actions. They were in no sense a denial of the importance of the community or of the value of all those mediating structures which are crucial to the well-being of society.

Choice and Responsibility

Archbishop William Temple in his book on *Christianity and Social Order* (1942) set out to develop what he called Christian social principles. His fundamental principles relate to God and man, but in introducing the three principles which are derivative of these – freedom, fellowship and service – he had this to say:

The primary principle of Christian ethics and Christian politics must be respect for every person simply as a person. If each man and woman is a child of God, whom God loves and for whom Christ died, then there is in each a worth absolutely independent of all usefulness to society. The person is primary, not the society; the State exists for the citizen, not the citizen for the State. The first aim of social progress must be to give the fullest possible scope for the exercise of all powers and qualities which are distinctly personal; and of these the most fundamental is deliberate choice.

On the basis of this remarkable statement, Archbishop Temple went on to argue that:

society must be arranged to give every citizen the maximum opportunity for making deliberate choices and the best possible training for the use of that opportunity. In other words, one of our first considerations will be the widest possible extension of personal responsibility; it is the responsible exercise of deliberate choice which most fully expresses personality and best deserves the great name of freedom.

Since 1979, extending choice has formed a central aim of government policy. In most areas it has been an outstanding success, in the teeth of fierce opposition. Since 1979, about 1.4 million council houses and flats have been sold by local authorities in Great Britain – roughly twenty per cent of the total stock of eleven years earlier. Large numbers of employees have bought shares in privatised state companies. Trade union members have been granted choice over the election of officials and decisions about strikes. Parents' rights to choose schools for their children in other education authorities have been enshrined in law. More than seventy schools have so far sought or are seeking to opt-out of local authority control. To judge by the demand for places, parents and teachers keenly value the choice afforded by the newly created grant-maintained schools and city technology colleges. Some eighty major hospitals have sought independent trust status as part of the health service reforms. The full impact of this extension of choice has not yet been felt in society, but it will emerge during the 1990s as it becomes embedded in the ordinary course of affairs.

Whether in private or public sectors, choice is an important counterbalance to the entrenched power of producer interests. Choice forces producers to be more responsive to the short-term needs of those they serve. Consumers, parents, patients and tenants will all receive a better quality of service as the range of choices with which they are provided is widened. Choice encourages innovation and variety, although choice will be more restricted in the public than in the private sector.

One objection to extending freedom in this way is that the increased choice of some is seen as a restriction of choice for others. What if extending parental choice leads to certain schools being identified as inadequate and so liable to cruel rejection? What if council house sales reduce affordable housing for others? It is important to notice that when choice is extended in the public sector, certain checks and balances have been built in to prevent those kinds of unsatisfactory outcome. Take, for example, the case of education. Parents will choose those schools they think best for their children. The result is that governors and the local education authority will no longer be able to do nothing about the schools which have serious problems that need to be addressed. Under the previous system in which choice was limited, the weaknesses of poor schools were not exposed, and so parents would have no choice but to put up with inadequately-run schools. Increasing choice certainly means that good schools are in immediate demand, but it also means that problem schools will be highlighted, so exerting pressure on governing bodies and local education authorities to make improvements and hence raise standards throughout the authority. In a world of choice this becomes a major function of the LEA.

It is important to recognise that the case for extending choice is not just concerned with efficiency and money. Council houses have been sold not with an eye on the revenue which sales raise, but so that families can gain independence and provide for their children. Share ownership has been extended not just to strengthen accountability but to give as many people as possible a direct share in wealth creation. Choice in education has been widened not just so that schools can be run more efficiently but as a way to raise standards of achievement – in examinations, sport, arts and at a personal and moral level. Trade union reforms have been implemented not just to improve productivity through more flexible work practices, but to prevent the intimidation of individual trade union members. In other words, extending freedom of choice is not simply freedom from certain types of state provision and control, but freedom for schools, hospitals and housing trusts better to satisfy the individual aspirations of those they serve.

Archbishop Temple also recognised that extending choice cannot be divorced from extended responsibility. The extension of personal choice is at the same time an extension of personal responsibility. Choice for parents implies more direct responsibility for their children's progress. Freedom for head teachers means more direct accountability for the way they run their schools. Alongside the right to buy goes the responsibility of ownership. A more independent status for hospitals means greater accountability for the service they provide to patients.

Extending choice and responsibility changes the ethos of a society. It encourages greater private and voluntary initiatives elsewhere in the community. The 1980s have seen the business community in the UK accept major new social responsibilities over and above their contributions to charity. The first enterprise agency was started in 1978. Today there are over 300 local enterprise agencies which provide a comprehensive national advisory service for small businesses.

Business leaders have come to recognise that their enterprise, energy and skills must be put to wider use if urban regeneration is to be more than charity. The quality of local leadership is crucial to creating confidence both within the community and with investors. This confidence will affect investment and development. For example, Business in the Community has grown rapidly over the past decade and, in collaboration with the CBI and the Phoenix Initiative, business leadership teams are now established in more than twelve cities, bringing together senior business leaders and representatives of government, trade unions, education and the voluntary sector, to help in economic regeneration, the development of enterprise, partnerships and compacts between business and schools, community projects and training. When parents and business people were given the opportunity to be school governors, there was widespread scepticism whether sufficient numbers could ever be found. The response has been outstanding, as has the readiness of business leaders to direct the new Training Enterprise Councils.

Such initiatives to strengthen community neighbourliness and responsibility have not been confined to business. Neighbourhood Watch schemes were started in 1982. Now there are over 80,000 covering three-and-a-half million homes. They are now also being extended to other Watches covering pubs, schools, hospitals, farms and industrial buildings. In total, these Watches are growing at the rate of roughly 400 a week. Also in the field of crime there are now more than 350 Victim Support schemes which cover most of England and Wales – another rapidly expanding movement.

Markets and Welfare

The third element of the Bishop's Quadrilateral is 'the market'. In discussing this the Bishop raises the question 'How much faith should we have in the market?' and answers with complete certainty, 'None whatever.' To him 'there is no such thing as the market' because it is a theoretical abstraction and even if it did exist it would not be a proper object of faith. The market should be something we can handle, not something which controls us.

In this answer 'the market' is being used in three separate senses. If the market stood for a political philosophy of unchecked individualism and libertarianism, in which the only criterion for change was removal of restrictions by government, then the Bishop would be right to answer that we should put no faith in such a system. But by his own response, he seems to use the market in a second sense, namely as a shorthand for the analytical tools of economics. Like any scientific discipline, economics involves abstraction from the real world. But such a method should not be judged invalid simply because it involves abstraction: its usefulness depends on how well it can explain actual phenomena such as shortages and rationing, price changes and unemployment. Economics is subject to severe limitations but remains a powerful tool of analysis.

Where, however, the Bishop's certainties are most misleading is in using 'the market' to refer to an economic system characterised by widespread property rights, and free enterprise tempered by quite extensive government intervention in economic life and then claiming that we should have no faith whatever in this kind of arrangement.

Wherever markets are allowed to work, the result is an increase in prosperity and jobs. The remarkable contrast in economic performance between Asia-on-the-Pacific and Latin America over recent decades can be traced to the superior wisdom of faith in the market over faith in the state. Most dramatic is the contrast between East and West Europe in the period after the Second World War. The prosperity of Western Europe is due to innovation, high productivity and high investment as the result of private enterprise. In Eastern Europe the comprehensive reliance on state planning to direct economic life has been nothing short of a catastrophe, with the results being most tragic where the beliefs are strongest and the controls most comprehensive. In the USSR the shops are empty, the morale of workers low, enterprise has virtually disappeared and innovation has to be imported.

In the midst of its difficulties one source of inspiration for East Europe has been the present Conservative Government. They remember that in the 1970s the British economy was characterised by high inflation, rapid growth of the public sector, marginal rates of income tax of ninety-eight per cent, extension of state ownership of industry, increased legal privileges for trade unions and arbitrary wage and price controls. And they also remember that the result was the 'British disease', namely low productivity, inefficiency and growing unemployment. Against this worsening background, the turnaround in the last decade has been dramatic – the growing juggernaut of government halted, enterprise encouraged, taxes cut and controls lifted. And they also know that the result has been a growth in the national income of approximately 25 per cent, the creation of nearly 3 million new jobs and a fall in unemployment of nearly 1½ million. The East Europeans' interest in privatisation, the growth of small businesses and retraining schemes are because they aspire to turning around their own economies in the same way.

The success of the market economy in creating wealth and jobs should not come as a surprise. The market derives its strength from the instincts and abilities of ordinary people. It works with the grain of human nature and provides a variety of ways through which the imagination, energy and talents of people can be fulfilled. It recognises powerful human motives and aspirations – to own, to save, to pass on, to improve one's lot – and allows them to be channelled productively.

We can also explain the success of the market economy in a theological context. All the essential elements which make for the success of the market economy can be found in traditional Jewish and Christian teaching – the physical world as God's world, the mandate to subdue and harness the earth, the significance of work in a context of vocation and calling, the need for private property rights and the rule of law, a recognition by the state of the creative and innovative character of people, and the importance of a government's role in enforcing justice.

Similarly, the ultimate reason for the failure of Socialist economies lies beyond economics. At one level this failure can be explained by widespread state ownership, control and planning. But what is critical is the philosophy out of which these have grown: a materialism which leaves no room for any spiritual dimension in the world of work, a failure to respect the dignity and therefore the freedom of the individual, and a 'fatal conceit', to quote Hayek, in the power of human knowledge and therefore in our ability to plan and control. Socialism is flawed by its view that the spiritual dimension is irrelevant to the material, the grudging concessions made to private property and the lack of opportunities which it gives for individuals to fulfil and express themselves.

The Market and 'the Poor'

One criticism of the market economy often made by spokesmen of the Churches is that the wealth it creates does not 'trickle down' to the poor. The energetic, the talented and the fortunate do well, but there are large sections of people, we are told, who are excluded from the fruits of wealth creation.

Three kinds of evidence are typically used to argue that 'the poor' have lost out under Mrs Thatcher's Administration: the growth in the number of those on low incomes, the widening of income differentials between high and low income categories, and the alleged fall in the real value of benefit in the 1980s compared with the 1970s. In the next chapter of this book Frank Field goes further than this. He talks about 'the poor' having been expelled from full citizenship and excluded from rising income during these years by the four horsemen of the apocalypse, the most powerful having been unemployment. The result has been a growing underclass who live under a form of political, social and economic 'apartheid'.

A number of comments need to be made about this.

First, insufficient credit is given to the power of the market economy in creating jobs. If growing unemployment was a major factor in increasing 'poverty' in the early

1980s, the subsequent fall in unemployment must be a major factor in reducing 'poverty'. We have had eight years of sustained growth in Britain at an annual average rate of over three per cent, and the creation of more than 2¾ million new jobs since 1983. Unemployment has fallen since July 1986 by 1¼ million in total, and in all regions of the country.

At the same time, part-time work has flourished. Over 6 million people are now employed on a part-time basis, and less than eight per cent of these say it is because they could not find a full-time job. Such increased flexibility of working clearly suits the needs of those who prefer to work on a part-time basis. A growing economy provides opportunities for people of all income levels, including low ones, to improve their position and directly reduces those categorised as 'poor'. Wealth creation is by far the most enduring method of job creation – far more powerful in the longer term than job creation programmes.

Second, the real growth in the eighties would not have occurred if the thrust of government policy had been egalitarian. During the 1980s there was a dramatic increase in the purchasing power of income even though relative incomes widened. For example, between 1974 and 1979 a person on average earnings had, after tax and inflation, an increase in real take-home pay of 0.6 per cent. By contrast, a person on half-average earnings had an increase in real take-home pay of 4.2 per cent. Real income increased slowly but inequality was marginally reduced. Since 1979 a person on average earnings has had an increase in real take-home pay of 33.8 per cent and on half-average earnings an increase of 26.8 per cent. In recent years there has been a large increase in people's absolute levels of real income, but a widening of differentials between high and low income levels.

Third, the latest figures from the Department of Social Security show that, before housing costs, all groups in the income distribution experienced improvements in real income between 1981 and 1987; the median income of the lowest 10 per cent rose by nearly 10 per cent. Even between 1979 and 1987, that is including the period of the 1979–81 recession, each group saw its income improve before housing costs. Median incomes rose, too, for all groups between 1981 and 1987 after housing costs, although measuring income in this way takes no account of the choices people make about housing, and the substantial growth in owner occupation. (In 1987 people in mortgaged households comprised nearly a third of the lowest decile after housing costs.) This encouraging picture is not diminished by the assertion, based on references to basic rates and single components of social security benefits, that the poor became worse off during the 1980s. The Department of Social Security's data, which takes account of disposable income from all available sources, shows that between 1981 and 1987 the real incomes of those in receipt of income-related benefits in the lowest 10 per cent of the income distribution rose by between 4 and 8 per cent, depending on the measure used. Nor are the improvements measured before housing costs solely attributable to higher Housing Benefit consequent upon increased rents. In fact, increases in Housing Benefit account for only a very small fraction of the overall rise observed for the lowest decile before housing costs. Certainly the statistics do not present a single, unambiguous picture. They rarely do. But taken as a whole, the evidence hardly allows the argument that increased wealth resulting from sustained economic growth in the 1980s has done nothing to help the least well-off. On the contrary, all the indications are that 'trickle-down' had a significant and continuing effect throughout the decade.

Fourth, social policy is not helped by grouping millions of people together and labelling them as 'the poor', the 'expelled' or 'the underclass'. The problems facing the frail elderly, the long-term unemployed and one-parent families are all very different and call for very different responses. *Faith in the City* rightly pointed to certain inner city areas and outer housing estates where unemployment has remained very high; few tenants have bought their council houses; truancy in schools is high; teenagers are exposed to a drugs culture; and the proportion of one-parent families is well above average. In these situations families are more than usually dependent on the state. Therefore it is in these areas in particular that the Government's education and housing reforms and inner cities policies offer the greatest hope. Policy has not been premised on some vague faith in the market solving all the problems of those on low incomes. The Government has sought to strengthen the market economy; but at the same time it has also sought to ensure that people from all backgrounds are able to benefit. Hence these particular reforms.

The initial task is to encourage wealth creation: to develop enterprise through establishing small workshops linked to training programmes. Children can be helped by directly improved standards through the national curriculum, and overall standards raised by greater parental choice, different kinds of schools and increased contact between the business community and the schools. At the same time estates can be improved, homes provided with gardens and improved security, through a diversity of ownership and the use of Tenants' Choice. All of these changes will give an increasing number of people a direct and meaningful stake in their communities. Getting this to happen is hard work but it is something to which the Government is totally committed and there is no doubt that it is working. The full fruit will emerge in years to come.

Wealth and Trusteeship

For the past eleven years creating the conditions in which wealth creation can flourish has been a vital objective of government policy.

This stems from a belief that every person should find it rewarding to be able, in Adam Smith's words, 'to better his condition' if he chooses to do so. By extending home ownership, share ownership and occupational pension schemes, families are becoming more financially secure and less dependent on the state, and hence in a better position to cope with the contingencies of life as well as to reach out to help others. Increasing wealth also means increasing resources for government: the more rapid the growth of income the greater the resources government receives and hence the greater the resources available for improving education, welfare, the Health Service and affordable housing. And then, as we have just seen, wealth creation is a crucial source of job creation.

One point which should not be underestimated is the effect which the successful regeneration of the corporate sector has had on its ability to play a wider role. As we saw earlier, the 1980s have seen the company sector in the UK assume a wholly new role in the community. Were it not for their commercial success this would never have been possible.

One objection frequently raised against the creation of wealth is that it encourages a materialistic philosophy of life. Usually this is made as an obvious assertion – the 'loadsamoney' society and the 'yuppie' culture. The reasons for linking wealth creation with materialism are seldom specified but would probably include the claims that: wealth creation satisfies personal needs but has little regard for the wider community; the methods used may be questionable as people see the possibilities of cutting corners; the competitive pressures on those working in successful companies tend to create an imbalance between work and everything else. Some would also probably argue that increasing prosperity is almost by definition an increase in materialism – possibly using as evidence John Wesley's great sermon on 'The Use of Money' which, while advocating 'gain all you can', 'save all you can' and 'give all you can', also observed: 'the Methodists grow more and more self-indulgent because they grow rich'.

The Bible has a good deal to say about wealth and materialism. Indeed, both figure quite prominently in the teachings of the Old and New Testament. The task of wealth creation is a description in contemporary language of God's command to man to 'subdue the earth' and to rule over it. The Hebrew words for 'subdue' (*rabash*) and 'rule' (*radah*) are particularly strong: the former literally means to stamp on or bring into subjection while the latter is frequently expressed as dominion. Man is given the responsibility to harness the resources of the physical world. Although originally applied in the context of agriculture, this command easily extends to extraction, manufacturing and services. The implication is not simply that wealth creation is a legitimate activity. The command surely implies that the task of wealth creation is fundamental to our trusteeship of the world and that in responding to it we also discover how work is basic to human fulfilment. Far from having a sense of guilt, therefore, about advocating wealth creation we should acknowledge that it is basic to our understanding of the creation order.

But the command to subdue and rule is not the freedom to destroy and waste. Our enthusiasm for wealth creation must be balanced by an equal enthusiasm for environmental protection. Man is a trustee for God's world. Although there may be extensive debate over the causes and effects of the risks to our planet and the precise policy choices which have to be made, there can be no doubt about the moral basis from which we start and in which the debate must take place.

It is above all clear that wealth creation can be sharply distinguished from materialism. According to St Paul it is the love of money which is the root of all evil because 'they that will be rich fall into temptation and a snare and into many foolish and hurtful lusts'. Jesus's censure of wealth is addressed to the rich: 'Woe to you that are rich . . .'; 'How hard it is for those who have riches to enter into the Kingdom of God'; and to the rich young man, 'Sell all you have . . .' Jesus and his disciples were probably neither very rich nor very poor and would today be categorised as self-employed tradesmen or craftsmen, or small businessmen. Jesus warns against 'covetousness' but this is quite distinct from the normal world of work and it is wrong to interpret warnings addressed to the very rich as a blanket condemnation of the whole process of wealth creation.

Although wealth creation cannot be labelled materialism, when Jesus does speak on economic issues he introduces a distinctive standard of values: 'Be not anxious about the morrow . . .'; 'Seek ye first the Kingdom of God and his righteousness . . .'; 'You cannot serve God and Mammon . . .' It is hard not to miss the meaning of injunctions such as these but infinitely more difficult to keep them. As Dean Inge remarked, 'Christ sits very lightly to all this paraphernalia of life'; and after making the case for social concern he concluded the argument with a statement which almost seems foreign to the Church today:

> However long may be our lease of our present home; however splendid may be the possibilities which applied science seems to promise us, this earth is but the shadow of heaven, an imperfect copy of the eternal and spiritual world which surrounds us and penetrates us, closer than breathing and nearer than hands and feet, but invisible and impalpable. There, in the eternal world, is the home of the ultimate values – Goodness, Truth, and Beauty – which give to our visible world all of worth that it possesses; there is our heart's true home; there is the presence of God. Against this spiritual world, as a background, is set all that we admire and love here on earth. And so, with all our enthusiasm for making life a better and happier thing for our brethren, we must never forget the words of St Paul: 'We look not at the things that are seen, but at the things that are not seen. For the things that are seen are temporal; the things that are not seen are eternal.'

Values in Society

In this essay I have sought to show that the Bishop of Durham's Conservative Quadrilateral is a caricature of modern Conservatism. Any serious discussion of wealth creation must confront the need for individual choice and the freedom of markets. But modern Conservatism cannot be understood within the narrow confines of economics, let alone economic libertarianism. Alongside its advocacy of the market it is concerned to defend those values which are at the heart of a responsible society – on the one hand a sense of personal duty and self-reliance and on the other a personal obligation to those in need, to future generations and to our environment. At the same time the Conservative vision of society is not just an atomised collection of relentlessly self-seeking individuals pursuing their narrow self-interests. It seeks increasingly diverse and strengthened communities in which individuals feel at home and through which they can fulfil their widely different individual preferences.

This essay has been about Christian values in relation to the market. Yet the importance of values applies to all aspects of our society. The one issue which remains is the source of such values. Hayek freely admits that a free society in itself is no guarantee that it can generate those values which are necessary to its survival. The one institution which more than any other should be the keeper of those values is the Church. Events in Eastern Europe have shown just how great a power the Church has to influence politics, when it remains true to these values. Religion alone provides meaning to our lives. Christian values in this type of a society are a strong basis for both freedom and prosperity. In terms of responsible wealth creation, the building of communities, creating public/private partnerships to deal with inner city regeneration, developing the potential of children in school through what is taught to them, the Churches have enormous opportunities to realise their values in action. But the question remains whether our spiritual leaders still have the will to proclaim them.

12

How Well Have Britain's Poor Fared?

Frank Field, MP

IT was the question, posed by David Edwards in a General
Synod debate, about why there had been a growing tension
between the Church and the present government which led
to the consultations behind this book. Of particular concern
to the Government has been the charge that, in general
terms, its behaviour has been unchristian and that, specifically, this is most clearly shown in its treatment of the poor.
Professor Porter's chapter is therefore the natural starting
point for this contribution. What does Scripture teach is the
right attitude to wealth and poverty?

Roy Porter emphasises, in my view quite rightly, the
danger of selecting those texts from either the Old or New
Testament which merely support the writer's particular
political prejudice. Instead, one must look at the whole
record and attempt to deduce the main lessons from it. But
another difficulty then confronts the politician or voter who
seeks to use Scripture as a map or compass. This is the great
logistic problem of attempting to extrapolate from established principles what our daily political conduct ought to
be. However, the main tradition in the Old Testament is
clear. Far from condemning the production and acquisition
of wealth, riches are seen as a sign of God's blessing. As
part of his creation, the world is here for our enjoyment, or,
as Roy Porter suggests, for us to luxuriate in. But the right to
acquire and to use wealth is not unrestricted. The story of

the wandering tribes, blessed by God and brought into the Promised Land, illustrates a fundamental part of Jewish and subsequent Christian teaching. The good things of this world are God's gifts. Ownership is conditional, not absolute. And from this conditional ownership stems a range of rights and duties. Moreover, clear ground rules are laid down for the acquisition of wealth. Not only is there a danger of idolatry, of being obsessive about the acquisition of wealth; acquisitiveness can result in the denial of property rights of others. Concern for the dispossessed and the poor is one of the themes of the Old Testament.

Property was seen, then as now, as a way of guaranteeing freedom and independence for the individual. There can, however, be no doubt that the denial of those rights did take place. The prophets rose up to condemn not the acquisition of wealth itself but the means by which it was often acquired. Moreover, because of our fallen nature, institutional mechanisms to redistribute wealth towards the dispossessed were established. These ranged from the small to the dramatic, from immediate relief such as leaving the corner of the fields for widows and orphans to garner, through to more substantial relief contained in the Laws of the Jubilee, where property was restored to its rightful owners every fifty years. The point at issue here is not whether the Laws of the Jubilee were ever enacted, but that there was recognition of the necessity to go beyond personal charity in order to establish justice.

The establishment of institutional redress does not excuse the individual from right conduct. It does, however, set the framework within which the Government's record on the poor should be considered. This is not a debate, as Lord Hailsham suggests in his contribution, about the 'rightness' of the swing of the pendulum, from collectivism to individual and communal responsibility. It is, rather, a debate about the effects which such swings have had. While shifting this pendulum, has the Government protected the poor in the way directed by Scripture? More precisely, how have the poor fared over the past decade, when the pendulum has undoubtedly swung away from collectivism towards a greater emphasis upon individual responsibility?

Of course, the Government is keen that it should itself define what is meant by the term 'poor'. Ministers have also attempted to reserve the right to determine the yardstick by which we measure how well or how badly this group has fared. So I shall offer a review of how the terms 'poverty' and 'low income' are now used. Changes in the collection and presentation of data on both the numbers on low income and changes in their standard of living will then be considered. This will be followed by a consideration of whether the living standards of those on low income rise faster under periods of high economic growth, or during those periods when growth is much more sluggish. This takes the discussion on to the issue of whether or not we have witnessed the birth of an underclass in Britain at a time of record economic improvement. The concluding section is concerned with the direction in which I believe a restatement of individual and collective responsibility should move during the 1990s.

Numbers on Low Income

The Government steadfastly refuses to use the term 'poverty'. In a letter to the Leader of the Opposition on 30 May 1989, the Prime Minister wrote: 'I have too much respect for ordinary people to belittle those who receive Income Support by the use of labels like "poor". I firmly believe that the best way to help *everyone* is through encouraging them to take pride in themselves and to make use of their talents rather than alienating them, making them feel helpless and encouraging dependency upon the state.'

It is interesting that the Prime Minister shuns the term poverty, not because she believes poverty to be non-existent, but rather in deference to the feelings of those who have ended up with the very least in our society. That said, I do believe that the Government is right to try and draw a halt to a debate which has rumbled on over the last two decades, with those on incomes of up to 140 per cent of the Supplementary Benefit rate, or as it is now known, Income Support rate, being termed 'poor', or 'on the margins of poverty'. Given the distribution of income in this country, with a very large number of people skewed towards the bottom, such a definition includes almost a third of the entire population. The claim that a third of the population in Britain today is poor is regarded by most people as simply absurd. Moreover, the argument is far too important to get bogged down at this level.

The Government asserts that those on benefit should be regarded, not as living in poverty, but as existing on a low income. Until they were renamed Income Support in 1988, Parliament approved each year the Supplementary Benefit scale rates. People who are not in work and have meagre financial resources are entitled to have their incomes brought up to a level prescribed by those rates. As nobody disputes that these rates give rise to only a modest standard of living, I too have taken the numbers on Supplementary Benefit or Income Support as a broad measurement of low income in Britain. Accepting the Government's framework for the debate, what has happened to the numbers on low income in post-war Britain?

A significant feature of the post-war period has been a steady rise in the numbers claiming Supplementary Benefit. From 1948 until 1979, the number of those claiming supplementary benefits (called National Assistance until 1966) rose from one million to 2.9 million. By May 1989, the total stood at 4.2 million, after peaking in 1987, when the total number of claimants reached 4.9 million. Even more dramatic, however, has been the increase in the numbers *dependent* upon Supplementary Benefit, a figure which includes both the claimant and his or her dependants. In 1948, the total number in that category was 1.5 million. By 1979, this had risen to 4.4 million. By May 1988, it had fallen to 7.4 million from the peak of 8.2 million in the

previous year. The increase in the number of dependants upon Supplementary Benefit since 1979 has been
greater than that experienced during the previous thirty
years.

While these numbers are large, they do not represent a
complete census of those existing on low income. Significant numbers of people live on incomes which are below
the Supplementary Benefit/Income Support level. In order
to determine the size of this group, a special analysis has
been carried out on the Family Expenditure Survey (FES).
The data were published as part of the *Low Income Families*
statistical survey and appeared for the first time in 1972. In
that year, the total number living on an income below the
Supplementary Benefit level stood at 1.8 million. This
figure fell, first to 1.6 million and then to 1.4 million in the
following two years. Since then, however, there has been a
steady increase in the size of this group, peaking in 1983,
when the total number of people existing on incomes below
the safety net benefit rates reached 2.8 million. By 1985, this
figure had fallen back to 2.4 million. (For details of these
figures and the basis upon which they were constructed,
see the House of Commons Social Services Select Committee report *Families on Low Incomes: Low Income Statistics*,
House of Commons Paper 565, 1988.) It was not until 1988
that the 1985 figures were published.

Simultaneously, the Government announced that it intended to dispense with carrying out the usual special
analysis of the FES data. Unless a private organisation
carries out this analysis, and the Social Services Committee
has asked the Institute of Fiscal Studies to do just that, it will
be impossible in future years to provide a comprehensive
account of the numbers on low income, measured against
the current benefit levels. In place of the *Low Income Families*
statistics, the Government now publishes a series entitled
Households Below Average Income. Here, the Government is
concerned with the numbers registered as living below half
the average income, and in measuring changes in the living
standards of decile groups. But as well as deciding to play

on a different pitch (by refusing to publish data on the numbers of people living at different levels of income in relation to current benefit levels), the Government has shifted the goal posts. The calculations were made on the basis of the family unit – which remains the basis of entitlement to benefit. Now, the calculations are made on a 'household' basis. This change has important conse-quences for the numbers on low incomes. The numbers shown to be living at below half the average income stood at 4.5 million in 1985, a million less than if the more conven-tional basis of family unit had been used to calculate the result. (See Paul Johnson and Stephen Webb, *Counting People With Low Income*, IFS, 1989.)

Paralleling the enormous increase in the numbers draw-ing Supplementary Benefit has been an equally important change in the type of person listed on the welfare rolls. Unlike in earlier post-war years, the vast majority of those now dependent upon Supplementary Benefit are the un-employed and their families. This category has risen from 27 per cent of all claimants in 1978, to more than 44 per cent in 1987 (*Hansard*, 4 July 1988, vol. 136, col. 453). Accom-panying the rise in unemployment has been a large increase in the number of single-parent families. In 1970, the num-ber of single-parent families drawing Supplementary Ben-efit stood at 220,000. By 1974, this had risen to 269,000, and had risen again to 322,000 by the end of the Labour Govern-ment in 1979. Since then, the numbers have more than doubled, rising to 727,000 in May 1988. The number of dependants stands at 1,570,000 (*Social Security Statistics* 1989, Tables 34.82 and 37.25, and earlier editions). The decline in the proportion of pensioners drawing Sup-plementary Benefit does not mean that the number of pensioners on low incomes has fallen to an insignificant level. After a rise during the immediate post-war period, the number of people over retirement age in this category claiming Supplementary Benefit has remained almost constant in the past decade.

Another change which should be emphasised is the

length of time for which people are dependent upon Income Support. If, for the sake of illustration, long-term dependency is determined by the continuous drawing of benefit over a five year period, the data indicate that the numbers below retirement age have more than trebled during the six-and-a-half years after 1979; up from 431,000 in November 1979 (the number includes dependants) to 1,345,000 by February 1986 (letter from the DHSS, 7 December 1988). What has happened to the living standards of this group will become an important part of any evaluation of the present Government's record.

Why is it that the numbers on low incomes have increased, particularly in the recent past? The Government claims that the real increase in the value of Supplementary Benefit accounts for 40 per cent of those claiming benefits since 1979. Likewise, 40 per cent of the increase in those living below the Supplementary Benefit level can be accounted for by the real increase in the value of the Supplementary Benefit rates (DHSS letter to the Child Poverty Action Group, 31 December 1986). A much more significant reason has been the dramatic increase in the numbers of unemployed and, to a lesser extent, the increase in the numbers of single-parent families.

The increasing vulnerability of these two groups to low incomes is apparent in the Government's own figures relating to the composition of those living on incomes that bring them into the lowest quintile (the bottom twenty per cent) of income distribution. In 1971, over half of all income-receiving units (that is, households for Income Support and tax purposes) in the bottom quintile were pensioners. By 1982, the proportion had fallen to around a quarter. This change is even more dramatic if people rather than income units are taken into account: around twenty per cent of the lowest quintile are now pensioners. The changing composition of the lowest quintile is accounted for by the fact that, over the past thirty years, pensioners *as a group* have become significantly better off (*Reform of Social Security: Background Papers*, vol. 3, Cmnd. 9519, HMSO, 1985, p. 11).

However, this overall increase in the income of pensioners disguises two trends. The increase in income for the groups has not been shared fairly throughout the whole period. Between 1973 and 1978, old-age pensions were increased by twenty per cent in real terms, thereby benefiting all pensioners. Between November 1979 and April 1989, however, the National Insurance pensions fell by 1.4 per cent, relative to the Retail Price Index. The continuing increase in the share of income going to pensioners has come solely from occupational pensions, from which the poorest pensioners are excluded (*Hansard*, 26 July 1988, col. 205).

Shadowing this increase in the absolute and relative incomes of pensioners has been a fall in the incomes of people who were previously employed. The record post-war level of unemployment has been said to be 'the single most important reason why more working-age families or income units now appear in the bottom quintile of the national income distribution than at any time in the post-war period' (*Reform of Social Security*, p. 12). The change since 1979 has been dramatic. Unemployment accounted for more than half of all income units in the lowest quintile in 1982, compared with a mere twenty per cent in 1979.

The rise in unemployment has overshadowed the increase in the number of single-parent families that has occurred in the past fifteen years. Even so, the increase here has also been significant. The proportion of single-parent families in the bottom quintile has increased from 5.5 per cent in 1971 to 7.5 per cent in 1981. This change reflects the increase in the overall numbers of these families. Between 1971 and 1986, the number of families headed by a single parent rose from 570,000 to 1,010,000. In 1986, single parent families represented around 14 per cent of all families with dependent children, compared to only 8 per cent in 1971 (*Population Trends*, 55, pp. 27–33).

Who Gains from Growth?

Many commentators would insist on judging the Government's success on a wide canvas – covering the numbers on low income and the length of time people are dependent on welfare, as well as changes in the real incomes of those at the bottom of the income distribution. Others would insist that the question, 'Who gains most from economic growth?' cannot be answered without considering whether the gap between those on low incomes and the rest of the community has widened. None of these considerations is of importance to the Government. It insists that the only relevant criteria in judging how well the poor or those on low income have fared are whether the living standards of this group have grown faster under their stewardship than under previous administrations.

The overall rate of economic growth since 1981 has been around two to three times the historic growth rate of the British economy and, during the latter part of 1988, it was almost four times that rate. We are therefore ideally placed to test whether or not the so-called 'trickle-down' theory works most favourably for those on low incomes during periods of rapid economic growth. Does the income of those at the bottom grow faster in a period of rapid expansion, even if, as a consequence, the gap between the top and the bottom widens? The claim that the poorest sector of society has indeed benefited at a significantly greater rate is central to the Prime Minister's defence of how the poor have fared since she came to power in 1979. What is the evidence?

Strange as it may seem, the Government has never, to my knowledge, published data that would allow this question – which, after all, is the crux of the debate about the 'trickle-down' or universal distributive effect of economic growth – to be answered. Indeed, far from publishing comparative data, it ordered the cancellation of the only comprehensive series on the numbers of poor. In its place, as we have seen, the Government's substitute is a new series of data on comparative changes in the living standards of decile groups. It claimed, with some justification, that this gave a more meaningful measurement of what was happening to low-income groups. Yet it has resolutely refused to extend these data to include the 1970s, so that at least one comparison could be made on changing living standards during different periods of economic growth.

Between 1979 and 1985, real incomes rose by an average of nine per cent whereas the poorest ten per cent experienced a rise of only six per cent. At the other extreme, the richest ten per cent romped home with a massive eighteen per cent increase in real living standards (*Hansard*, 11 July, 1989, col. 422). Not only did the richest ten per cent outperform the poorest by a rate of three to one, but the average earner also managed significantly to dwarf any progress by those at the bottom of the pile.

National income fell between 1979 and 1981. A period of rapid economic growth occurred from 1981 onwards. However, in this period, and taking the Government's data before they published major revisions to it, it could be claimed that the bottom ten per cent registered an 8.3 per cent increase in income, compared to a 6.4 per cent increase for the total population (*Households Below Average Income: A Statistical Analysis 1981–85*, Government Statistical Service, May 1988, Table A2).

The House of Commons Social Services Select Committee asked the Institute of Fiscal Studies to extend the Government's decile analysis and, during this work, two errors were discovered in the treatment of housing costs, which particularly affected the 1981 HBAI analysis and, to a lesser extent, the 1983 analysis. The revised data show that, after housing costs, the gain of the bottom ten per cent, registered as 8.3 per cent in the original figures, falls to 2.6 per cent, a total well below the gain of 5.4 per cent in real income for the total population over the 1981–85 period.

Even without these major revisions, questions ought to be raised about how appropriate it is to measure increases in living standards of those on low income by using this decile analysis.

This chapter has earlier drawn on published government data on the lowest quintile of the population. This showed significant changes over a period of time for the groups which found themselves in the poorest twenty per cent of the population. It is therefore very likely that the membership of the bottom ten per cent will fluctuate, perhaps significantly, even on an annual basis. A large number of those counted as part of the lowest decile in any one year may not belong to the same group in a subsequent year. The Government has not published any information on the changing composition of the lowest decile over the 1981–85 period. However, an analysis was carried out on the new earnings survey to cover the five years from 1970 to 1974. This showed that, of all male manual workers surveyed, 21.4 per cent were in the lowest paid ten per cent in at least one of the five surveys, but only 2.9 per cent were in this tenth on all surveys: 'This confirms a considerable two-way movement across the boundary of the lowest tenth; and of those who are in the lowest tenth at one particular time, less than one-third are in the lowest tenth every time' ('How Individual People's Earnings Change', D. E. Gazette, January 1977, p. 23).

A more accurate measure of the living standards of those on low income would be to assess the performance of those who are permanently trapped at the bottom. Here we return to that group singled out earlier who remain in benefit for long periods of time. Over 2.5 million claimants (including pensioners) have been drawing Supplementary Benefit continuously for more than five years. It is on this group of long-term claimants that our attention should be firmly fixed in any rational determination of what has happened to the living standards of the disadvantaged during a period of rapid economic expansion. Moreover, data are readily to hand, which allow a contrast to be made on how the poor fared during contrasting periods of economic growth. During the period of modest economic growth, from 1970 to 1978, the value of Supplementary Benefit payments increased, in real terms, by 9.1 per cent, or an average of 1.1 per cent per annum. If the period when national income fell, from 1979 to 1981, is excluded, the real increase in the Supplementary Benefit/Income Support rates over the November 1981 to April 1989 period, shows a fall in real terms of 3.7 per cent, or an annual fall of 0.4 per cent.

The reason for this fall (in real terms) in the value of Supplementary Benefit/Income Support during the period of perhaps the most rapid economic growth since the industrial revolution, can be explained quite simply. Under the new Income Support regulations, claimants are expected to meet twenty per cent of their rate contribution. While the Government has allowed a set sum in the weekly scale rate, which is supposed to cover these rate contributions, average payments by claimants are well in excess of this allowance of £1.30 a week. Since April 1988, claimants have also had to meet their water-rate bills.

On both sets of data, the Government is hard-pressed to demonstrate that the trickle-down theory is about to work, let alone that it has worked over the past decade. Taking its own analysis of changes in living standards for decile groups, we have seen that the poorest group has experienced increases in its living standards which are significantly below those for the group on average income. No similar analysis exists for the previous decade which would allow a comparison between changes in the living standards of those in the lowest decile during a period of modest economic growth with their living standards during the period of Mrs Thatcher's stewardship. Over a longer time span, from 1981 to April 1990, and looking at the real increase in the value of benefit levels for the millions who have continually been on benefit throughout that period of time, we find that real living standards have fallen. This is in marked contrast to the 1970–78 period, when real living standards for those on benefit actually rose.

An Underclass

Three groups, above all others, are more likely to find themselves among those who are dependent, year in, year out, on welfare payments. These groups include the very frail elderly, single mothers who have no hope of escaping welfare, and the long-term unemployed. The fall in living standards for these groups lays the basis for what I believe has been the emergence of an underclass in Mrs Thatcher's Britain.

The key to this change lies in the Government's systematic recasting of the concept of citizenship. Over the past 300 years, British governments have not only extended the basis which underlies citizenship, or full membership of the community, but have also, admittedly in fits and starts, extended this status to an ever-growing proportion of the nation. Over the last decade, however, the established idea of citizenship as an incorporating force has been thrown into reverse. Four main factors have virtually expelled many people from full citizenship. (This argument is presented fully by the author in *Losing Out: the emergence of Britain's underclass*, Basil Blackwell, 1989.)

The primary factor has undoubtedly been unemployment. The brief era of full employment which followed the Second World War provided, for the first time, a universal escape from a poor law culture where poverty, personal failure and shame were inextricably interwoven. Full employment provided an income independent of welfare for all who wished to work, and ensured a greater degree of equality in income distribution than has been effected at any other time. Being in work automatically ensured that workers and, to some extent, their families, would benefit from specific rights, such as social insurance entitlements. More recently, this has also acted as a gateway to a range of company welfare programmes. In contrast, unemployment has not only countered these trends, but has also had a crucial effect on the direction of social mobility. Studies since the 1930s have shown a rapid social rise for a significant proportion of children born to working-class parents. This trend continues, but is now accompanied by a downward mobility for those denied access to the labour market.

Secondly, there has been a widening of class divisions. A dominant characteristic of British society has been its polarisation along class lines, although this tendency was countered by a conscious bipartisan political approach designed to prevent a deterioration in class differences in life chances (see Peter Jenkins' *Mrs Thatcher's Revolution*, Jonathan Cape, 1987, which questions how long into the post-war period this bipartisanship lasted). This is also no longer the case. It has been the deliberate aim of governments led by Mrs Thatcher to reshape British culture around an enterprise ethos. One of the unplanned consequences of this policy has been a widening of class divisions for the first time in the post-war period. (The data are not published which would allow one to define just how extensive this trend is but such data as are available are reviewed in *Losing Out*, pp. 34–41.)

Thirdly, there has been the exclusion of the poor from rapidly rising living standards. In the late 1950s, the Conservative Government decided that those on lowest incomes should share in the increase in national income apparent at that time. This policy has now been reversed, despite the fact that living standards have been rising at a record rate over the 1981–89 period. Instead of keeping the living standards of this group in line with rises enjoyed by other groups of the population, the present Government has reverted to the more limited approach of protecting only benefit levels from rising prices. Yet, as we have seen, because of changes in what claimants have to meet out of their Income Support payments, the weekly benefit rates have not even kept pace with price increases. A policy of linking increases in basic welfare payments to price rises at a time of rapidly rising real living standards would anyway have resulted in a widening gap between the standards of living of welfare recipients and the rest of the community. But for this group to experience real *cuts* in the value of their weekly benefit at an exceptional time of record advances in real living standards for the rest of the community must mean an even greater distancing in money terms of those on welfare income from the rest of the community.

A reference must also be made to two other groups who have become, literally, destitute. Changes were made to the entitlement to Income Support of young people in 1988. In an attempt to ensure that parents do not willingly divest themselves of their responsibility to maintain their late teenage offspring, the weekly rate paid to independent under-25-year-olds was reduced, compared with the entitlement for older people. In addition, no Income Support payments are made for those young people who are eligible for a YTS place, or who might otherwise be at school or college.

That some parents are unwilling, or unable, to meet the financial responsibilities of their teenage children has been testified by the children's societies, Barnardo's, and the Citizens' Advice Bureaux (see for example, 'Too much pressure: young people's experience of the social security and related systems', *Children's Society*, January 1990). The result, for some young people, has been destitution. There is much hearsay evidence that some of this group, once denied benefit, and unable to gain a YTS place, have resorted to crime or prostitution in order to gain money. It is likely that some at least of these tales are true. What is incontrovertible, however, is the extent of homelessness among some of these young people. The nightly scene of the camp fires of those sleeping rough turns parts of Britain's city centres into a mirage of the Third World.

Similarly destitute are some of the huge army of mental patients who have been discharged from hospital. This policy of closing what are now euphemistically called long-stay hospitals, more commonly known as mental hospitals, is an example of a noble intention turning into a living nightmare for the ex-patients. Hospitals have been closed without any appropriate accommodation being offered, let alone secured, for these hospital inmates. Since 1979,

41,229 inmates have lost their homes in a hospital, but only 12,562 have been offered alternative accommodation. Late in 1979, a stop was placed on what was, in effect, the dumping of patients into the community. Now, each hospital inmate has to be offered a 'home' in the outside world before being discharged. But, so far, no attempt has been made to trace the 29,000 who are likely to be part of the large army of homeless and destitute people in Britain.

Fourthly, there has been a significant change in public attitudes. This has led to a psychological and political separation of the very poorest from the rest of the community. There are obvious dangers which arise from any attempt to plot shifts in public attitudes, especially as one of the peculiarities of the British is to exaggerate the apparently positive aspects of the past. Siegfried Sassoon, writing in the trenches during World War One, encapsulated this tendency in his remark that, for the British, promotion from Inferno to Paradise would only lead to a harking back to the good old days.

However, despite the danger of over-sentimentalising the past, communal solidarity does appear to have played an important part in working-class life. That value is much less evident today. Many people from working-class backgrounds who have profited in this more affluent society exhibit that unpleasant tendency in human nature which is keen to ensure that once the advancing group's own social mobility has been guaranteed other people do not benefit to the same degree. Feelings of solidarity have thus been replaced by a drawbridge mentality.

Large numbers of people currently find their status as citizens under attack from one or more of these four expelling forces. Some find themselves in retreat from simultaneous assault by all four, and to such an extent that they are being relegated to what amounts to an underclass. They live under what is increasingly a subtle and insidious form of political, social and economic apartheid. Today the very poorest are separated, not only from other groups on low incomes, but, more importantly, from the established working class. This latter group shares with more affluent social classes the hope of ever-rising living standards and opportunities, and such common aspirations now appear to be more forceful than the personal and political differences arising from the continuing and massive disparities in income and wealth (although such disparities are increasingly evident). This realignment producing a voting coalition of the hopeful has reduced the underclass to political impotence.

Where Does Responsibility Lie?

Clearly, the Government has to assume most responsibility for these developments. This is a particularly unpalatable fact for an administration which prides itself on its strategy of switching responsibility from the state to the individual. The Government sets the ground rules by which individuals live their lives. This Government has been a leading agent in fashioning each of the factors described above as expelling from full citizenship. While a reversal of government policy in these areas would have important repercussions, this alone would be insufficient to eradicate the existence of an underclass. These four horsemen of the apocalypse have knitted into other economic and social changes occurring simultaneously in Britain today.

What is happening to the number and composition of single-parent families is a case in point. My concern, in this instance, lies not with those who are widowed and on Income Support, nor indeed with those who have been divorced or who are separated. My particular concern lies with the single, unmarried mother who begins her family while still a teenager and whose children are born to different fathers. While this group remains the smallest constituent element of single mothers on welfare, regrettably it is the fastest growing.

With the decline in institutional religion, people draw their values from a variety of sources. Television soap operas are one such unlikely source. Less immediate, but arguably no less influential, is the language of state action. If single mothers are allowed to claim welfare with few if any questions asked about the whereabouts of the father, then society is subtly undermining the traditional norm of two-parent families. This is plainly courting disaster. The state is seen as conferring its blessing on the status of the single mother.

The Right claims that something should be done about the growth in single-parent families because this is a guaranteed way to leapfrog the housing queue. The implied suggestion is that single mothers have rather an easy time on welfare. I am anxious for this subject to be debated more publicly for entirely opposite reasons. Single mothers do jump the queue, but only into a flat on 'sink' (i.e. the worst) housing estates. The more important aspect, and one readily ignored by the Right, is that once a single parent is weighed down with the responsibility of one or more children, the chance of a life other than one entirely dependent upon welfare becomes remote.

We need to block the supply routes to becoming a single mother on welfare. It is crucial that young single mothers are encouraged to go into our schools and talk to thirteen-, fourteen- and fifteen-year-old girls to tell them about life on welfare, housed on a 'sink' council estate. Let them explain what it is like to be responsible, twenty-four hours a day, mostly alone, for young children. Let them discuss how it feels to exist on a meagre allowance from Income Support. One-Parent Families is supporting the Barton Hill Young Mothers' Group in Bristol who are doing just this, and this initiative needs to be spread and become part of the curriculum in all secondary schools.

I also firmly believe that schools should be teaching both young male and female adults not only about the range of birth control techniques, but also of the need for individuals to respect one another, physically and emotionally. This is an ignored aspect in the drive towards personal responsibility. Even more important, if we intend to change the climate of opinion in which people take their individual actions, it must be stressed to young males that the social security rules are being changed. They must be made aware that the act of begetting children is regarded by the state as one of the most important decisions which the individual is able to take. One of the most effective ways of underscoring this importance is to attach appropriate financial obligations to it. Today's youth needs to be made conscious of the fact that these responsibilities will be enforced by the state and that they will be expected to meet the cumulative costs of such payments. Maintenance audits also ought to become part of the secondary curriculum. An audit, giving the likely costs of maintenance over the time for such payments will be made, must become part of the thinking of young males. A very modest nine pounds a week maintenance payment, for eighteen years, comes to a cumulative cost of £8,424.

The Government must offer a scheme whereby single mothers can make over to the state the responsibility to collect any maintenance order. The Government should undertake to pay the mother the maintenance each week, while accepting the responsibility for gaining the contribution from the father. The orders for payment should not be attached to wages. All too many men find this procedure easy to avoid by changing their jobs. Rather, the order should be attached to the National Insurance record which follows the worker automatically to his new job.

Mothers would be confident that maintenance payments would continue to be collected and paid by the state, even if they have left the welfare rolls and are back in work. After this chapter had been drafted, the Prime Minister announced the Government's intention to increase the numbers of fathers who pay maintenance towards the cost of their children. However, the Government's intention, so far, is only to increase the number of maintenance payments made for mothers on welfare. If this limited plan goes ahead, it will have the ironic effect of increasing welfare dependency. Unless the offer of collecting maintenance payments is given to both mothers on welfare and in work, the disincentive to leave a regular welfare income, and the certainty of maintenance payments, for a much more uncertain income from work, with the resumed responsibility for chasing fathers for maintenance payments, will deter most mothers from making a return to work, as and when the opportunities arise. In contrast, knowing that maintenance payments will continue to be made until the dependent child has completed his or her education will help open up for many single mothers the option of working. In return, the fact that fathers pay their payments should be one, but only one, of the considerations when the question of access to the children is considered. Of course, those fathers who have a record of potential violence to the mother and/or the children would remain excluded as they currently are. What is required is that the overall balance should be one which results in a child-centred strategy. This strategy rests on the assumption that it is desirable for children to know both of their parents, even if those parents no longer live together. Of course, other changes are needed, such as providing day-care facilities and training courses designed to help young single mothers, but no reform which bucks the issue of financial responsibility is likely to be successful.

Conclusion

How has the Government lived up to the Scriptural demands of protecting the poor? Have the mechanisms of institutional redress to safeguard the poor been enhanced or retarded under their stewardship? These questions have no easy answers, not least because of obscurantism on the part of the Government. It is not interested in calculations as to whether the numbers of those on low incomes have increased. Nor is it concerned about the difference in the gap in living standards between those at opposite ends of the income scale. On each of these criteria, the Government undoubtedly has a case to answer. Its defence rests solely on the belief that, in a free market economy, while the discrepancies between earnings may widen, the income of those at the bottom will rise at a faster rate than it would otherwise have done.

Even on the basis of this limited criterion, the Government cannot claim a success. The poorest ten per cent have experienced increases in living standards which are well below those gained by people on average income. If the long-term claimant is considered – a stable group compared to the fluctuating population which comprises the lowest decile – then the Government's record is even worse. Benefit rates have fallen in real terms over the 1981–90 period. It is remarkable that this should have occurred at a time of record growth in the British economy. Moreover, for the first time, an underclass, debarred from even the most paltry benefits of economic growth, is being created. This is assuredly the aspect of the Government's record which would most have aroused the Old Testament prophets.

13

The Limits of the Market

John Atherton

IGNORANCE is not a virtue in coming to terms with the contributions of religious and political traditions to contemporary society. The sudden re-emergence in Britain in 1979 of 'conviction politics' has made this task even more difficult. Its appearance has generated more heat than light, not least in the Churches. Their pronouncements on current affairs have been punctuated by inaccuracies and misinterpretations, particularly with regard to government policies and philosophies. Combined with a long-term inadequacy in economic matters and a general reluctance to face new developments, they have reduced the effectiveness of the Churches' witness in contemporary society. But the response of the Conservative Party to hostile Church pronouncements has not been characterised by any greater understanding. Undiscerning criticisms of government have generated equally undiscerning pro-government reactions. Too often the results have had all the appearance of a dialogue of the deaf.

In such a situation, there is something to be said for consulting an established tradition of relating Christianity to social affairs. It could assist the Churches and the Conservative Party to come to terms with contemporary change in ways more morally and theologically adequate. Sadly, amongst churchmen and politicians alike there is a lack of familiarity with developments in recent Christian social thought and ethics. Yet it is this strand of theology which could have the experience and potential for illuminating political and economic debate in helpful and creative ways.

Obviously there have been many different ways of relating Christianity and society; one classic analysis may be found in Richard Niebuhr's book of 1951, *Christ and Culture*. As a supplement to the historical chapters in the present book, I simply note that there has been a continuing concern in British Christian social thought to take seriously the insights and experiences of a variety of political, social and philosophical traditions. From the Anglican F. D. Maurice in the mid-nineteenth century to the Quaker John Mac-Murray in the mid-twentieth century, there has been a growing commitment to conversations with other disciplines and traditions as integral parts of the religious quest. The present dialogue should be regarded as a proper extension of these concerns. Indeed, the Churches have a particular responsibility to come to terms with a political and economic movement which has governed and reshaped British society in the 1980s. This is especially the case if these changes are also seen as representative of social and economic trends deeper than Thatcherism and wider than Britain. Addressing such signs of the times has always been a priority for those with a faith which centres on the incarnation.

What could be the consequences of such a dialogue for the Churches and the Conservative Party?

The Challenge to the Churches

A greatly changing social context and the emergence of Thatcherism, although separate realities, represent a convergence which challenges Social Christianity and its influence on the relationship of the mainstream Churches to contemporary political and economic affairs. As changing context, the trend to more market-oriented economies has become particularly prominent since the late 1970s. In Western societies the drift has affected the UK and the USA under Conservative administrations, but also France, Spain, Australia and New Zealand under Socialist governments. What has been even more pronounced has been the conversion of Communist countries to market mechanisms, particularly in the Eastern bloc and China. 'It has become worldwide, uniting rich and poor, capitalist and socialist countries in a common language and the beginnings of a common practice.'[1]

Widespread as these developments are, they have reached their sharpest and most unequivocal form in the emergence of Thatcherism in Britain and 'Reaganomics' in the USA. Often described as the New Right, they have been associated with the resurrection of free market economics, social policies and philosophies after a generation of Keynesian collectivism. They are a clear sign of a change of direction in the governing of societies and economies.

It is the New Right[2] which has presented such a sharp challenge to the Churches in Britain. Yet this should not distract attention from the wider and potentially more significant challenge to the Churches of more market-oriented economies. It is proposed therefore, for brevity of argument's sake, to regard the New Right, and its commitment to free market economics and philosophies, as representative of this broader movement into more market-oriented societies but in its more 'extreme' form. It is an acknowledgment that Thatcherism is symptom as much as cause of contemporary change.

The response of the Churches to the challenge of this evolving context is reflected in their criticism of many of the principal values and outcomes of government policies

---

[1] Robert Skidelsky, *The Social Market Economy* (The Social Market Foundation, 1989), p. 4.

[2] For further definitions of the New Right, see J. P. Wogaman, *Economics and Ethics* (SCM, 1986), pp. 15–16; R. H. Preston, *The Future of Christian Ethics* (SCM, 1987), pp. 135f.; John Atherton, *Faith in the Nation* (SPCK, 1988), chs. 3 and 5.

when seen to be overinfluenced by New Right policies and philosophies. Three parts of the life of the Churches have been associated particularly with this reaction. Whilst they do not represent the whole of Christian social witness, they are nonetheless manifestations of the developing social mind of the Churches. They influence the Churches' public stance and relationships with the established orderings of society, including government at national and regional levels. The three parts of the Churches' life are:

(1) The 'official Churches' acting through their governing bodies as synods and councils. For example, the Church of England's General Synod has criticised a wide range of government policies on the National Health Service, education, social security, taxation, inner cities, broadcasting, housing and the economy.

(2) The Churches' 'social action curias',[3] a term which refers mainly to Social Responsibility departments at national level. Their reports on social affairs have been critical of some of the principal values and programmes of the present administration. From the rejection of the free market over-emphasis on economic values and systems by *Perspectives in Economics* (1984) to the subsequent dismissal of the New Right option for welfare policies by *Not Just For the Poor* (1986), there has been a persistent unwillingness to accept major trends in government thinking since 1979.

(3) The leaders of the major Churches have intervened effectively and substantially in social affairs. More unusually, they have also rejected some of the chief values and practices of a Government dominant in Britain for over a decade. For the Archbishop of Canterbury, the Moderator of the General Assembly of the Church of Scotland and the President of the Methodist Conference to agree in such a way and at the same time, cannot be regarded as

---

[3] I owe this provocative concept to Professor Henry Clark, University of Southern California, in his unpublished work on the Board for Social Responsibility.

coincidence.[4] Nor can Conservative leaders treat them as isolated phenomena. Convergences over a wide spectrum do not suggest eccentricity. They indicate something more substantial and widespread.

Each of these three parts of the Churches' public life and witness have responded to government policies in very similar ways. Firstly, they reject many of the social consequences of government programmes. They are particularly concerned for the growing numbers of poor people and families, and over the increasing divisions between people, communities and regions. Secondly, they question self-interest and economic materialism as moral preferences for the individual. Thirdly, they reflect unease with the tendency to elevate the free market into a hard determinist ideology. To begin to organise areas of human living like education, health, culture and religion by reference to such an ideology has met with widespread condemnation. Fourthly, they have expressed concern over the erosion of collective provision by the state in its local and national forms.

The cumulative effect of the agreements between these three areas of the Churches' life produces a criticism of government as influenced by the New Right which is remarkable for its coherence and consistency. So notable is this collaboration and agreement as to suggest a common religious source. Examination of an important tradition in Western Christian social thought confirms the existence of such a basis. This particular tradition has been described as 'the mainstream liberal perspective' or as 'Social Christianity'. The former concept was coined by the American theologian J. P. Wogaman in his *Christian Perspectives on*

---

[4] The Moderator of the Church of Scotland, address to Kirkaldy Rotary Club, 17 February 1989; the Archbishop of Canterbury, report of address to the One Nation Tory Dining Club in the *Observer*, 5 March 1989; the President of the Methodist Conference, address to the Methodist Conference in the *Methodist Recorder*, 30 June 1988.

Politics.[5] It refers to a type of 'generating centre' of Christian political thought which is neither a majority point of view nor 'liberal' in the sense of *laissez faire* economics. Nevertheless, it does produce commonly held theological convictions of a 'progressive–orthodox' kind; it expresses mainstream church opinion on social affairs; and it promotes a reformist attitude to change. This, Wogaman argues, distinguishes it from other types of 'generating centre' including the Christian pacifist, liberationist and neoconservative. 'Social Christianity' is, however, my preferred concept for describing the theological basis for the British Churches' critique of the New Right, because it relates more precisely to historical developments and present phenomena and avoids the confusions associated with the concept of 'liberal'.[6]

Social Christianity emerged as a critical response to the harmful consequences of industrialisation and urbanisation in the nineteenth century in Britain and the USA. In the former, it developed as Christian Socialism. Although not significantly socialist in any secular sense, it did represent a theologically-based critical appraisal of major trends in society. It was dominated by some of the most influential Anglican theologians in the last one hundred years, including Maurice, Westcott, Gore and Scott Holland. In the USA, Social Christianity evolved as the Social Gospel through the contributions of such Protestant theologians as Mathews, Gladden and Rauschenbusch.

Together, the two movements became the principal influence on the development of Christian social thought's involvement in advanced economies. By the end of the First World War, if not before, much of Church opinion on contemporary social affairs, including that held by official Church bodies, social action curias and leaders, was also shaped increasingly by Social Christianity. This growing

---

[5] J. P. Wogaman, *Christian Perspectives on Politics* (SCM, 1988), ch. 6.

[6] This concept will be developed in my forthcoming reader, *Social Christianity: From Christian Socialism and the Social Gospel to Christian Social Ethics* (SPCK, 1993).

influence was confirmed and extended by the great ecumenical conferences which addressed the social signs of the times with a maturing power and sophistication. Beginning with Stockholm in 1925 and particularly Oxford in 1937, they fed into the World Council of Churches' Assemblies at Amsterdam in 1948 and Evanston in 1954. All were greatly influenced by the theological heirs of Christian Socialism and the Social Gospel, including William Temple, Reinhold Niebuhr and John Bennett. They and their successors continue to occupy dominant positions in the development of Social Christianity and contemporary Christian social ethics in the USA through Bennett, Shinn, Stackhouse and Wogaman, and in the UK through Preston. Together, they represent a marked convergence and development of theological contributions to the method and content of moral judgments on complex social issues.

Reflection on this influence on the Churches' relationship to the social order highlights two insights of importance for its further development. These are brought into sharp relief by the nature of the present dialogue.

First, it reveals the continuing importance of contemporary social context for the formation and development of Social Christianity as a significant form of Christian engagement with complex modern societies. It made creative and discerning use of disciplines and movements evolving in that context. Philosophical, historical and sociological disciplines were combined to ensure the growing significance of social data and theories in the formation of Christian social thought through their interaction with developing Christian beliefs. Indeed, by 1900 in the USA, the Library of Congress categorised theological writings in this field as 'Christian Sociology'. But a contemporary example of this recognition and use of context in Social Christianity is the acknowledgment of the importance of the change to more market-oriented economies and societies. This would take seriously the discipline of economics in the Christian response to the modern context. It would represent a development compatible with the role of sociology in the earlier history of this impressive theological movement.

Secondly, a brief survey of Social Christianity's evolution suggests not only the continuing importance of context, but also the continuing impact of inadequate earlier reactions to it. It is important to acknowledge the distorting influence of Social Christianity's original rejection, in the nineteenth century, of many of the principal features of *laissez faire* capitalism. The persistence of this unease over market economies is noted by Skidelsky in his comparison of British and German experiences. He observes how in Britain 'old fashioned capitalism, socialism, the welfare state and Keynesian macro-economics were wrapped in an ill-assorted package labelled the "mixed economy". The consensus which sustained this mixture proved to be highly vulnerable, because it concealed a basic ambivalence about the justification of markets, and indeed about the private enterprise system itself'.[7] It is this early unequivocal criticism of free market capitalism's philosophies, policies and social outcomes which has continued to influence Social Christianity's stance towards market economies in general as well as free market economies in particular. This has been despite a growing recognition by the leading theologians of Social Christianity, including Bennett, Niebuhr, Preston and Wogaman, of the need to distinguish between an unacceptable *laissez faire* capitalism and a qualified acceptance of welfare capitalism. This failure has prevented the Churches from accepting the need to separate the criticisms of current manifestations of *laissez faire* capitalism from the need to take account of the significance for human living in today's world of the market and its associated properties. Recognising the value of the market involves accepting it as a most effective and legitimate economic mechanism for the production and allocation of scarce and finite resources. It also includes affirming

---

[7] Skidelsky, *The Social Market Economy*, p. 7. I am much indebted to Lord Harris for this reference, and for much else in the field of free market thinking.

the legitimacy of value-laden 'properties' intimately associ-ated with the effective operating of the market as mechan-ism. These include self-interest as a key incentive for economic endeavour, competition, enterprise or creativity, profit, inequalities, a strong but limited state, private prop-erty, and the individual with a high degree of freedom.[8]

It is by inspiring the Churches and Social Christianity to come to terms in more discerning ways with the market and its properties that the current dialogue may make its most important contribution. In other words, the encounter between Churches and Conservative Party, particularly where the latter appears to be unduly influenced by New Right thinking, has a wider significance if it also challenges the Churches to creative dialogue with the drift to more market-oriented economies as a dominant feature of our greatly-changing context. It offers the opportunity of recalling the Churches and Social Christianity to a reconsideration of what it means to take seriously the contemporary context.

The consequences of such a reappraisal could be con-siderable. It would preclude the unequivocal condem-nation of the New Right if this also includes rejection of the market and its properties. (Recent signs of the emergence of such a discriminating response to market economics have been apparent in appraisals of the New Right by Mostyn Davies and Alan Suggate.[9]) Instead, a positive understand-ing would recognise the value of the market as a principal economic mechanism and affirm the value-laden properties integral to its effective performance. This would involve promoting social market capitalism or market socialism as legitimate options for Christian economic discipleship.

---

[8] This argument about market economies is developed further in my 'Christian-ity and the Market in the 1990s', Industrial Christian Fellowship Annual Lecture, ICF Theme Pamphlet 39 (1989).

[9] Mostyn Davies, 'The New Conservatism', William Temple Foundation, Occasional Paper no. 16 (1987); Alan Suggate, 'The New Right', in *Crucible* (Oct.– Dec. 1988).

This affirmation of market economies as a preferred option for Christian social thought in its response to advanced contemporary economies would represent a major change in the development of Social Christianity. Unfortunately, the persistence of an ambiguous relationship to market economies continues to be reflected in Social Christianity's undeveloped and limited acceptance of wealth creation, in contrast to its highly developed and extensive acceptance of wealth distribution. It is revealed, too, in its reluctant recognition of the right of Christians to be Conservatives. In contrast to developments in the USA, in Britain this recognition has never been expanded into a comprehensive theological justification of democratic capitalism as a legitimate option for Christian discipleship. In terms of acknowledging this Conservative option, it is disturbing to note how recent church reports either neglect it (*Faith in the City*) or reject it (*Not Just for the Poor*).

The Challenge to the New Right

In this dialogue the challenge is equally to the Conservative Party, especially when under the influence of a movement such as the New Right.

The tradition of Social Christianity, although justly criticised for paying insufficient attention to a market-influenced context, does have a considerable experience in engaging advanced societies. It possesses in this field an adequacy not found to the same extent in other theological traditions. This is particularly the case in the development of theological method and in the content and quality of moral judgments on social affairs. The importance and credibility of the latter is heightened by their convergence with similar judgments generated by different theological methods and traditions. For example, there is a strong agreement, in Western Christian social thought, on a clear presumption for democracy in the theological appraisal of political systems. However, from this tradition of Social

Christianity certain questions arise about contemporary trends. These point beyond areas of possible convergence between the partners in the present dialogue, for example over the contribution of the market, to areas of likely conflict.

Of the areas of likely disagreement, five stand out for serious consideration. Obviously, different groups, traditions and theologians formulate them in different ways and, indeed, ask different questions. However, these five do arise out of Social Christianity's continuing tradition of criticism of *laissez faire* capitalism, including in its contemporary form as New Right Conservatism. Obviously, the Conservative Party is broader than the New Right, and includes a variety of traditions. The following critical questions therefore relate only to those tendencies in Conservatism which follow a more unequivocal free market thinking (including much in the New Right). However, any serious commitment to market economies will also need to be aware of their likely appearance.

First, free market or New Right Conservatism has a tendency to elevate the market into a hard determinist ideology. This can claim, like classic Marxism, to be a scientifically objective ideology (as elaborated by Von Mises). Or it can develop into a closed philosophical variant (of which Professor F. A. Hayek and Lord Harris are exponents). Reacting against the collectivism and corporatism of the 1930s to the 1960s, such Conservatism has the dual tendencies of romanticism by overestimating and idealising the powers and virtues of free market economies, and of an exclusive ideology, by rejecting the feasibility and indeed legitimacy of alternative economic and political systems. In the hands of their disciples and collaborators, including politicians, these tendencies warrant R. H. Tawney's judgment on Marx: 'petrifaction by the elect'.[10] It is this which reinforces the inclination to idolatry and

---

[10] Quoted in R. H. Preston, *Religion and the Persistence of Capitalism* (SCM, 1979), p. 87.

authoritarianism, and so attracts the strongest criticism of Social Christianity.

Secondly, and linked to the elevation of the market into a hard determinist ideology, is the problem of developing philosophies and policies to remedy the significant deficiencies and limits of the market. These include 'social goods' such as education, health care, housing and transport, especially for the less able and prosperous, and 'externalities' such as the environment in its increasingly all-embracing and international dimensions. Indeed, it is this heightening awareness of the ecumenical, of the whole inhabited world, which may well raise such profound limits to the operating of market systems as to require their supplanting by as yet undiscovered systems. Living together in what will be seen increasingly as a finite world raises profound questions about market systems with their innate tendencies to promote competition for scarce resources and to avoid protective regulation and strategic planning. Social Christianity's historic understanding of finitude and sin in relation to corporate realities and activities, and its equal concern for distributive justice in the allocation of resources, reinforce these grave questions about market limits. They will also come to suggest, in as yet unconceptualised form, guidelines for possible ways forward out of these predicaments.

The third question concerns the persistent and increasingly significant issue of the marginalised in Britain and other developed nations, and in the underdeveloped Third World. By the former is meant those who are effectively excluded from effective participation in increasingly prosperous societies. This can amount to up to a fifth of a population. By the latter is meant those who are excluded effectively from any serious possibility of fulfilled human living, sometimes lacking even the basic minimum necessary for sustaining life itself. This can amount to a majority of a population. Such marginalisation has traditionally presented a sharp challenge to the New Right and its antecedents. This is not least because free market definitions, explanations and related policies have not appeared to be commensurate with the sheer gravity, extent and empirical reality of marginalisation. Symptomatic of this historic deficiency in free market thinking and practice are current arguments over whether poverty actually exists in Britain, and their related confusions over inequality. For example, moderates like Professor Brian Griffiths pay a heavy price by continuing to separate marginalisation and the problem of felt inequality, and then ignoring the latter, or, in the case of the more extreme free marketeers, actually encouraging it. Although clearly and necessarily distinguishable, poverty and inequality have been regarded by most social and theological commentators as complementary realities in modern societies, the two sides of the same coin. This relationship was recognised by an astute observer of British social history earlier in this century. He recommended that the student of poverty would be advised to start much higher up the stream; that what the rich call the problem of poverty, the poor, with equal justice, call the problem of riches.[11] That judgment reflects a deep theological concern. For the empirically measurable reality of inequality as deeply damaging divisions between persons, communities, regions and nations, if contrived in any way by advantaged people or structures, and if borne unduly by the marginalised, and benefited from by the prosperous, stands in clear and unequivocal conflict with Social Christianity. That which the biblical witness has seen to be related – poverty and unjust inequalities – no political ideology should be allowed to put asunder. This remains the presumption of Christians and Social Christianity. It represents one of the sharpest challenges to New Right Conservatism.

Fourthly, there persists a serious reservation about the nature and extent of the free market's commitment to democratic politics. This grave unease arises out of the strong support by Social Christianity and most major

[11] J. M. Winter (ed.), R. H. Tawney, *The American Labour Movement and Other Essays* (Harvester, 1979), p. 112.

Western theologians for democracy as a theologically valued and preferred political system. Reinhold Niebuhr's famous aphorism sums up this commitment: 'Man's capacity for justice makes democracy possible; but man's inclination to injustice makes democracy necessary.'[12]

Reservations about the New Right's commitment to politics arise because of its overemphasis on economics and the free market as the principal vehicles for expressing people's preferences. These relate to its correspondingly low estimate of the state and political democracy as means for delivering greater citizen participation in the governing of society. Essentially, it overemphasises the consumer's work in the market and underplays the citizen's political vote. So to extend involvement in society by market means in education, health, social services, housing and industry, valuable as this is, is a policy which still suffers from the already acknowledged limitations and defects of the market. It is also no substitute for the extension of democratic participation by political means. For example, the latter could involve developing more effective local, regional and European Community government to complement national government and introducing some form of proportional representation and greater employee participation in the decision-making of economic enterprises. The present Government's distancing itself from the European Community's Social Charter is a sign of this ambivalence in New Right thinking. What is more significant is that the cumulative effect of these political limitations, when taken in conjunction with questions relating to ideology, marginalisation, social goods, externalities, and moral values, suggest that the constraint on the capitalist market of democratic politics needs to be supplemented by other social restraints in addition to democracy. I have come to see that 'democratic capitalism' which was developed as an option for Christian political discipleship by Michael Novak

---

[12] Reinhold Niebuhr, *The Children of Light and the Children of Darkness* (Nisbet, 1945), p. xi.

in the USA and in my *Faith in the Nation* in the UK, now needs major modification into 'democratic social market' capitalism. The restricted commitment of free market capitalism to political democracy requires the development of further social supports and restraints of market operations.

The overemphasis on economic, as against political, mechanisms and values for extending citizen participation has another defect. It neglects two arguments traditionally used by supporters of market economies to justify the value of democratic decision-making in market economies. On the one hand, recent events in Eastern Europe and China reveal the obstacles encountered by those attempting to restrict market-oriented reforms to purely economic affairs. It is becoming more and more apparent that the extension of citizen-choice by market-led means in the end invariably spills over into, and needs to be supported by, concerns for greater participation in the running of society through representative democracy. On the other hand, one has become increasingly aware of the correlation between Adam Smith's recognition of the value of the free market as the least bad way of operating an economy, and Social Christianity's view of democracy as the least bad way of governing a society; for both positions are realistic. The New Right's over-optimism about the free market and its lack of realism about democratic politics combine to cast serious doubt on the Conservatives' claim to be the party of original sin.

These two arguments linking market and democracy add up to a strong criticism of New Right thinking and practice on democracy. They confirm the importance of holding together market economics and democratic politics. As a consequence, they also convict the New Right of not maintaining this balance. This is because of its propensity to overemphasise free market economics, to the detriment of democratic politics, as the principal means for operating a modern society. It is this deficiency which is also highlighted by New Right Conservatism's reluctance to accept democratic socialism as a legitimate if not preferred option for Christian discipleship. Its unwillingness to embrace fully a social market system, as democratic social market capitalism (as already noted), only compounds this major political defect.

The fifth and final question relates to moral values. Social Christianity has argued for generations that Christian involvement in the social order is seriously impaired by New Right and free market understandings of the nature of moral values and by their concentration on particular values. There is a concern that the overemphasis on the free market, as developed by Von Mises, Hayek and Friedman, generates a profoundly determinist view of life. This is seen as eroding dangerously the freedom of human decision-making supported by strongly-held values and visions. Besides contradicting Christian beliefs about free will and moral intentions, such economic determinism even conflicts with the interpretations of Adam Smith, the founder of free market economics and philosophies. He recognised clearly the need for non-market systems and values if the market was to operate morally and therefore effectively. People, he thought, 'could safely be trusted to pursue their own self-interest without undue harm to the community, not only because of the restrictions imposed by the law but also because they were subject to built-in restraint derived from morals, custom and education'.[13]

This overemphasis on the free market and undervaluing of human freedom also influences the promotion of particular values and the rejection of others. For example, New Right Conservatism places an undue emphasis on the value of the person as individual, on freedom as relief from external interference, and on unrestrained private property as underwriting that view of individual liberty. Consequently, there is insufficient appreciation of the Christian understanding of the individual as a person in community, the related and wider view of liberty as both freedom from

---

[13] A. W. Coates (ed.), *The Classical Economists and Economic Policy* (Methuen, 1971) containing Adam Smith's 'Theory of Moral Sentiments'.

illicit restrictions and freedom to pursue self-chosen purposes, and the acceptance of private property as qualified by accountability to God and the neighbour. Conservative theologians like Brian Griffiths tend to avoid these wider, social dimensions of human living under God, partly by a heavily politicised reading of the Scriptures. This restricted theological realism is also reflected in the New Right's overemphasis on self-interest in a market context, and a lack of appreciation of its inevitable tendency to degenerate into individual and corporate selfishness.

It is important to note that this highly selective choice of values is exacerbated by the neglect or rejection of values now accepted by wider Christian social thought as central to its task. There is a disturbing avoidance of the determining norm of justice in corporate affairs (for instance in the work of Hayek and Nozick). Clearly, the New Right's criticisms of social justice need to be taken into account when developing a more adequate theory of justice. However, what cannot be countenanced by responsible Christian opinion is any evasion of the non-negotiable demand of justice in biblical and wider Christian tradition. The New Right's indifference with regard to the regulative norm of justice is confirmed by its demotion of the value of equality, frequently through its misinterpretation. Again, this flies in the face of Christian social thought's persisting presumption in its favour. For there has been a growing recognition in Social Christianity of the necessary, if at times uneasy and confusing, relationship between the determinative norm of justice and the supportive and regulative demands of the fundamentally equal valuing of all human beings in the eyes of God. 'Equality,' declares Hobhouse, 'lies at the foundation of justice in the sense that every person and every function capable of harmony must be equally taken into account in framing the plan of harmony.'[14]

---

[14] Reinhold Niebuhr, *Moral Man and Immoral Society* (SCM, 1963), p. 159, quoting L. T. Hobhouse, *The Elements of Social Justice*, p. 172.

The theologically unnatural separation of justice from equality, and the demotion of the latter in the face of an overvaluing of inequality, may well erode the power of justice to generate that moral legitimation for a market system of political economy which only a sense of fairness can provide. It is this addition of justice which produces the dividing line between the unacceptability of 'democratic free market' capitalism and the acceptability of 'democratic social market' capitalism. For a social market economy, unlike a free market economy, is 'one which is embedded in social arrangements regarded as "fair"'.[15] This is certainly accepted by American theological apologists for democratic capitalism, like Bennett. It has yet to be acknowledged by their English counterparts.

The cumulative effect of these five questions out of the tradition of Social Christianity confirms the value of the market in its own right but also recognises its substantial defects and limitations. Taken together, they reinforce Wogaman's judgment that the market is a good servant but a bad master.

After the Dialogue

Given the benefits of dialogue for the formation of future Christian social involvement, what more can Social Christianity and Churches learn from the encounter? As someone involved in the development of Social Christianity but not a member of the Conservative Party, I feel that this question warrants my attention and that Christian members of the party are better placed to address similar questions to their own constituencies. It seems to me that there are two areas for further work.

First, a greatly changing context requires a major change in Social Christianity, and therefore in the Churches' use of it. It means recognising the value of the market as a princi-

---

[15] Skidelsky, *The Social Market Economy*, p. 4.

pal mechanism for the production and allocation of scarce resources, and affirming the value-laden properties associated with its effective operating. In such a changing context, restating the mainstream liberal tradition of Social Christianity will be no longer sufficient. Consequently, the more undiscerning and unequivocal criticisms of the Government which have characterised many recent Church pronouncements on social affairs will no longer be acceptable. They do not take seriously a positive recognition of the market as mechanism, and the affirming of the value-laden properties associated with it. To do this requires not merely restating Social Christianity but reformulating it in ways sensitive to such a changing context. It is to pay careful attention to contemporary context as Social Christianity did in the nineteenth century. It would involve also addressing key questions to the context out of Christian understandings; it would involve seeking to 'Christianise' it in the way Rauschenbusch sought to do in early twentieth-century America. Out of such an interaction between contextualising Christianity and Christianising the context, the reformulation of Social Christianity could occur. Interestingly, it is such reconstruction of tradition in the light of contextual changes which has been occurring in other fields of political endeavour. Both the Communist Party with its *Facing up to the Future*, and the Labour Party with its Policy Review documents, have been struggling to take account of the trends towards market economies and greater participation. The results are beginning to look like variants of a more democratic market socialism. The changes in Eastern Europe are on a much more dramatic scale. It is on such a similar road of reconstructing tradition that the Churches are being called by the present dialogue.

A reformulation of Social Christianity would, then, involve recognising the value of the market as mechanism and affirming the properties associated with it. Yet it would also mean facing up to those key questions which are intimately related to the struggle for human living at the end of the twentieth century, which are also raised by historic Social Christianity in dialogue with the Conservative Party. These include struggles to develop wider democratic participation in decision-making, remedying the gross injustice of the marginalised in Britain and the wider world, and incorporating the increasingly international and ecological dimensions of human living into more and more political, economic and social activities.

It is out of such a dialectical relationship between trends to more market-oriented economies and questions representing the predicaments and hopes of human living on this planet, that a possible synthesis could occur. It would suggest a reformulated Christian *oikonomia*, a Greek New Testament concept from which is derived our concern for managing the household as economy and for the whole inhabited world as ecumenical. For it is that concern for feasibility as represented by market economics, and for radical hope as the persisting moral concerns of the human, which continue to form the agenda of Social Christianity. What is not clear, as yet, is whether the questions are so radical that in the process of interaction with market economies a future reformulation will lead beyond the theory and practice of traditional economics. Perhaps this is what Tawney sensed when he speculated how future generations would look back in wonder at the nineteenth and twentieth centuries' obsession with economics. But that is a legitimate possibility for Social Christianity only because it will have been achieved through taking seriously economics as market in a wider social framework.[16]

The second area for future work relates to the implications of dialogue for the Churches' witness and ministry in and to society, in the light of the reformulation of Social Christianity. This has a particular significance for the

---

[16]These arguments will be developed further in my forthcoming book, *Christianity and the Market: The Reformulation of Social Christianity for the 1990s* (SPCK, 1992).

Church of England and its relationship with the established orderings of society including government.

The consequences for Church–society relationships begin to emerge out of a recognition of the inadequacies of two alternative models, 'critical solidarity' and 'confessional separation'.

The traditional response of the Church to society has been described as 'critical solidarity' with the established orderings of society.[17] This stance has characterised the official Churches, their social action curias and their leaders. But it does not continue to be either appropriate or acceptable theologically in the emerging contemporary context, if 'solidarity', however 'critical', implies collaboration with a free market or New Right Conservatism with its tendency to develop persisting and fundamental deficiencies and limitations. Accepting the challenge of market economies does not override the equally decisive critical questions raised of free market economies by Social Christianity. Nor, indeed, is the model of critical solidarity appropriate for Church relationships with established orderings in an increasingly plural and secular post-Christendom and a post-industrial society. The emergence of free market capitalism and state socialism, as well as of non-Anglican denominations and other faiths, suggests even more the inappropriateness of an Anglican Church–State relationship based on 'solidarity'. The need for independence to enable criticism and solidarity to emerge freely from the Church, as its positive contribution and commitment to society, would be true to much of the spirit of Anglicanism whilst amending some of its inadequacies.

On the other hand, the future relationship of the Churches to our changing context should not be described as a radical stance *against* established orderings and trends. For example, the critical questions asked of the Conservative Party concerning the limits of the market could, it is

---

[17] G. S. Ecclestone, *The Church of England and Politics* (CIO Publishing, 1981).

argued, be institutionalised into a 'Confessing Church' form following the model of the Confessing Church's stance against Hitler. This is being advocated within the World Council of Churches on the initiative of Ulrich Duchrow, a Lutheran theologian.[18] Yet this would probably produce a marginalised sectarian Christianity unwilling and unable to take seriously present realities and achievements, including the value of markets and their properties. It would therefore constitute a clear departure from the tradition of Social Christianity's concern to generate a public theology, to address the central determining realities of the contemporary context through their midst, however critically.[19]

This need to reject established models such as 'critical solidarity' and 'confessional separation' should not disturb us in our search for a reformed relationship between the Christian Church and society. Promoting a reformulated Social Christianity out of the synthesis between the market and these questions about its limits has positive implications for Church–State relationships. It suggests a necessarily independent Church, promoting a Christian *oikonomia* which acts, in the best tradition of Social Christianity, both as a critique of existing society and as guidelines for society's future. This would provide the basis for deciding between the appropriateness of solidarity and criticism in each situation in relation to each social question. And such a learning experience would show more fully why a dialogue between the Conservative Party and the Church of England is a worthwhile enterprise.

---

[18] Ulrich Duchrow, *Global Economy: A Confessional Issue for the Churches* (WCC, 1987).

[19] On public theology, see Max L. Stackhouse, *Public Theology and Political Economy* (Eerdmans, 1987).

14

Christians, Conservatives and Europe

Timothy Raison, MP

IT would be odd for a symposium to discuss the future relationship between Christianity and Conservatives without looking at the development of the European Community, yet to analyse this triangle may be as difficult as juggling with three balls. It is tempting to say: what is this all about? Is there any specifically Christian dimension to questions like whether or not we should join the Exchange Rate Mechanism of the EMS, what we should do about the Common Agricultural Policy, or even whether a federal Europe should be our ultimate objective? People can, and do, talk about these matters endlessly without ever having to consider that question. But at the very least the topic needs some probing by Conservatives.

Let us start with the problem of how far there was a specifically or implicitly Christian impetus behind the formation of the Common Market. Jean Monnet is generally credited with having been the father of the European Community, so it is worth looking at his valuable *Memoirs* (translated by Richard Mayne, 1978) for insight into this. It must be said that this remarkable man says almost nothing about religion, his or anyone else's. He had a passionate belief in unity in all sorts of spheres, together with a firm conviction that the way to bring this about, as far as Europe was concerned, was through the practical creation and operation of effective economic institutions. Thus the

Common Market's goal of ending the wars which had torn Western Europe apart was to begin with the merger of coal and steel policy through the European Coal and Steel Community. The problem was intimately tied up with that of the Saar and the Ruhr, critical areas of tension in Franco-German relations. Adenauer in 1950 had actually postulated in a newspaper interview a merger of France's and Germany's economies, parliaments and citizenship, drawing on Churchill's offer to France in 1940. But of course to the French this seemed unthinkable and Monnet and, crucially of course, the French Foreign Minister Robert Schuman were able to press on pragmatically with the creation of the ECSC. Monnet quotes Schuman as saying, 'We must doubtless envisage some transfer of sovereignty, but not yet.' He also quotes a comment of de Gaulle's: 'If one were not constrained to look at matters coolly, one would be dazzled by the prospect of what could be achieved by a combination of German and French strength, the latter also embracing Africa . . . Altogether, it would mean giving economic, social, strategic and cultural shape to the work of the Emperor Charlemagne.' But to Monnet the matter *had* to be looked at coolly and the dream of an immediately integrated 'Carolingian' Europe was rejected in favour of the practical work of binding not only Germany and France, but the Benelux countries and Italy, into the ECSC. Britain, of course, stood aside.

If the pragmatic seemed to override the romantic in this crucial episode that does not quite mean that the Carolingian dream – with its Catholic essence – had no significance. Adenauer, the Christian Democrat, was a devout Catholic, although not a man whose whole approach to politics was permeated with Catholic ideas. He was, however, a Rhinelander, not a Prussian. French politics were more secular than German politics, but Schuman was not afraid to speak in terms of Christian morality and the third great statesman in the triumvirate who launched the Community – the Italian Alcide de Gasperi – was very much a *Christian* Democrat. There does seem to have been some sense of drawing on the legacy of the distant past to tackle the terrible conflicts that had scarred the recent past.

It is worth here drawing on Ernst Haas' book *The Uniting of Europe* (1958). He describes the enthusiasm for unity in Europe in the French Mouvement Republicain Populaire, which Robert Schuman led, by contrast with the Gaullist RPF:

> If faith in the nation constitutes the bedrock of RPF thinking, doctrinal rejection of this very notion is the basis of thinking in the Christian-Democratic MRP (Mouvement Republicain Populaire), the only French party for which European federation is the unanimously accepted first principle of modern politics. Favoured by the long incumbency of its leader, Robert Schuman, in the Quai d'Orsay, the MRP was enabled to press for general Franco-German rapprochement on the basis of the natural unity of Western European Christian (i.e. Catholic) values. In addition, union would prevent German political and economic hegemony. Catholic theory reinforces this political penchant. Human associations are pictured as a natural hierarchy, rising from the family unit to the universality of mankind. Hence, the nation as the major claimant for loyalty is considered a usurper, to be overcome by supranational federation of the like-minded. While this doctrine would logically lead to world federation, in the immediate future Western European unity is actually predominant in MRP thought. Finally, the Catholic doctrine of pluralism with its emphasis on co-operation and harmony among distinct social groups further favours and conditions a political orientation toward permanent union with erstwhile rivals and competitors. Hence, union with Germany is all-important, while the inclusion of Protestant Britain in such a grouping is not a major concern to the MRP. Conviction on these points not only made possible the Schuman proposal for ECSC, but solid MRP support for its adoption and consistent activity for its expansion since.

Haas then refers to similar Christian Democratic ideas favouring the European idea in Italy, Belgium and Luxembourg. He points out that during the crucial period of

1950 to 1952 Christian Democrats were influential in all six governments of the future ECSC:

> On the level of doctrine there was commitment to a united peaceful Europe, commonly shared by all six parties and cemented with Church teaching. Further, it must be stressed that in 1950–52 in all six countries, Christian parties were represented in the cabinets, with Christian Democratic prime ministers presiding in all but Holland and France. Convinced that Europe's ills demanded a new approach and unpalatable steps these men were hesitant to take within the national framework, they tacitly agreed to shift the burden to a supranational agency . . . Christian doctrine and opportunity combined to suggest the creation of a new type of 'pre-federal' organisation to solve problems considered economically too difficult and politically too dangerous to tackle in the national setting.

Haas, however, accepts that the Christian Democrat parties were not strong enough by themselves to clinch parliamentary ratification of the ECSC treaty in all six countries and that its success was due to a convergence of different interests. The same point is made by Uwe Kitzinger in *Diplomacy and Persuasion* (1972):

> Even the historic cleavage of clericals and anticlericals was bridged by the European idea. Certainly three of the men in the van of the movement were devout Catholics born in Lothair's middle kingdom, an area where the liberal conception of the world and its denizens as naturally divisible into neat nation states appears unsophisticated in the extreme: Robert Schuman, a German during the First World War and then Prime Minister of France; Alcide de Gasperi, a Deputy in the Vienna Diet while Austria–Hungary was at war with Italy, and then Prime Minister of Italy; and Konrad Adenauer, the non-combatant anti-Prussian mayor of Cologne who flirted with the idea of separating the Rhineland from Prussia after the First World War. To them, the restoration of Charlemagne's empire of a thousand years before, with the cultural unity it implied, had an emotional appeal. But the

stalwarts of the movement came also from the ranks of the anticlerical Left, organised, in the early post-war years, in the Social Movement for a United States of Europe. The Socialist Paul-Henri Spaak, a former Belgian Prime Minister, provided the personal driving force in the drafting of the Rome Treaties, and the French Socialist leader Guy Mollet was Prime Minister during the critical phases of the Common Market negotiations and secured the votes of 100 out of the 101 French Socialist deputies in favour of their ratification.

Perhaps the best one can say is that the ideas behind the European Community were partly Christian but that the instruments were strictly secular.

A Christian Market?

As well as the question of how far the Common Market was Christian in its inspiration, there is also the wider question of how far the politics of those who made up the Community have been influenced by Christianity (in its various forms) and how far one can see those influences being expressed in the way in which the Community is evolving. It seems certain that Europe will not be Marxist. But will it be inspired by the liberal market ideas more often associated with the Protestant tradition or will it reflect the in-some-ways more collectivist approach of Catholic social thinking? How far will the argument between Conservatives led by Mrs Thatcher, who believes that we need to put more stress on the *individual's* responsibility, and church leaders, who are arguing for greater emphasis on social or community action, be reflected in the European forum? The development of the Social Charter has given particular topicality to this – as in a way does the conversion of the British Labour Party to membership of the Community and the belief that the Community can promote, if not socialism, at least the social democracy towards which it has recently apparently been moving.

In some ways, the Protestant impact on politics over time seems harder to define than the Roman Catholic. Its origins clearly had to do with some sort of revolt against authority and the Establishment of the day: Protestantism was equated with freedom, although the critics would say, freedom for whom?

The link between Protestantism and capitalism was of course analysed in two famous works – Max Weber's *The Protestant Ethic and the Spirit of Capitalism* (1905, translated in 1930) and R. H. Tawney's *Religion and the Rise of Capitalism* (1926). Tawney was stimulated by Weber's argument, and he provides a summary of it in the foreword which he wrote for a reissue of Weber's book in 1970:

> The pioneers of the modern economic order were, he [Weber] argues, parvenus, who elbowed their way to success in the teeth of the established aristocracy of land and commerce. The tonic that braced them for the conflict was a new conception of religion, which taught them to regard the pursuit of wealth as, not merely an advantage, but a duty. This conception welded into a disciplined force the still feeble bourgeoisie, heightened its energies, and cast a halo of sanctification round its convenient vices. What is significant, in short, is not the strength of the motive of economic self-interest, which is the common-place of all ages and demands no explanation. It is the change of moral standards which converted a natural frailty into an ornament of the spirit, and canonized as the economic virtues habits which in earlier ages had been denounced as vices. The force which produced it was the creed associated with the name of Calvin. Capitalism was the social counterpart of Calvinist theology.

In his preface to the 1936 edition of his own book, Tawney points out where he differs from Weber: 'Puritanism helped to mould the social order, but it was also itself increasingly moulded by it.' Indeed, the picture that comes over from both is one of capitalism and Protestantism moving hand in hand.

But of course there was more to the story than that. Wesley may have said: 'We must exhort all Christians to gain all they can, and to save all they can; that is, in effect, to grow rich' (though he added that they should also give all they can); but in the nineteenth century the English Nonconformist Churches tended to move away from *laissez faire*. It is generally agreed that the growth of the British Labour movement owed more to the Free Churches than to Marx. Even so, many nineteenth-century Nonconformists would still have accepted the views of one person who grew up in a Nonconformist household, Mrs Thatcher, as she expressed them in her speech printed as an appendix to this book. Though she made clear that the state has to provide for education, pensions and the sick and disabled, she laid particular stress on the individual's responsibility, and on using our talents to create wealth: '. . . it is not the creation of wealth that is wrong but love of money for its own sake.' As earlier Protestants had believed, it is not wrong to be rich, so long as you use the money well and charitably.

So much for an English view, but it is also necessary to say a little about German Protestantism and its political impact. With the loss of Prussia after 1945 Germany (West Germany, that is) lost a major element in its Protestant life. But Protestantism had anyway not been a very dynamic force in political life over time. In his *The Churches and Politics in Germany* (1973), Frederic Spotts writes:

> By instilling a sense of the inwardness of religion and the vanity of human effort in its adherents, Lutheranism had given rise over the centuries to a political passivity that in turn led to a deification of the state, whose agents were entrusted with responsibility for all public affairs. In this way Lutheranism – inherently without specific political content – not only pliantly accommodated itself to any form of government, but even became the central foundation of the prevailing political philosophy. As a result, Lutheranism in most of Germany became thoroughly conservative, patriarchal, and authoritarian. For four hundred years Luther's

catechism and his commentary on the thirteenth chapter of the Epistle to the Romans were instruments of political no less than religious indoctrination, the effect of which was to inspire a submissive political temper.

The practical consequence, as Troeltsch had observed, was both the political emasculation of Lutheranism and the inculcation in the German character of deep contradictions – the linking of Christianity with conservatism, piety with love of power, freedom of conscience with fanatical nationalism. Far from being a politically neutral element in society, German Protestantism was the main buttress of a patriarchal, militarist Prussia as she expanded her dominance over the rest of Germany. Since it was bound to the *status quo* and against democracy and progress, Troeltsch fairly concluded that 'Lutheranism opposed the modern development of the State only one degree less ardently than Catholicism'. Written at the beginning of the twentieth century, Troeltsch's words were a terrible prophecy of the disaster to which German Protestantism was helping to lead the nation.

There were, however, dissenting voices. When Hitler came to power the majority of Protestant leaders welcomed his accession, some of them enthusiastically, as bringing an end to chaos and free-thinking. But others thought differently. Concern began to grow among some about Nazi racism. Pastor Niemöller founded a league of pastors to oppose state interference in ecclesiastical affairs and in 1934 a synod took place at Barmen in the Rhineland. Influenced by the great theologian Karl Barth, a 'Confessing Church' was organised, based on the belief that the supremacy of Scripture could not be changed to suit prevailing ideology or politics. The traditional Lutheran subservience to the state was undermined – for those brave people who followed this path. According to Spotts, during the Third Reich three thousand pastors were arrested, at least 125 sent to concentration camps, and twenty-two were known to have been executed for their beliefs. The most famous, of course, was Dietrich Bonhoeffer, who after his death came to be seen, particularly abroad, as an exemplar of the good in Germany that had been so overshadowed by Hitler.

Gradually after the war the Lutherans began to agree on what had gone wrong and also to move from their traditional passive conservatism or acquiescence into a rather more active concern with social policy, but it seems fair to say that the Catholics operated in this field with a longer tradition of social doctrine behind them. Interestingly, though, the move by Cardinal Frings to establish a Catholic trade union was blocked, first by the British Control Commission, who favoured one union movement, and then by a whole range of people and groups ranging from Adenauer and the CDU to various Catholic workers' groups. And in fact the tradition of social doctrine did not mean that all was clear-cut.

This was particularly true of the question of worker participation in industrial management, which has a bearing on the contents of today's Social Charter. 'Co-determination' – by which workers were given a place on management bodies – had in fact been introduced in 1947 by the British Military Government into the Ruhr coal and steel industry. This had been widely accepted – including by both Churches – on the grounds that the concentration of economic power had damaged democracy and helped Hitler. In 1949 the Catholic lay assembly had gone on to call for co-determination in all German industry. This produced a reaction. Some of the Catholic bishops were disturbed by this; Cardinal Frings said that better results could be achieved if employers were guided by Christian charity. In June 1950 Pope Pius sought to end the argument by laying down his disapproval of co-determination. He insisted that it endangered private property rights, especially when outside bodies (i.e. trade unions) were involved.

This set the cat among the pigeons. On the one side were the Catholic bishops who felt that they could not oppose the Pope, together with German industrialists and many of the CDU who were influenced by Protestant-like economic liberalism. On the other side, however, were the Evangelical Church, the Protestant press and Catholic workers, as well as many others in the CDU. In the event Adenauer came down in favour of maintaining co-determination where it had been brought in. The argument continued to rage in German politics, but worker participation and the two-tier board have become a familiar part of the German industrial scene. As far as social policy generally is concerned, the Churches – particularly the Catholics – have been active in promoting social security and the search for a family policy.

Thinking and experience in Germany – the most powerful although perhaps still not the most assertive of the Community's members – are bound to be very influential in the development of European social policy; but of course these arguments have gone on in other member countries as well. For all its secularist tradition France has in fact a Catholic trade union movement. Jacques Delors, the President of the Commission and protagonist of the Social Charter, grew up in this movement. It is interesting to read the assessment by Ernst Haas of social thinking among Catholic trade unionists in the 1950s when 'Europe' was being created:

> For the CFTC, Catholic social doctrine provides yet another strong motive for increasing supranational loyalty. The federation is opposed to nationalisation of industries if this process merely entails state management. Its notions of industrial harmony include a corporatist, anti-class struggle and social harmony component, which it seeks to achieve in practice through tripartite commissions in all major phases of the economy, representing labour, industry and the public. As with the DGB [the German trade union organisation], but for different reasons, economic democracy was held out as the answer to the problems of modern industrialism. And as in the case of the German unions, the institutions of ECSC and of the future organs of integration provide for far more representation of trade union leaders in responsible positions of equality than do the institutions pre-

valent within the national framework. Supranationalism once more becomes the means for achieving social and economic respectability.

When it comes to Italy, Haas comments: 'the basic doctrine of the Christian-Democratic, Liberal, Republican and Social Democratic parties is unflinchingly committed to the principles of economic integration and political federation in Europe . . . Catholic doctrine supports Christian-Democratic thinking in this field, while the more mundane consideration of the expanding market doctrine appeals to the smaller parties'. But overall Haas does not argue that Christian Democracy on its own sufficed to create the ECSC: that was fundamentally due to the convergence of a range of national interests.

The Social Charter

So far in this essay I have tried to examine the extent to which the creation of the European Community has been influenced by Christian ideas and experience; I have also touched on one or two areas where Christian thinking has had an impact on politics – the nexus between Protestantism and capitalism, for example, and the influence of Christian ideas on the development of worker participation. It would be possible to take this further – for example, by examining the encyclicals of Pope Leo XIII in 1891 on *Capital and Labour* and of Pope Pius XI forty years later on *The Reconstruction of the Social Order*, and subsequent Catholic thinking. The former encyclical was marked by a fierce anti-socialism and defence of property; the latter was partly concerned to repudiate the argument that the former took the part of the rich against the non-owning workers. Pope Pius also looked sympathetically at the corporatist approach by which syndicates of workers and employers might be brought together to try to achieve harmony, though he clearly implied that Mussolini's version of corporatism was marred by too great a subservience to the state. To go into this in detail would, however, perhaps be to move too far from the questions that face us today. Yet it is worth making the point that at the heart of the change in policy brought about in the Conservative Party by Mrs Thatcher and Sir Keith Joseph after 1975 was a rejection of the corporatism that Mr Heath seemed to espouse in his 'tripartite' approach to incomes policy, and that Labour followed with its Social Contract between government and the unions. Economic liberalism became the order of the day in Britain – and that was something that neither of the two Popes would have been prepared to accept, any more than are the contemporary Catholic radicals who argue for a real shift of power from management to workers.

This brings us back to the Social Charter. There is little doubt that one reason why Mrs Thatcher has been so opposed to it is that to her it smacks not simply of socialism but also of corporatism. And for Conservatives this in turn raises the question of whether the European Community will develop as essentially a manifestation of the liberal, market economy or whether it may become a vehicle for socialism, even if only of a latter-day, social democratic kind. There are other important questions to discuss, to do with loss of national sovereignty, relations with the outside world, and competition policy generally – on all of which the Churches may have something to say; but social policy seems inescapably the particular concern of all the Churches today, and the Social Charter is therefore something of a touchstone in the Christian and the Conservative view of Europe.

What does the *Community Charter of Fundamental Social Rights* say? The preliminary draft of 30 May 1989 started with the usual European-style preamble. This referred to a variety of principles, including combating unemployment, the approximation of improved living and working conditions, improvements in the social field, combating discrimination, and various freedoms. It referred specifically to certain articles in the Treaty of Rome, as amended by the

Single European Act, covering among other things freedom of movement of workers, the right of establishment, improvement of the working environment, development of dialogue between management and labour at European level, equal pay, a common vocational training policy and economic and social cohesion.

Jacques Delors and others believe that a true internal market cannot be achieved while living and working conditions vary widely from one member state to another, and that this objective had been in the original Treaty. As a Commission press release (17 May 1989) put it, 'There will be no sustained economic growth in Europe without a social consensus.' Or as a resolution of the European Parliament stated: 'established social standards must not be undermined by the internal market. Market forces should not be allowed to determine the social framework conditions of the internal market.'

There were several areas which were likely to cause difficulty for the present British Government. One was the draft proposal that all employment should be 'fairly remunerated' and that either the law or collective agreements should ensure a 'decent' wage and a method of equitable payment for workers on part-time or temporary contracts. This could clash with the proposed abolition of wages councils and the end of any mechanism for settling minimum wages. Next, the charter proposed a right to strike such as exists in France and Italy. Britain does not have such a right, based on the automatic suspension of contracts of employment, but only a limited series of trade union immunities.

The draft also proposed a 'maximum duration of working time per week', a right to annual paid leave and a weekly rest period. Annual leave is a statutory right in all EC countries except the UK and Italy, and there is a statutory limit on working hours in all except the UK and Denmark. Most controversial, however, was the right to information, consultation and participation of workers. The draft proposed that forms of worker participation should be developed, 'in such a way as to take account of the laws, contractual agreements and practices in force in the Member States'. Nine out of twelve of them provide legally for works councils representing employees who must be informed of major developments. Ireland, Greece and the UK do not.

Britain's objections to all this were stated very firmly by the Secretary of State for Employment, Norman Fowler, and then the Prime Minister in June 1989. Mr Fowler said that to sign the charter would be to sign a blank cheque before anyone had defined what the rights would be and what they would cost'. Since the charter is said to be seen as a quarry for legislation in Brussels, this reaction is understandable. The Prime Minister had already said in her Bruges speech of September 1989 that 'we certainly do not need new regulations which raise the cost of employment and make Europe's labour market less flexible and less competitive with overseas suppliers,' and she reiterated this view when she reported to the House of Commons on the Madrid Summit where the charter was briefly discussed. The CBI expressed its concern that the charter should assist, not hinder, the creation of jobs and wealth. Not surprisingly the Labour reaction was very different.

Another dimension to the question of the social role of the Community has been raised by Jacques Delors. In the *Guardian* of 6 October 1989 he is quoted as saying that the revival of the European Community has already proved to be a magnet attracting the people of Eastern Europe, nourishing their hopes and giving them the courage to implement necessary reforms. But it was not just the economic vitality of the Community which was doing this; it was also its political and social ideals: 'Think of the effect it has in Prague, in Warsaw, in Budapest, in East Berlin and in Leipzig, when the Community declares solemnly, by means of a Social Charter, that it will not subordinate fundamental workers' rights to economic efficiency.' This was one reason why he and his colleagues would do all they could to implement the proposed Social Charter.

The question for Conservatives was whether resistance to all this is the wisest stance. In an article in *The Times* (7 September 1989) Ronald Butt accepted that the Social Charter as it stood would mean backdoor socialism, vitiating genuine managerial judgments, and be 'an economic and political disaster'. Even if it remained 'simply an approved list of generalised descriptions, it could be enforced only by an international court of judges who (in the deplorable Bill of Rights manner) would have to adjudicate between the imperatives of one ringing generality and another according to their own say-so'. But in fact it would almost certainly be translated into laws imposing specific modes of employee participation, 'fair' remuneration, 'decent' wages and other social 'rights' – which the Government would then have to force through Parliament in Britain, without the possibility of amendment.

Clearly an unappealing prospect: nevertheless, Mr Butt asked: 'is it wise simply to damn it and stand aside, leaving it to the TUC, Labour, M. Delors and the Brussels bureaucrats to lead the argument about "social Europe"? . . . Would it not be better for Mrs Thatcher and the Government to be fighting for their own version of what the Community can say about social matters?' Specifically, might it not make sense to support an approach based on the German emphasis on consultation within workplaces? This could help promote workplace bargaining, as opposed to blanket national pay awards.

There is, in my view, considerable force in what Mr Butt has to say. I certainly would be opposed to any move back to the corporatist ideas which were fashionable in the 1970s or to pile unnecessary costs on to industry. But it is very doubtful whether 'social Europe' will – or indeed should – go away. For one thing, social policy is firmly entrenched in the Treaty of Rome. Article 117 states that 'Member States agree upon the need to promote improved working conditions and an improved standard of living for workers, so as to make possible their harmonisation while improvement is being maintained . . .' Article 118 lists the various areas where the Commission has 'the task of promoting co-operation between Member States in the social field . . .' Both the Economic and Social Committee of the Community and the European Parliament have formally supported movement in the social dimension, which preceded the publication of the draft charter. When the latter was brought forward in May 1989, only the UK opposed it outright, although Denmark asked for more time in which to consider it. It will clearly be very difficult for Britain to block all development.

There is also a certain logic in the argument that some degree of harmonisation of those social policy elements which impose costs on industry is a legitimate element in competition policy. This could apply to safety and working conditions, occupational hygiene and environmental factors, social security and perhaps training. It is important to note that social policy is still – as it was when the Community began – essentially related to the area of employment. It does *not* cover the whole gamut of health, housing, education and social security policy, however much it might be thought that M. Delors would like to move into those realms.

But there is another aspect which it is particularly important for Conservatives to consider. Although the Social Charter is thought of as a vehicle for socialism, this is not necessarily so. The charter would certainly recognise the right to strike and the right to belong to a union – but it would also recognise the right of any individual *not* to belong and not to be penalised for his decision. Thus it would appear to rule out the closed shop – pre-entry and post-entry. Over the years, Conservatives have had at least as much to offer in the realm of social policy and working conditions as Labour has. It would be a mistake to refuse to contemplate continuing to do this on a European scale. This can be perfectly compatible with the principle of 'subsidiarity' reiterated by Mr John Major at the 1989 Conservative Party Conference: namely, that collective European policy decisions are only justified when there is a real reason for taking them at European level rather than at national level. Indeed, 'subsidiarity' is accepted too in the draft charter.

Of course, there are some Conservatives who would prefer to go beyond the mere notion of subsidiarity, and like the idea of taking decisions on a European scale for its own sake. They are not frightened by the idea of a steady move towards a more cohesive and united Community, and respond more readily to the vision that inspired Monnet and his successors. But in Britain at least their hour has clearly not yet come: it is enough to concentrate on a more limited strengthening of certain Community powers.

The argument about the Social Charter continued during the latter half of 1989. In an attempt to achieve consensus, the Commission softened the text considerably: a number of controversial features were either watered down or accepted as being matters for national rather than community decision. By the time of the European Council at Strasbourg in December, European trade unionists were beginning to complain that it had lost its force. Nevertheless, Mrs Thatcher stood apart from her fellow heads of government by declining to accept the charter. Others had reservations – the Germans, for example; but they did not carry them through to the point of dissent. Yet Mrs Thatcher's opposition was not particularly ferocious: it was more in terms of agreement to differ. And since the charter is a quarry for legislation rather than itself a binding legislative instrument it was perfectly possible for the United Kingdom to take the view that it would judge directives and other measures flowing from it on their merits as and when they were put forward.

Only time can show how important the Social Charter really is. From the British point of view, perhaps the most surprising immediate consequence of it was the decision of the Labour Party not just to accept it in principle, but also to accept the right to join or *not join* a trade union – a dramatic change in Labour policy.

The European Future

I have concentrated on social policy because it is in this field that the interests of modern Christians are most obviously likely to be engaged. But there are other areas where questions for Conservative (and other) Christians arise.

One of them is certainly the Community's attitude towards the Third World or the developing countries. It has long been recognised in the Community that it should not simply be concerned with its own prosperity, and the fact that it includes all the former colonial powers has both helped and shaped this commitment. The main instruments have been the successive Lomé Conventions with, in effect, the former colonies in Africa, the Caribbean and the Pacific. On top of this, there is a programme of aid for the so-called 'non-associated' countries, for example in the Indian sub-continent.

Like many of the Community's activities, its aid programme has been characterised by a mixture of idealism and self-interest. Food aid has played a considerable part – and behind that has been the desire to find ways of mopping up the massive agricultural surpluses. Britain's Conservative Government has taken the lead both in tackling the problem of over-production and in opposing the indiscriminate use of food aid, which can so undermine indigenous food production. Food aid can help to support the labour element in development projects and of course the surpluses have proved valuable in tackling the dire famines that have arisen in East Africa and elsewhere. But overall the Community – like educated opinion generally – has come to see its drawbacks.

The Lomé approach is more genuinely developmental. The conventions are about trade as well as aid, which is clearly as it should be. By and large, Britain's position has been positive over trade – for instance over beef and sugar from our former colonies; but we have tended to be back-markers on the aid side. This has been partly a product of our desire to hold down Community expenditure, but also specifically a result of the system by which the Treasury docks the British aid programme of the amount deemed to be Britain's Community spending. For every additional pound of Community aid spending the Overseas Development Administration has one pound less to spend – which is not exactly a stimulus to greater ODA support for the Community's programmes.

In spite of this, Britain has become more sympathetic to, and involved in, the Community's aid efforts than it was a few years back. We have stressed the need for greater cost-effectiveness (and naturally done what we can to achieve a greater share of contracts for British companies); except perhaps on the question of Lomé funding, our approach is now seen as positive. Aid is, of course, an area where Christian involvement is considerable, and while the aid lobby is often critical of the scale of government spending on aid there is generally a good working partnership between government and the voluntary organisations – helped by increasing support by government for the latter, administered normally with a light touch.

The development of the Community's aid or co-operation programme is one where we may well see intensified Christian pressure and involvement in the future. The voluntary agencies may start to work increasingly on a pan-Community scale, both as pressure groups and as operational agencies. This might well be matched by a greater willingness by member countries to pool their activities, anyway in limited respects. We have to be realistic: aid is seen as both a political and commercial, as well as an altruistic, instrument and no member country is going to jeopardise significant bi-lateral relationships or commercial opportunities. But at the very least in some of the poorer and least influential countries – perhaps those in the Horn of Africa – there is a case for pooling the programmes of the different Community countries under one administration.

If social policy and aid are the matters in the Community where a Christian dimension seems most evident, what about the major topics of the completion of the internal market and the Community's part in a wider Europe? As we have seen, social policy impinges on competition policy: but what about the general question of whether there is a specifically Christian view on the free movement of people, goods and capital across national boundaries? Perhaps the Protestant might support this on grounds that would have appealed to his free market forebears, or the Catholic see in it some sort of revival of the easy movement that characterised mediaeval Christendom at its most ideal. They both have their appeal; but in contemporary terms the Christian concern will probably be to see that market policy does not bear heavily on particular groups or regions. But Conservatives will hope and believe that the greater ease of movement of people seems to embody the kind of freedom that Christians should uphold – while at the very least the free movement of goods and capital seems in line with the parables of the Sower and the Talents.

The question of the wider Europe – though again one that can perfectly easily be discussed without reference to Christian principles – is nevertheless one where the historic and cultural role of Christianity is of great significance: and Conservatives (following, for example, Burke and T. S. Eliot) should have a strong sense of these things. Clearly we must not allow our response to the developments in Eastern Europe to weaken either the economic gains that have flowed from the Common Market or our NATO-based security – and I do not believe that the West Germans ultimately differ from that view. But subject to that we should welcome any prospect of bringing the Eastern Europeans back into the true European fold. To both the Christian and the Conservative, Cracow, Chartres, Cologne and Canterbury must seem rich in shared resonances. And if we have to cede, as it were by contract, some of our independence of action to bring about these wider gains I do not see that that is a denial of either our Christianity or our Conservatism. A loss of national sovereignty is probably harder to stomach for Conservatives than for Christians. Catholics essentially belong to an international Church, and

Anglicans no longer simply the Church of England (even if still largely, around the world, an English-speaking Church). But Conservatives can be even less tied by dogma than Anglicans: in the event their attitude towards the evolution of a federal Europe is more likely to be influenced by a pragmatic weighing up of the pros and cons than by any inexorable principle other than what they see to be for the good of the British people.

15

Conserving the Family

John Gummer, MP

THE fact that two out of three marriages succeed ought not
to blind us to the growing problem of marriage breakdown
in Britain. We now have the highest rate of divorce in the
European Community as well as record figures for illegitimacy and abortion. The brave words of the sixties when
'liberal' laws on moral issues were seen as ushering in a
more tolerant and a happier society have an increasingly
hollow ring.

The Church has been at the centre of this major shift in
attitudes and cannot avoid some of the blame. It was the
report *Putting Asunder* which promoted the concept of 'no
fault' divorce where breakdown of marriage displaced the
matrimonial offence as the reason upon which a divorce
could be granted. That proposition inevitably led to a much
greater social acceptance of divorce. Now that there is no
need to prove any wrong-doing, divorce is increasingly
seen as a normal and acceptable way of arranging to take on
a second partner. It has become the 'right' of anyone who
could show that he no longer got on with a first spouse. It
has culminated in the proposition now being canvassed by
the Law Commission for England and Wales that agreed
divorces need no longer concern the courts at all but
become a mere matter of administrative arrangement to
tidy up an otherwise awkward situation. Indeed, it is
argued that the proposal to shorten the time before a

divorce may be sought to a single year in Scotland is a sign that the Law Commission there has spurned the radical proposal favoured in England! Even so it appalled many Conservative politicians and led to a free vote even among Cabinet Ministers – rare indeed on a Government Bill. Yet the idea of such 'quickie' divorces was supported by the Church of Scotland hierarchy.

This contrast between the antagonism of lay people in the Churches and the dedicated support for radical proposals shown by ecclesiastical activists has become increasingly marked. The Church of England General Synod voted overwhelmingly to ordain divorced and remarried men, yet its legislation was lost in the House of Commons on the first occasion and only passed finally on the strength of votes from atheists and agnostics.

Why then is there this real concern for the traditionalist view which is showing itself among lay Christians despite the course maintained by much of the Church Establishment? Some of it, of course, arises from the wider pressures which have given such impetus to traditionalist resurgence. Those who perceive Christian teaching to be undermined across the board by liberal interpretations of the gospels focus upon the 'new morality' as a prime example of their case. They look to a restatement of the Church's teaching on personal morality as an essential part of returning to a more vigorous defence of the historic faith.

Yet, even for those who are not so generally engaged, there is a growing concern at the practical effects of the liberalisation of attitudes towards marriage and divorce. This worry is perhaps concentrated on what has happened to the social welfare system. When the Finer Report gave form to the widespread pressure to help one-parent families in 1974 it was suggested that there were 620,000 such units. Today we are talking about nearly twice that number. With record illegitimacy rates – the eight per cent in 1971 had risen to 25 per cent in 1988 – we must expect even greater expansion. So the problems of poverty will increasingly be dominated by the plight of the lone-parent and child.

Many local authorities admit that their housing policy favours those who have children and are unmarried against those who have waited to start a family. Just as the inheritance laws in fiercely Roman Catholic Poland drove large numbers into the divorce courts in order that both partners could keep their inheritance, so our preference for aiding those with children born outside marriage or in a failed marriage is encouraging couples to order their lives so that they can qualify for state funding. Playing the system which Beveridge designed to help poor families bring their children up decently has increasingly made it a system which weights the scales against the family and encourages 'alternative' life styles. People have become convinced that it is their right to divorce, leaving the state to pick up the bill. In this they are encouraged by a Church which seeks to blame the Government for lack of spending in these areas rather than to ask itself what it can do to help change the underlying situation. The fundamental seriousness of the present position cannot be overstated. Every two families that stay together will be paying for the one that breaks up.

For the Christian that neighbourly cost might cheerfully be borne if it were not for the increasing evidence that the very existence of such provision itself contributes to the breakdown of marriage. Not that we ought to be surprised. The fact that marriage is commonplace does not mean that it is easy. Even those of us who have been granted very happy and stable marriages know that they pass through difficult periods and, indeed, real crises. Yet it is precisely that understanding which leads us to recognise that those who seek to uphold the excellence of lifelong union need the support of an institution which is clearly seen as indissoluble. We are far more likely to work out our problems in a situation where we recognise that we have to make marriage work than one in which it is possible to opt out when the going gets tough. There is no question that a tolerance of divorce leads to a growth in the divorce rate.

Yet Christians have become frightened of upholding the traditional view of the family lest we be accused of smugness or of failing to understand. The need to show sympathy to the unfortunate has led us to refuse to face the truth of our present position. As more and more marriages fail and resulting social stigma is a thing of the past people will increasingly accept divorce as a normal way out of their marital troubles and see less and less reason for working at marriage. The personal happiness of the partners who willingly entered the bond carries greater weight than the security of the children who had no say in the matter. And the egalitarian instincts of the British insist that the right to sequential marriage shall be available to all. Even though most people find it a struggle to bring up one family and meet the bills it is taken for granted that poverty should be no impediment to divorce and remarriage. Those who find it inconvenient to meet the cost are, for the most part, relieved of the responsibility by the tax-payer. It would, of course, be unacceptable to suggest that those who cannot afford to keep two families should not seek a second. Yet the assumption that everyone has a right to divorce and remarriage even if they have not also the means inevitably results in others paying for the children.

Indeed, in the richer sectors of society the problem of the cost of multiple marriage has long been addressed and it is only in very recent budgets that the tax advantages of paying for children of former marriages after divorce have been reduced. Even so, it is still true that it is cheaper for a rich man to educate children after divorce than before. Again, the poorer tax-payer, struggling to keep his own family, is asked to foot part of the bill of the better-off demanding the right to divorce.

Greater still is the cost to us all of the social security bill. Over 80 per cent of all single-parent families rely on benefits – almost all of them non-contributory and therefore funded entirely from general taxation. In 1979 only 43 per cent of such families received benefits. By 1988–9 the tax-payer was spending £3.4 billion – nearly three times as much as in

1981. The more those benefits are available and the greater the range of housing opportunities to which single parents are more readily entitled than two-parent families, the more people will see single parenthood as a real option.

All the evidence now points to the devastation which family break-up wreaks. Stability in the home is increasingly seen by research to be an essential part of the successful upbringing of the next generation. The mere presence of both parents in whatever circumstances seems to be of real importance. The work done by Professor Hind of Cambridge University graphically illustrated the damage done to children by marriage breakdown. I quote all this as if we need the proof of the scientists. Yet instinctively we have understood it for generations. We only doubt it at all because we are embarrassed to rely on anecdotal evidence and we prefer instead to seek other material to support the conclusions which experience has taught us.

A society does have to make up its mind whether it intends to safeguard marriage or not. It is not a subject upon which it can be neutral. At the moment our arrangements undermine the stability of the family with results which are increasingly recognised. If we decide that the state should support the family unit as an essential element in the stability of society then we have to ensure that our legislation recognises that concern and will reinforce that priority. It is not that we believe that divorce can be legislated out of existence or that marriages can be made happy by Act of Parliament. It is merely that we need to set a tone in society which will tend towards upholding the marriage bond, in place of the contrary attitude that recent legal changes have fostered. Lifelong marriage is the norm for which we must legislate. To steal a construction from Mazzini, divorce, *prima facie*, demands an apology. Marriages ought not to be ended merely by the couple living apart, nor should they be finished at the behest of one party. The law ought to insist that this contract cannot be broken unilaterally but only by due process in which the reason for the voiding of the contract is clearly recognised.

This would begin again to emphasise that divorce is the abnormal ending of a marriage and not an accepted and generally applied way out of a freely engaged contractual relationship. The one thing that the Permissive Society has done is to ensure that marriage can be fully voluntary and considered!

Yet the need to reassert the stability of marriage does not demand only that we make divorce more difficult. It asks also that we take the responsibilities of child-bearing more seriously. One of the most heartening and yet most humbling moments for a parent is when, late at night, he or she checks on the children asleep in their beds. Their vulnerability and utter dependence, their confidence that tomorrow you will be there – that is the point when the seriousness of what you have undertaken and the overwhelming importance of stability really strikes home. It is then a particular condemnation of the present state of marriage in Britain that the realisation of that responsibility is at an all-time low.

Among single-parent families the proportion which receive any help from the fathers has halved during the last ten years. The social security system makes it of little interest to the mother whether her income derives from the state or from the father. She loses benefit pound for pound and is often unwilling to pursue unpaid maintenance or even, increasingly, to name the father at all. Yet for society there is a world of difference. The growing number of men who believe it perfectly right that others should shoulder the burdens which they have chosen to create undermine any concept of a responsible society. The cost to the taxpayer is considerable and that cost is often borne by those who are already meeting their own family commitments. Yet more sinister, it is an attitude which further promotes the view that the baby is a concern of the mother and is her business alone.

All this points to the need to insist that provision for the children must be a central issue of divorce hearings and that some effective attachment of earnings and sharing in

income growth must be devised. Those who fear for the
effect of such pre-emption on any future relationship beg
the question. The prior responsibility of children must be
upheld. Divorce cannot continue to be a means of shedding
responsibilities. Instead it must confirm those responsibilities in a form which enables two people to live apart and
still fulfil the undertakings which parenthood implies. In an
age and society where conception is in almost all cases
voluntary, it must be reasonable to insist that people take
responsibility for their actions. Such an attitude to the
individual and his place in the family ought to be a natural
one for the Church. Yet little has been heard in Synods of
demands that fathers, divorced or never married, should
support their children. A rediscovery of the theology of
judgment would remind us that we are all called to account
at the Last Day and that to construct a society in which men
are encouraged not to be accountable is to deny one of the
most fundamental of Christian insights.

Here Conservative policies seem much nearer the traditional understanding of the gospels than much of contemporary Christian social comment. It seems that the
corporatist attitudes of the sixties have so far affected the
views of today's Church leaders that they fall over each
other in the rush to make the Government responsible. In
the past there would have been a clear call to the individual
to accept his own responsibilities and then to the community to create the conditions within which such acceptance would be most effectively ensured. Only then would
come the call to create a society which helps those for whom
the demands are too great to bear.

The primacy of personal responsibility comes from the
Christian understanding that choice is at the heart of being
human. God gave us the opportunity of choosing between
good and evil – between heaven and hell. The chance to
choose is therefore not peripheral but at the centre of any
Christian conception of the nature of man. It is, after all,
choice which distinguishes us from the rest of creation. We
are placed a little lower than the angels but we shall reign

with God on high. It is our privilege as loved beings to be given the responsibility to choose for ourselves and thereby the chance to join in God's own creative work. That very privilege has its cost. The chance to choose heaven implies the chance to reject it. So it is not given to Christians to deny personal responsibility merely because they fear that some will exercise it badly. Instead we must affirm that individual accountability is the most precious gift. It alone enables us to love and to be loved. Without it our actions and desires are the product solely of instinct and never of choice. So to take away individual responsibility and to lay all upon the state is to dehumanise humanity. We are all accountable and that is our glory.

To make those who choose to be parents bear the cost of that choice – even though it be to their own hindrance – is wholly in accordance with a Christian understanding of the nature of man. Yet it is not enough to rest there. We do have a duty so to construct society that people find it conducive to doing what is right. To force men and women to do right is not to love them but no more is it loving to make wrong-doing easy. It cannot therefore be sensible to have a system where there are positive advantages for the irresponsible. That is why we ought to reconsider our policy of providing priority housing to unmarried parents in preference to those who have sought to ensure stability first. So too the changes in taxation to remove the advantages once accorded to the unmarried couple over the married was an essential part in creating the conditions conducive to morality.

So we must make staying together easier than breaking up; we must insist that parents bear their responsibility outside as well as inside marriage; and we must ensure that the married state carries privileges and not disadvantages.

Such a policy makes a statement about marriage and its primacy which ought to be welcomed by the Church. Yet it will require commensurate action among Christians if it is to be successful. Just as the signals given by the Church in the fifties promoted the Permissive Society, so a change of heart among Church leaders can do much to signpost the return of the old morality today. What an example it would be if clergy whose marriage difficulties led to divorce invariably lived as celibate priests thereafter in order to uphold the sanctity of lifelong marriage! How real a support to those who sought to live out their marriage vows would it be if the Church of England insisted on that discipline as a matter of canonical course! Is it too much to ask of those who stand at the altar representing Christ?

Of course, the Church of England will need to look again at its more general marriage discipline. It cannot continue without some kind of nullity provision nor can it allow marriages of divorced couples to take place in some churches while the vast majority rightly refuses them. A sensible procedure about nullity makes a clear and unequivocal ban on second marriages in church both possible and principled.

A state which declares itself on the side of marriage has a right to expect that the Church will itself support an institution blessed by our Lord in Cana and central to all Christian views of society since. But it cannot end there. Both Church and State need to establish marriage as the norm and other circumstances as deviant. We must declare ourselves if we are to give men and women the chance and the encouragement to uphold the best. It is not intolerant so to dignify and distinguish marriage from other relationships. It is merely to trumpet abroad that society's future depends upon the stability brought about by marriage and that it is in its interest therefore to promote it. So too the Church, which prohibits sexual relationships outside marriage, has an even greater interest in making marriage an institution which society recognises as in its best interests and therefore to be encouraged.

That does mean that it is not possible for such a society to see alternative life styles in the same way as it sees traditional marriage. It ought, for example, to be tolerant of homosexual relationships but not suggest that they are in any way to be encouraged or recognised as parallel with marriage. A civilised society can properly draw a distinction between what it allows and what it encourages. It is not unreasonable to maintain a clear preference for the proper state of things while still not persecuting those who choose to behave differently. We have swung from the barbarity of locking homosexuals up to the moral anarchy of encouraging the subculture.

The inability of the Church to restate its traditional teaching on extra-marital sexual relationships has led to the present impossible position where for Anglicans the official statement of these matters is that heterosexual intercourse outside marriage is sinful while homosexual intercourse is 'less than the ideal'. Apart from this being a formulation unrecognised by any previous generation of Christians, it does indeed mean that it is less sinful to sleep with one's neighbour than with one's neighbour's wife – a position hardly consonant with Scripture, or indeed with reason.

Indeed it has been one of the real disappointments of the tolerant country, that decriminalisation is not enough. Since the enactment of the recommendations of the Wolfenden Report we have seen growing pressures from those who want tolerance turned to acceptance and acceptance turned to promotion and missionary zeal. It is a demand whose fulfilment would turn a society marked by civilised tolerance into one characterised by apathy and finally by immorality. A Conservative society recognises the need for communal standards as well as minority protection. In this it accepts the traditionalist Christian approach for the community to set a tone which promotes virtue and discourages vice.

The true promotion of that which society sees as good demands that we regain control of the language which has long been the object of radical attack. When the Department of the Environment issued its standard community charge registration form to serve as a guideline to local authorities it asked for the name of 'husband, wife or partner'. In extremist councils the word 'husband' and 'wife' were dropped and the nature of marriage immediately devalued to the level of living together. So too we have allowed that important family occasion – the naming of a child – to be devalued as government forms ask for 'forenames' instead of 'Christian names'. A tolerant society might ask for 'forenames' as an alternative. Only the apathetic would allow yet another element in the stability of the family to be removed by those whose commitment to multi-culturalism verges on the anarchic.

In the same way we must not allow the extreme feminists to press their case to the destruction of the family, and nowhere is that more important than in the usurpation of the language. Christianity is a family religion. Its God has a Son. That Son has a Mother. The images of *Abba*, Father (or more accurately Daddy), must not be destroyed by the advocates of inclusive language. The intolerance of liberalism is the real enemy of Christian civilisation. For the advocate of egalitarianism no other insight may be retained; all must be swept away in the cause of anti-sexism, anti-racism and anti-discrimination. Like all heresies these start with a dollop of truth and exaggerate into a mountain of mischievous nonsense.

Recapturing the language also means insistence on spades being called spades, even when civilised behaviour leads us to avoid bloody shovels. It may be too late to reclaim the word 'gay' for its original use. But we ought not to have allowed the language to be misused to dignify the deviant.

Christians and Conservatives ought to be as one in reclaiming marriage as the key institution for the stability of society and the nurturing of children. The carpenter's house in Galilee is the model for every Christian. The state cannot ensure by Acts of Parliament that all of us will even begin to imitate it. It can, however, seek to build a society which clearly recognises the superiority of the standards it portrays, and encourages all our people to reach after them.

16

Responsible and Accountable

Ruth Etchells

Before God thou shalt answer . . .
How thou hast spent thy life, and in what wise,
Before the Chief Lord of Paradise.

THOSE are some key lines from *The Summoning of Everyman*,
a popular play in mediaeval times, now studied regularly in
our schools and colleges. Reading that play with students
of the 1970s and 1980s, one thing has been very striking. For
them the ultimate threat and reward of hell or heaven are at
best questionable, at worst offensive; yet regularly these
children of a largely secular culture are gripped and com-
pelled by the play's tension, as the final judgment in it
approaches. Why? One reason is that this 500-year-old play
uses the same method as some of our greatest modern
playwrights, like Stoppard and Osborne and Pinter, for
exactly the same purpose: to expose the members of the
audience to that audience's hidden but inherent sense of
being 'under judgment', of being in some way individually
'accountable', with all the anxiety, even dread, that attends
it.

But accountable to whom, or what? The answer seems
clear enough in the mediaeval play. There, every individual
bears responsibility, for which he or she will answer to God
at a solemn 'summons' after death. How far is this a
mediaeval view, long abandoned by Christians? Or is there

behind it an irreducible element of Christian theology which might productively engage with that often formless, anxious sense of 'accountability' in a modern audience?

It was precisely this question about a Christian understanding of personal accountability which the Prime Minister raised when she made a remark which Professor Griffiths has explained in this book but which has been quoted with disfavour in more than one church report: 'there is no such thing as society'. She was asking, sharply and memorably, for a serious response on what we believe about the relative nature of individual responsibility and societal responsibility, about their inter-action, and about the role of an elected government within that. We are reminded that, though such a response may – or must – issue eventually in a political agenda, we have to start from theology, that is, from what the Christian faith teaches of human accountability within a universe created and sustained by the God and Father of the Lord Jesus Christ. Put simply, the question is one which faces Everyman – and woman: to whom or what, for whom or what, do Christians say each of us must answer?

To reply, we have to recover a fuller sense than has recently been the case of the Christian doctrine of Judgment in its individual as well as its societal application. For Christian beliefs about human accountability begin, where the Old Testament does, from an absolute affirmation that God is in charge, that he both owns his creation and cares about it, that he rules his people and prescribes for them, individually and corporately, a way of being and a destiny in accord with his righteousness; and that in some ultimate way he takes account of offence against this, and sets it right.

To the righteous Yahweh of the Old Testament the nations are accountable as nations, each carrying a collective responsibility – a concept alien to the thinking of many today, for whom such a notion of coherent collectivity, and hence accountability, has no clear content in a pluralistic society. Many today, too, would strongly question the parallel notion that God punishes nations for wrong-doing. But in the Old Testament the thought springs from the theological conviction that God is righteous, is ruler of all, and is not mocked. Hence the teaching of the prophets that if a nation sins it will suffer. This stark 'rewards and punishments' view, however, is in the later books of the Old Testament, for instance in Job and in the Suffering Servant passages of Isaiah, balanced by a profound exposition of the theological dilemma of innocent human suffering and the prosperity of wrong-doers. And this gives depth to that which always distinguishes the Old Testament God, as Judge, from contemporary religions: that he is a God who seeks a relationship, expressed in personal terms, between himself and his people. Their accountability to him and his care of them are the two sides of the 'Covenant', the relationship which the Commandments express for the nation in personal language ('Thou shalt'), using personal pronouns of God ('I', 'Me').

It is this Covenant which, later, is behind the Gospel understanding of God as 'Judge', and the 'Judgment' that therefore lies between God and man. The uniqueness of Jesus's own message has this 'judgment', this covenanted human accountability to a righteous and caring God, at its very heart. The Synoptic Gospels describe him as teaching that a new kind of covenanted 'Kingdom of God' is *come*, one in which God's righteousness still holds total sway, and yet in which, against all the odds, human accountability can answer to it. The Gospel of John describes this in another way: God's righteousness is actually, materially present in the world, because it is 'made flesh' in Jesus himself; and therefore Jesus's own presence is, itself, the dreaded 'Judgment'. Any goodness always is, of course, a 'judgment' among us because we see and know the truth about ourselves by its light; but in this case, uniquely so. The Gospel – the 'Good News' – that Jesus declares is that God's 'Judgment' should be looked at with hope and thanksgiving, because we shall find in it not terror but deliverance from our deepest fears and griefs. God who is

Ruler as well as Judge, the God who is ultimately 'in charge', has, through Jesus, provided a way of matching the requirements of his absolute justice with our inadequate human responsibility.

All the Gospel descriptions of Jesus's life and teaching and acts of healing are about this astonishing paradox: that God treats human accountability with complete and transforming mercy at the same time as he meets the requirements of absolute justice. For us, however, standing this side of Calvary, it is supremely the Cross and Easter which give what Jesus said and did power and authoritative content: they are the 'how', the means by which mercy and truth can meet together. For Easter following the Cross means that when God shares human accountability in the person of Jesus, he takes to himself the grief and distress of our failure as responsible beings, and touches that failure with new and transforming life. Jürgen Moltmann put it powerfully in *The Crucified God*:

> God humbles Himself and takes upon Himself the eternal death of the Godless and Godforsaken, so that all the Godless and the Godforsaken can experience communion with Him. Whatever proceeds from the event between Father and Son must be understood as the spirit of surrender of the Father and the Son, as the spirit which creates love for forsaken men, as the spirit which brings dead men alive.

If we are to hear what Christians have to say about individual and social responsibility, then above all we must grasp this central part of the Gospel. It says, quite simply, that, yes, human beings are accountable, and to a God whose nature is absolute good, before whose just and pure scrutiny fallible, sliding humanity knows itself in the wrong. Such a knowledge of failed accountability carries with it fear and destructiveness. By sharing that, taking it upon himself to the utmost in the abjectness of the Cross, and then defeating the death in it through the mystery of the Resurrection, God has given humanity, even the most godless and rejected of us, new and confident life. This is not simply a way of 'picturing' what God has done in that mighty act. It is not 'like' being given a new heart and new life: it actually 'is' a new heart and a new life, and it creates a new way of being before God.

For many people today, as a recent Nobel prize-winner put it, 'God doesn't rule over men as He used to, and for a long time people haven't been able to feel that life was firmly attached at both ends so that they could confidently stand in the middle' (Saul Bellow, in *Mosby's Memoirs*). Many have yet felt 'accountable', but to no purpose. As Arthur Miller describes it through one of his characters, there seems little point to the struggle for quality of living if there is not going to be any verdict on it anyway. When his experience was that God's 'bench was empty. No judge in sight,' then all that remained was 'the endless argument with oneself – this pointless litigation of existence before an empty bench.' But a Christian theology of accountability has something powerful to offer in the face of such loss of significance. It restores to humankind, even to the most humble and marginalised of any society, a sense of human worth. For such a doctrine of Judgment declares the personal investment in our destiny of the Supreme and Most High God, and it therefore affirms that our doings, indeed our very being, not only matter but are the object of the most intimate, unforgetting and caring scrutiny by the Creator God himself, not to our destruction but to our good.

For Christians understand God's activity in Judgment, in holding humanity finally to account, as two-fold: a 'right discerning' and a 'setting right'. In the Bible a judge is not primarily punitive, but the one who creates order and restores what has been destroyed. But any final 'setting right' by the Divine Judge has to be trusted in beyond time, secured by our certainties about the nature of God, since we by no means always perceive its operation within time. Hence the concept of 'the Day', 'the Last Day', 'the great and terrible Day', 'the Day of Judgment'. It is the Day on which the persecuting nations will get their deserts. It is also the point at which those within the community who have by their sins weakened and burdened the nation will meet their due. It is a Day to be looked for eagerly by the pious, when God's justice will be seen, vindicating them in all its awful power. It is also the Day on which the nation will itself be held to account; and the Day when each individual will know his reckoning, whether he or she is counted amongst the righteous or the sinful. So the Day is one of terror or hope, of potential total loss or potential total joy.

Jesus's parables about such a Day of accounting, as we have them in the gospels, sometimes cast it in the form of a trial; for instance, the story of the final tribunal, dividing humanity like sheep and goats to left and right, allocating eternal reward or loss as deserved. But they also give us with equal power other very different pictures of this final gathering up. It is a feast to which all are summoned – and guests not there are absent by their own choice. It is a sheep-gathering for which the lost lamb is tenderly sought that it might be part of the flock. It is above all a home-coming, at which the prodigal and penitent child is received joyfully and tearfully and with utmost celebration by a longing and loving Father.

It is in the light of these pictures that we should understand the 'trial' parables of Judgment. Karl Barth reminds us that 'the Judge who puts some on the left and others on the right is he who has yielded himself to the judgment of God for me and has taken all malediction from me'. Hence though our final accounting is to be understood as a real event, and to be contemplated with awe, yet through the mercy of God we may look to it 'with head erect', as the Heidelberg Catechism puts it.

We need to pause over what this implies about time and eternity. 'Accountability' is not a matter of taking responsibility for either this life or hereafter, one or the other: for the Christian, the two are firmly bonded. We live this life in the intersection of eternity with time, and to be human is to be finite yet already admitted, in some sort, to 'beyond time', a condition of infiniteness given content and shape through the grace of Jesus Christ. One might wonder whether our feebleness as a Church in the face of disaster and – particularly – bereavement, lies in our diminished certainties about this eternal dimension to our existence. The power of Jesus Christ for our right living of this life is constrained if we do not recognise that his good news is not only for time but for eternity. Time and space and our role in them, society and the world and our role in them, our nation and our family and our role in them, our Church and our most private and inner relationship with God and our role in them – all these can only be fully valued, responsibly and effectively lived, as we view them and live them in the eternal dimension of which Christ has made us free.

There will come to each of us, in some way, a point where we must answer to God for our lives in the times in which we are placed, with all their local challenges to right living. Even if till that point the truth has not really seized us, there is no avoiding at some time the awful cost which gives us the pass. 'Sometimes it causes me to tremble, tremble, tremble . . .' the old negro spiritual goes. Indeed it must! We need to recover our sense of being accountable, not as some suppressed sense of unease, but as a thoughtful perception of reality which will affect the way we live. If the nation is to do this, then the Church itself needs to take a fresh grasp of it, having itself come dangerously close at times to offering a 'cheap grace' almost wholly social and time-bound in its consequence.

Being 'responsible' to that ultimate extent must begin from developing the capacity to discriminate, to judge the basic distinctions between good and evil and to apply them. This capacity to know 'good', and name it, and to know 'evil', and name it, to our personal lives and that of our nation, is fundamental to our human identity as accountable beings, and some consider that its loss is one of the more dreadful experiences of our present culture. A society which disregards this in its education system, in its legal system, in its public affairs, let alone in its spiritual life, would be at serious risk of disintegration, because it would have drifted into the corruption of irresponsibility. A government and a Church which took no action amidst such drift would fail in their own accountability to their people.

This raises sharply for us the fact that today our society must establish for itself 'good' and 'evil', must find a mode of accountability which does not depend on assent to explicit Christian doctrine. There is nevertheless a role here for the Church. For it can in its present condition in the nation provide an 'intermediate institution' between the individual and the state. In earlier centuries the Church was politically an 'involuntary society' to which every citizen was required to belong, with penalty for default. Now, the nation is the 'involuntary society', and the Church is a voluntary one within it, with great historical reserves of thought and devotion to offer.

There is, first, the accountability of the nation for its poor and needy. Throughout the Bible such national responsibility, to be accepted both personally and corporately, is given the strongest possible emphasis. This is often focused upon the responsible leaders of the nation. They will answer to God for their usage of the marginalised and destitute, for God's very nature is compassionate, caring always for the remnant and the broken. We must note, though, that the Bible never implies that the 'poor' are necessarily morally righteous because they are poor. What it does insist is that the poor are always in the right as over against their oppressors. In such cases those accountable are identified and God's Judgment is clear. Those responsible for creating or allowing or sustaining unjust structures – economic, political, social – bear accountability not only for the good and evil of their own personal lives, but for the pressure towards wrong which they have placed on those who suffer as a consequence of those structures. 'Am I my brother's keeper?' carries the clearly implied response, 'Yes'. He who puts at risk even one of these 'little ones' (the vulnerable of any kind, not simply the very young) is indicted. Although the whole nation is thus accountable, any government is accountable to God as no other group is in society, for the pressures or support it creates for those who are in any way disadvantaged.

But in the Bible such corporate responsibility never removes its individual counterpart. As individuals we live within God's Judgment whatever the social or political conditions. At no point does the Bible suggest that responsibility for personal moral integrity can be shuffled off as no longer applicable because of the unjust social structures.

The recent political emphasis on personal accountability is arguably very profoundly grounded in wholly orthodox Christian doctrine. Its neglect in recent times makes its recovery important now, for it is correlate with the created nature of humankind as accountable; and it is correlate with the Christian view of history as the outworking of God's relation with humanity in a Judgment that is both just and gracious, which weighs in the balance and yet saves. Whenever and wherever accountability ceases to be a matter of felt obligation and, thus depersonalised, is attributed to a theoretical concept called 'society', then our grasp on moral reality becomes defective, for there is loss of that inner conviction of personal accountability which is a part of the created nature of human beings. The dignity and worth of such a society will be diminished to the degree that its individual members lose such conviction. Nevertheless, this doctrine of personal responsibility is falsified and becomes a parody of itself if it is used to undermine or disregard the obverse responsibility, of individuals bonded together in a society, so as to meet their corporate responsibility. For that is correlate with the Christian recognition of humankind owning a corporate as well as individual existence, answerable to God for the justice and mercy of its societal life.

How may the biblical teachings about God as merciful Judge be expressed in a secular society which on the whole relates to God only in the most peripheral or emergency sense? I would propose some possible ways forward.

The first is that even in the most secularised society there remains a large majority who recognise the need for commitment, and who relate this to a sense of accountability to oneself at least, and one's own conscience. Such an attitude is available even when God is not part of the equation. It can elicit a discrimination between good and evil in measuring one's life. This caring about what one does or becomes was voiced powerfully in *Jane Eyre*: 'I care for myself. The more solitary . . . the more unsustained I am, the more I will respect myself. I can meet my own eyes in the mirror, even if I have no God whose gaze I have to confront.'

Balancing this is the possibility of being answerable to society. This is fraught with difficulty of definition, since it can be misread as a demand for uncritical acceptance of whatever goals a government may set, in the name of the nation, for its citizens. But we need to recognise that every state has a responsibility about the kind of citizens it is encouraging its nationals to be. So any government which, in the name of the nation, through furthering its development in a particular political or economic direction, creates in its citizens a motivation of greed or laziness, dependency or ruthlessness, is failing in its accountability to its citizens.

It is in a nation where a government itself acknowledges the law of accountability, and knows itself answerable to its citizens, that those same citizens are most likely to lay upon their hearts, and know, these truths about their own accountability. Within us all is this knowledge, though it may be buried very deep. A great modern novelist, Saul Bellow in *Mr Sammler's Planet*, summed this up in a prayer one of his characters spoke over a dead friend

> who as willingly as possible, and as well as he was able . . . and even as death was coming, was eager . . . to do what was required of him. He was aware that he must meet, and he did meet – through all the confusion . . . of this life – the terms of his contract. The terms which, in his inmost heart, each man knows. As I know mine. As all know. For that is the truth of it – that we all know God; that we know, that we know, we know, we know.

17

Towards an Understanding

David L. Edwards

NO attempt is being made to provide a comprehensive or an agreed summary of this book. It may be most useful if I set down very briefly a few reflections about some of the lessons to be learned from our dialogue. These are my personal reactions, in my own words, after editing the essays and listening to the many conversations which preceded them.

(1) When we use the term 'the Church' in relation to social questions, inevitably we have in mind mainly the statements of ordained church leaders, reports by church committees and resolutions passed by church synods after debates. Similarly when we use the term 'the State' we think immediately of politicians assisted by civil servants, the police and the rest of the apparatus which the Government controls. But no one should say of Church or State, *c'est moi*. It is dangerous to forget that, properly understood, 'the Church' includes masses of laity and many pastors, Christians who are not active (and perhaps not interested) in politics, just as a democratic state means in the last analysis the whole electorate, many of whom are not supporters of any party's ideology. It is the responsibility of the leadership in Church and State to express opinions based on knowledge about the urgent questions of the day. But these opinions do not necessarily reflect the

whole life and thought of the Church or the state. Indeed, not many years have to pass before historians can reckon that many of the leadership's opinions were wrong. We must not get the arguments at the top out of proportion, thinking that 'the Church', meaning its leadership, says all that Christianity has to say or that 'the state', meaning its leadership, says all that the people has to say. What is being discussed by the leadership is the relevance of Christianity to political and economic realities which are prominent for the time being and in this field no one is either infallible or entirely authoritative.

(2) In recent years the leadership of Britain's Churches, but particularly of the Church of England, has been widely felt to have the wrong priorities. This feeling is strong among church members as well as among citizens (two categories which, of course, overlap). It is felt that church leaders ought to be far more positive and clear about personal religion (belief, spirituality and morality) and somewhat more hesitant about pronouncements on politics and economics. It is widely agreed that church leadership (including synods, etc.) has a duty to be concerned about the problems of the society in which it is set. In Britain this is a very old tradition; bishops, for example, have been summoned to Parliament since its origins. Theologically, the reason for being creatively interested in politics or economics is that God himself is working to transform society 'on earth' into his 'Kingdom' under his government, a government of liberation, justice, peace and love. In human terms, the reason is that the poor and marginalised are God's children. To ignore them is to insult their Father. Accordingly, the recent 'bias to the poor' in the British Churches is rightly praised. But many still feel that religious leadership ought to be different from political leadership.

The feeling that church leaders should concentrate on their own job is likely to be particularly strong in a time such as our own. Such leaders, if intelligent and sensitive, are likely to refuse to oversimplify questions of theology, ethics and church organisation which in our time seem specially difficult. They are therefore accused of failing to give a lead. But the criticism grows if, when discussing politics and economics, they themselves oversimplify the problems with which professionals in those spheres wrestle. For it cannot be claimed that the Bible, on which the teaching of church leadership should be based, simply lays down the law in our current political and economic controversies.

Instead of repeating the criticisms made of attempts to identify the Christian Gospel with a Conservative, Socialist or other political programme, I submit a comment on one of the ablest and most independent discussions of the basic questions to appear in recent years, *Economics Today: A Christian Critique* by Donald A. Hay, Fellow of Jesus College, Oxford, published by the Inter-Varsity Press in 1989. This distinguished scholar tries to persuade his fellow-Christians to adopt the 'principles of biblical social ethics' which he presents (pp. 70–79). These are:

> Man must use the resources of creation to provide for his existence, but he must not waste or destroy the created order. Every person has a calling to exercise stewardship or resources and talents. Stewardship implies responsibility to determine the disposition of resources. Each person is accountable to God for his stewardship. Man has a right and an obligation to work. Work is the means of exercising stewardship. In his work man should have access to resources and control over them. Work is a social activity in which men cooperate as stewards of their individual talents, and as joint stewards of resources. Every person has a right to share in God's provision for mankind in their basic needs of food, clothing and shelter. These needs are met primarily by productive work. Personal stewardship of resources does not imply the right to consume the entire product of these resources. The rich have an obligation to help the poor who cannot provide for themselves by work.

The trouble about such principles is not that they are wrong. As ideals they are, I think, beyond criticism and I am one of those (the vast majority of the British electorate) who in principle like the middle way between the market economy and the planned economy which these principles lead Dr Hay to take. (On the one hand, 'the singling out of individual freedom as the overriding value in assessing social arrangements is incompatible with biblical criteria'; on the other hand, 'the totalitarian characteristics of Communist regimes are not unrelated to the attempt to plan for distributive justice' – pp. 162, 196.) The trouble comes if specific policies are derived from these principles and are then controverted – policies about the protection of the environment, state interference in the economy, 'co-determination' in the workplace, 'workfare' instead of unemployment benefit without work, rights of property, levels of taxation and benefits, terms of international trade and aid, etc. Then the nature of the biblical or ecclesiastical authority claimed for such principles is scrutinised; it is seen that 'the biblical revelation is set in an historical context which is remote from our own' (Hay, p. 12); it is emphasised that even the regulations in the Hebrew Scriptures are not precise answers to all our questions (for example, 'the Law has nothing to say directly about the regulation of markets', p. 36); and it is concluded that 'few economic issues can be settled by direct appeal to Scripture' (p. 71). Therefore I believe Professor R. H. Preston was right to offer a more modest alternative to reliance on 'principles of biblical social ethics'. He has advocated *discernment* as a Christian method for doing social ethics, saying that it is 'achieved by putting one's understanding of human life, drawn ultimately from the biblical witness to Jesus Christ, alongside a diagnosis of what is going on' (quoted by Hay, p. 65). This source of guidance is much less 'clear-cut' than many people want. But it seems to be the only source available to Christian realists. From it may come shrewd commentary, as illustrated by Preston's Maurice Lectures on *Religion and the Persistence of Capitalism* (1978) and by his later publications such as *Church and Society in the Late Twentieth Century* (1983).

(3) The relevance of Christianity in the ordering of society has been expressed in many different ways in the course of history. In Europe including Britain, the influence of ideas proclaimed in, or related to, the Bible has been far greater than is always recognised. But social conditions change, largely because their economic basis changes, and Christians ought not to connect the everlasting Gospel too closely to a vanished era for which nostalgia is felt, for example mediaeval Christendom, Anglican England or Calvin's Geneva. What history can do is to set standards of social achievement which challenge us to do better, together with a reminder that the Christians who achieved these standards in the past were human enough to make many mistakes, for example by not allowing enough liberty. In both these ways history can encourage us as we make our mistakes.

(4) It has been discovered in modern times that the most effective way to create wealth, ultimately for the benefit of all, is to allow individuals and enterprises to compete in a free market, retaining most of their profits to add to their private property. The ownership of the means of production, distribution and exchange by the state or by the firm's employees is less likely to be progressive in the creation of wealth. A Bible-based Christianity (including both Testaments) teaches that the Creator blesses wealth creation provided that it does not become an obsession and is properly used. Therefore in modern times Christians may rightly regard the free market as something mainly beneficial and even as something given by God, like the state and the family. In the language of traditional theology, these are 'orders of creation'. They deserve affirmation and celebration.

(5) But the market has its limits. Unless they are guided and modified by the whole community acting partly through the state, market forces do not do enough for job creation, for the dignity of the worker, for health, education and social security, for the arts and for other causes which Christians value. It is impossible to quantify 'success' or

'efficiency' in such causes if one relies solely on the criteria of the market. A flourishing market may leave many people feeling poor, marginalised and underdeveloped – and they are not much consoled by being informed that people in other times and places have been worse off. Therefore there must be limits to the sphere which the market is allowed to dominate. The Christian conscience is right to insist on this ethical control of market forces. The exact limits of the market are, however, a matter for political argument.

(6) The chief purpose of wealth creation through the market (thus limited) is to make easier, and to encourage, a richly human life. This must involve the strengthening of family life as the greatest earthly source of human happiness, the strengthening of many other communities on a human scale and the strengthening of the individual's sense of being responsible and accountable for making the most of the fragile gift of life. The Christian will add very emphatically that every person is responsible and accountable to God, who as holy love both demands and enables an ultimate perfection. It is by its witness to the will of God in such matters, rather than by participation in political argument, that the Church makes its main contribution to the welfare of society.

(7) A greater unity and a higher prosperity seem to be attainable in Europe including Britain during the 1990s. It appears to be possible to create a society better as well as richer than any in the past. The necessary work will provide profoundly exciting and challenging opportunities for Christians – chiefly the laity – to make theoretical or practical contributions. These contributions may be made within what is somewhat oddly called the Conservative tradition. They may also be made in other ways.

Appendix

A Speech by the Prime Minister
21 May 1988

I AM greatly honoured to have been invited to attend the opening of this 1988 General Assembly of the Church of Scotland; and I am deeply grateful that you have now asked me to address you. I am very much aware of the historical continuity extending over four centuries, during which the position of the Church of Scotland has been recognised in constitutional law and confirmed by successive Sovereigns. It sprang from the independence of mind and rigour of thought that have always been such powerful character-istics of the Scottish people. It has remained close to its roots and has inspired a commitment to service from *all* people. I am therefore very sensible of the important in-fluence which the Church of Scotland exercises in the life of the whole nation, both at the spiritual level and through the extensive caring services which are provided by your Church's department of social responsibility.

Perhaps it would be best if I began by speaking person-ally as a Christian, as well as a politician, about the way I see things. Reading recently I came across the starkly simple phrase: 'Christianity is about spiritual redemption, not social reform.' Sometimes the debate on these matters has become too polarised and given the impression that the two are quite separate. Most Christians would regard it as their personal Christian duty to help their fellow men and women. They would regard the lives of their children as a precious trust. These duties come not from any secular legislation passed by Parliament, but from being a Christian. But there are a number of people who are not Christians who would also accept these responsibilities. What then are the distinctive marks of Christianity?

They stem not from the social but from the spiritual side of our lives. I would identify three beliefs in particular. First, that from the beginning man has been endowed by God with the fundamental right to choose between good and evil. Second, that we are made in God's image and therefore we are expected to use all our *own* power of thought and judgment in exercising that choice; and further, if we open our hearts to God, he has promised to work within us. And third, that our Lord Jesus Christ the Son of God when faced with his terrible choice and lonely vigil *chose* to lay down his life that our sins may be forgiven. I remember very well a sermon on an Armistice Sunday when our preacher said: 'No one took away the life of Jesus: he chose to lay it down.'

I think back to many discussions in my early life when we all agreed that if you try to take the fruits of Christianity without its roots, the fruits will wither. And they will not come again unless you nurture the roots. But we must not profess Christianity and go to church simply because we want social reforms and benefits or a better standard of living – but because we accept the sanctity of life, the responsibility that comes with freedom and the supreme sacrifice of Christ expressed so well in the hymn:

> When I survey the wondrous Cross
> On which the Prince of glory died,
> My richest gain I count but loss,
> And pour contempt on all my pride.

May I also say a few words about my personal belief in the relevance of Christianity to public policy – to the things that are Caesar's? The Old Testament lays down in Exodus the Ten Commandments as given to Moses, the injunction in Leviticus to love our neighbour as ourselves and generally the importance of observing a strict code of law. The New Testament is a record of the Incarnation, the teachings of Christ and the establishment of the Kingdom of God. Again we have the emphasis on loving our neighbour as ourselves and to 'Do-as-you-would-be-done-by'. I believe that by taking together these two elements from the Old and New Testaments we gain a view of the universe, a proper attitude to work, and principles to shape economic and social life.

We are told that we must work and use our talents to create wealth. 'If a man will not work, he shall not eat,' wrote St Paul to the Thessalonians. Indeed, abundance rather than poverty has a legitimacy which derives from the very nature of creation. Nevertheless the Tenth Commandment – 'Thou shalt not covet' – recognises that making money and owning things could become selfish activities. But it is not the creation of wealth that is wrong but love of money for its own sake. The spiritual dimension comes in deciding what to do with the wealth. How could we respond to the many calls for help, or invest in the future, or support the wonderful artists and craftsmen whose work also glorifies God, unless we had first worked hard and used our talents to create the necessary wealth? And remember the woman with the alabaster jar of ointment. I confess that I have always had difficulty with interpreting the biblical precept to love our neighbours 'as ourselves' until I read some of the words of C. S. Lewis. He pointed out that we don't exactly love *ourselves* when we fall below the standards and beliefs we have accepted. Indeed we might even *hate* ourselves for some unworthy deed.

None of this, of course, tells us exactly what kind of political and social institutions we should have. On this point, Christians will very often genuinely disagree, though it is a mark of Christian manners that they will do so with courtesy and mutual respect. What is certain, however, is that any set of social and economic arrangements which is not founded on the acceptance of individual responsibility will do nothing but harm. We are all responsible for our own actions. We cannot blame society if we disobey the law. We cannot simply delegate the exercise of mercy and compassion to others. The politicians and other secular powers should strive by their measures to bring out the good in people and to fight down the bad: but they can't create the one or abolish the other. They can only see that the laws encourage the *best* instincts and convictions which I am convinced are far more deeply rooted than is often supposed.

Nowhere is this more evident than the basic ties of the family which are at the heart of our society and are the very nursery of civic virtue. It is on the family that we in government base our policies for welfare, education and care. You recall that Timothy was warned by St Paul that anyone who neglects to provide for his own house (meaning his own family) has disowned the faith and is 'worse than an infidel'.

We must recognise that modern society is infinitely more complex than that of biblical times and of course new occasions teach new duties. In our day the only way that we can ensure that no one is left without sustenance, help or opportunity, is to have laws to provide for health and education, pensions for the elderly, succour for the sick and disabled. But intervention by the state must never become so great that it effectively removes personal responsibility. The same applies to taxation, for while you and I would work extremely hard whatever the circumstances, there are undoubtedly some who would not unless the incentive was there. And we need *their* efforts too.

Moderator, recently there have been great debates about religious education. I believe strongly that politicians must see that religious education has a proper place in the school curriculum. In Scotland as in England there is a historic connection expressed in our laws between Church and State. The two connections are of a somewhat different kind, but the arrangements in both countries are designed to give symbolic expression to the same crucial truth – that the Christian religion, which of course symbolises many of the great spiritual and moral truths of Judaism – is a fundamental part of our national heritage.

I believe it is the wish of the overwhelming majority of people that this heritage should be preserved and fostered. For centuries it has been our very life blood. Indeed we are a nation whose ideals are founded on the Bible. Also it is quite impossible to understand our literature without grasping this fact. *That* is the strong practical case for ensuring that children at school are given adequate instruction in the part which the Judaeo-Christian tradition has played in moulding our laws, manners and institutions. How can you make sense of Shakespeare and Sir Walter Scott, or of the constitutional conflicts of the seventeenth century in both Scotland and England, without such fundamental knowledge? But I would go further than this. The truths of the Judaeo-Christian tradition are infinitely precious, not only, as I believe, because they are true, but also because they provide the moral impulse which alone can lead to that peace, in the true meaning of the word, for which we all long.

To assert absolute moral values is not to claim perfection for ourselves. No true Christian could do that. What is more, one of the great principles of our Judaeo-Christian heritage is tolerance. People of other faiths and cultures have always been welcomed in our land, assured of equality under the law, of proper respect and of open friendship. There is absolutely nothing incompatible with this and our desire to maintain the essence of our own identity. There is no place for racial or religious intolerance in our creed.

When Abraham Lincoln spoke in his famous Gettysburg speech of 1863 of 'government of the people, by the people, for the people', he gave the world a neat definition of democracy which has since been widely and enthusiastically adopted. But what he enunciated as a form of government was not in itself specifically Christian, for nowhere in the Bible is the word democracy mentioned. Ideally, when Christians meet, as Christians, to take counsel together, their purpose is not (or should not be) to ascertain what is the mind of the majority but what is the mind of the Holy Spirit – something which may be quite different. Nevertheless, I am an enthusiast for democracy. And I take that position, not because I believe majority opinion is inevitably right or true – indeed, no majority can take away God-given rights – but because I believe it effectively safeguards the value of the individual, and, more than any other system, restrains the abuse of power by the few. And that *is* a Christian concept.

But there is little hope for democracy if the hearts of men and women in democratic societies cannot be touched by a call to something greater than themselves. Political structures, state institutions, collective ideals are not enough. *We* Parliamentarians can legislate for the rule of law. *You* the Church can teach the life of faith.

For, when all is said and done, a politician's life is a humble one. I always think that the whole debate about the Church and the State has never yielded anything comparable in insight to that beautiful hymn: 'I vow to thee my country'. It begins with a triumphant assertion of what might be described as secular patriotism, a noble thing indeed in a country like ours:

> I vow to thee, my country, all earthly things above:
> Entire, whole and perfect the service of my love.

It goes on to speak of 'another country I heard of long ago' whose King cannot be seen and whose armies cannot be counted, but 'soul by soul and silently her shining bounds increase'. Not group by group, or party by party, or even church by church – but soul by soul and each one counts.

That, members of the Assembly, is the country which you chiefly serve. You fight your cause under the banner of an historic Church. Your success matters greatly – as much to the temporal as to the spiritual welfare of the nation.

Index